Yugoslavia

Yugoslavia

Socialism, Development and Debt

David A. Dyker

Routledge
London and New York

First published 1990 by Routledge
11 New Fetter Lane, London EC4P 4EE

Simultaneously published in the USA and Canada
by Routledge
a division of Routledge, Chapman and Hall, Inc.
29 West 35th Street, New York, NY 10001

© 1990 David A. Dyker

Phototypeset in 10pt Times by
Mews Photosetting, Beckenham, Kent
Printed and bound in Great Britain by
Biddles Ltd, Guildford and King's Lynn

British Library Cataloguing in Publication Data

Dyker, David A., (David Alexander), 1944–
    Yugoslavia: socialism, development and debt.
    1. Yugoslavia. Economic development
    I. Title
    330.9497

    ISBN 0-415-00745-3

Library of Congress Cataloging-in-Publication Data

Dyker, David A.
    Yugoslavia: socialism, development, and debt / David A. Dyker.
        p. cm.
    Includes bibliographical references.
    ISBN 0-415-00745-3
    1. Yugoslavia – Economic policy – 1945– 2. Yugoslavia – Economic
conditions – 1945– 3. Debts, External – Yugoslavia. 4. Balance of
payments – Yugoslavia. I. Title.
HC407.D94   1990
338.9497–dc20   89-24036
                                                             CIP

To the memory of Maria Lambor

Contents

Map and Tables

Preface

This book represents the culmination of over twenty years of research on the Yugoslav economy. Over that period I have watched the (rather old-fashioned) card-index system grow to almost threatening proportions, and it was indeed a relief finally to attack the task of putting it all together. The reader will find that I have not specifically referenced every fact, every detail – that would have made the book unreadable. But he can rest assured that every unreferenced piece of data was taken from one of the two main Yugoslav business weeklies – *Ekonomska Politika* and *Privredni Vjesnik*. I am grateful to the Economic and Social Research Council, the British Academy and the University of Sussex for the financial support which enabled me to complete the research. I am also deeply indebted to Saul Estrin of the London School of Economics and Dubravko Matko of the Institute of Soviet and East European Studies, University of Glasgow, for their detailed and helpful comments on the typescript. I hope the final product is worthy of the attention they devoted to it. Dragana Gnjatović of the Economics Institute of Belgrade was kind enough to allow me to use material from her admirable *Uloga Inostranih Sredstava u Privrednom Razvoju Jugoslavije*. Finally, I must thank Peter Hollies for the gift of his invaluable library, and Naomi-Jane Dyker, who drew the map.

Chapter one

A Young State and a Developing Economy

The dilemmas of Yugoslav statehood

The creation of Yugoslavia in 1918, in the aftermath of the Balkan Wars
and the First World War, marked the final victory in a century-long
struggle by the South Slavs to create a 'Southslavia' (the literal meaning
of Yugoslavia) in the Balkans, following on the collapse of the Ottoman
and Austro-Hungarian Empires. But while the other newly-independent
states of Eastern Europe could all claim the status of nation-state, in the
sense that each contained a single, dominant national and linguistic group,
Yugoslavia was from the start a multi-national state, more of a microcosm
of the ramshackle empires it succeeded than any tribute to the Wilson
Doctrine. It did have a large measure of linguistic unity with around
70 per cent of the population speaking some form of Serbo-Croat as their
first language (Hoffman and Neal 1962: 29), but Croatia, with its
Habsburg past and Roman Catholic religion, was as self-consciously
different from Serbia (Orthodox and still smarting from the memory of
the Ottoman yoke) as is the Protestant, French-speaking part of
Switzerland from France. The Serbo-Croat-speaking Muslims of Bosnia
and Hercegovina and the people of Montenegro – Serbo-Croat-speaking
and Serbian Orthodox in religion, but with a long history of independent
statehood – further complicated the picture. Outside the Serbo-Croat-
speaking heart of the new state lay a periphery populated by Slovenes
and Macedonians – Slav nations, but with distinctive national languages
– and substantial minorities of Albanians, Hungarians and, at that time,
also Germans. The biggest single ethnic group – the Serbs – accounted
for about 40 per cent of the total population of some 12 million people.

But Serbia, the self-styled 'Piedmont of the South Slav area' was
politically quite dominant in the Kingdom of the Serbs, Croats and
Slovenes, as it was known until 1929. It was Serbia which had managed
to develop some kind of a modern state apparatus during the 19th century,
having wrested a degree of autonomy from the Turks in 1815 and
complete independence in 1878. It was Serbia which had set a pattern

1

of territorial expansionism as it struggled to reclaim anciently Serbian lands from the Turkish Empire in a series of wars through the period 1815–1918. It was the assassination of the Habsburg Archduke Ferdinand in 1914 by a Serb, Gavrilo Princip, which started the First World War, and it was Serbia which, as an ally, battled through to victory in 1918, though at the cost of appalling loss of life. Finally, it was the Serbian royal family, in the person of King Alexander Karadjordjević, that was to rule the new kingdom, after 1929 through a royal dictatorship.

These circumstances created a complex of political problems which threatened to tear the Kingdom of the Serbs, Croats and Slovenes apart, and which do, indeed, still impinge in present-day Yugoslavia. The Serbs, naturally, felt that they had 'earned' the right to run the new show, and they were, *though economically a good deal less advanced than the Slovenes and Croats of the North and West*, the only group with an existing administrative elite. Thus 'the new state amounted to a Serbian hegemony, with not only king and court, but also administration, army and police predominantly Serbian, and therefore tending to be anti-Croat. Under a government dominated by Serbs, Croats had less to say about their affairs than before the war. . . . Croat passions, not unnaturally, began to burn. . . . The Serbs handled the problem with a remarkable lack of finesse. By 1923–4 Croatia was virtually in a state of insurrection' (Hoffman and Neal 1962: 59–60). When King Alexander proclaimed his royal dictatorship in 1929 he imposed a new system of administrative territorialization which was expressly designed to deprive Croatia of a territorial identity within Yugoslavia. Repression, needless to say, made things worse rather than better, and by the late 1930s, with the German menace looming, public opinion started to swing towards reconciliation. In 1939 a deal was struck which gave the Croatians their own *banovina*, or province, and a degree of autonomy. The new arrangement did not work particularly well, but in any case the old Yugoslavia was destroyed by German invasion in 1941. Germany imposed a brutal occupation on Serbia, but permitted the formation of a puppet fascist state in Croatia under the *Ustaše*.

The wartime period 1941–5 was characterized at once by the depths of atrocity and the heights of heroism. The *Ustaše* launched genocidal attacks on Serbian populations, and to a degree the Serbian Chetnik movement, originally formed in 1941 to resist the Axis occupation, replied in kind. But the Chetniks offered little immediate challenge to the Germans, preferring to keep their forces intact for the power struggle they expected after the end of the war. For the Chetniks, then, the ultimate restoration of the Karadjordjević monarchy remained a central priority. Meanwhile it was the communist-led Partisan movement – predominantly Serbian in personnel but led by a Croat, Josip Broz Tito – which soon came to dominate effective resistance to the occupiers, and indeed to fight a heroic guerilla campaign, holding down dozens of German battalions and contributing significantly to the allied cause. The Partisans were recognized by Winston Churchill as the 'official' resistance in Yugoslavia as early as 1943, and thenceforth received substantial support, material and moral, from the Western Allies. But the Partisans were just as interested as the Chetniks in taking power after the end of hostilities, and joined battle with the latter as trenchantly as with the Germans. Thus civil war was layered upon civil war, with little quarter offered by any of the protagonists. Partisan treatment of Chetnik personnel after the end of the war does them little credit. The Chetnik leader, Draža Mihailović, was executed in 1946 for alleged collaboration with the Germans.

There can be no doubt that the Partisans, with their appeal to traditional warrior-hero attitudes and their genuinely pan-Yugoslav and ultimately universal ideology, struck a deep chord amongst Yugoslavs for whom the Serb-Croat bickerings of the inter-war period had turned into the most horrific nightmare. But the Partisan leaders, at this time at least, were no democrats and no decentralizers. They had gained power by defeating and repressing their rivals, and aimed to extend that power through the imposition of a Stalinist police state. Willy-nilly, they would have to use as their instruments Partisan cadres, predominantly Serbian. It went without saying that Belgrade, the capital of Serbia, would continue to be the capital of Yugoslavia, and that meant that the main administrative centre of the country would continue to be in some sense alien to Croats and Slovenes at least.

For that reason, and perhaps also for more concrete financial and career reasons, the northern nationalities signally failed to take positive initiatives to roll back Serbian domination of the administration and the coercive forces through the post-war period. Serbs, together with their close cousins, the Montenegrins, continued to dominate the officer corps, and indeed the proportion of that corps made up by members of other nationalities seems to have fallen steadily up to the early 1970s (Paver 1973). In 1970 61 out or 100 'leading personnel' of the Federal Ministry of Internal Affairs, i.e. the police, were Serbs, and another 9 were Montenegrins (Dyker 1977). Most striking of all are the following figures for national composition of membership of the federal bureaucracy in 1969 (Poen . . . 1969):

Serbs	4335	Montenegrins	424
Croats	504	Slovenes	187
Macedonians	145		

We should certainly be very cautious about attributing these patterns to any *policy* of Serbian domination, such as had been followed by the royal

3

regime before the war. Indeed the Belgrade government, as we shall see, has frequently taken steps to try to correct the imbalance. But the vicious circle of Serbian preponderance in the organs of the state, and 'agin the government' attitudes amongst the other nationalities, particularly the Croats and Slovenes, is a crucial factor affecting policy implementation in any area, but not least the economic area, and we shall return to it repeatedly.

The legacy of backwardness

On the eve of the Second World War Yugoslavia had a level of National Income per head of around 60 (1938) dollars (Gnjatović 1985: 43). The corresponding figure for the USA itself was $607 (Kuznets 1954: 153). The Yugoslav figure for 1938 represented but little progress over the inter-war period as a whole, with the average rate of growth of National Income only slightly above that of population. The period 1920–9 was a good one for Yugoslavia, as it was for other agricultural countries able to take advantage of the buoyant food markets of that decade. But the Wall Street Crash, and the ensuing Great Depression, changed all that. While Yugoslav GDP grew at a rate of 4.5 per cent during 1920–9, it could muster only 1.3 per cent during 1929–38 (Maddison 1976: 451). In 1939 agriculture accounted for around 80 per cent of the active population and 51 per cent of National Income. Industry and handicrafts employed 8.6 per cent of the active population and generated 29.7 per cent of National Income (Gnjatović 1985: 43). The distribution of income generated by this production profile showed a substantial but not overwhelming degree of inequality. Vinski found that in 1938 the 'proletariat', including the poor peasants, accounted for 34.6 per cent of the population, but only 18.2 per cent of National Income. For urban workers taken by themselves, however, the situation was much more favourable, with corresponding figures of 6.0 per cent and 5.3 per cent. The 'middle classes' – mainly the peasants – had 52.9 per cent of the population and 55.6 per cent of National Income. For the 'bourgeoisie' the corresponding figures were 5.3 per cent and 25.6 per cent (Vinski 1970).

What development there was was unevenly spread. Cobeljić quotes research which indicates that in 1918 less developed regions of Yugoslavia accounted for just 16 per cent of the work places outside peasant agriculture, 23 per cent of total invested capital, and 11 per cent of installed capacity (Cobeljić 1959: 79, quoting work by M.Jelić and R.Cvetković). It is not clear what the precise coverage of 'less developed regions' is in this research, but it must have accounted for around 50 per cent of the total population. Things got worse rather than better over the inter-war period, with industrial capital invested per head of population in Slovenia growing twice as fast as in Serbia, six times as fast as in Bosnia and Hercegovina, and nearly twenty times as fast as in Montenegro (Gnjatović 1985: 45).

Thus the Yugoslavia which the Communists inheritated in 1945 was in many ways a fairly typical developing country. Predominantly agricultural, it had discovered in the 1930s just how vulnerable agricultural exporters can be in times of international recession. To make matters worse, the pressure of rural overcrowding was increasing all the time, with total agricultural population increasing from 9 million in 1921 to 11.5 million in 1938 (Cobeljić 1959: 80) This kept agricultural labour productivity levels low and made it virtually impossible for the peasantry to generate enough money income to pay their heavy tax burden, purchase industrial inputs, etc.

The agrarian reform of 1918–31, a reform in the classic redistributional mould, ensured that the great majority of peasants had some land, but that few had enough. Almost 70 per cent of the number of farms in the 1930s were less than 5 hectares, and the dominant group of peasants, accounting for nearly 50 per cent of the total land stock, were those holding farms of 5–20 hectares (Mirković 1968: 209). After 1929 the peasant indebtedness problem grew rapidly, exacerbated by deflation and usurious rates of interest. The state tried to help by introducing various measures of partial moratorium, but the problem remained essentially unresolved on the eve of the Second World War.

Typical also of many contemporary developing countries were the ecological costs which the pressure of rural over-population started to impose on Yugoslavia. Large-scale destruction of forests, as land, often marginal land, was cleared for cultivation, was one of the major factors leading to the emergence of a serious erosion problem. It also led to increased aridity in an already rather dry area, and to increased volatility in the stock patterns of major rivers, with flooding after heavy rainfall an ever more common problem (Mihailović 1977: 105–7). Thus the pressures in favour of industrialization were as much of a general socio-environmental as of a specifically economic nature.

Development strategy between the wars

Yet the picture of an agrarian economy, rent by internal tensions and imbalances and buffeted by international trends over which it had no control, is a little misleading. The royal Yugoslav regime, and the Yugoslav public, perceived clearly the need to foster industrial development.

It was obvious, and with a few romantic exceptions generally recognized, that industrialization had become inevitable, that only through it

> would it be possible to develop the productive forces of the people, and indeed of agriculture itself, and that it was a necessary precondition if the Yugoslav peoples were to progress, or even just to survive.
> (Mirković 1968: 350)

Mirković pin-points three key characteristics of inter-war industrial policy – a high degree of protectionism, free access for foreign capital, and substantial direct state support for domestic industry through subsidized rail tariffs, tolerance of tax evasion, defence contracts on very favourable terms for the private contractor, etc. However, he perceives no great master plan for development behind these specific measures.

Bićanić shares Mirković's implicit cynicism, judging that

> state policy was predominantly in the hands of people whose outlook had not developed beyond the mentality of what Marx called primitive accumulation and who considered the state apparatus and state economic policy not as instruments with which to build modern capitalism, but as means for private accumulation by extra-economic means, i.e. using the state machinery and the state budget instead of capitalist economic machinery.
> (Bićanić 1973: 18)

But he does also identify 'objectives of the policy of state monopoly capitalism', in terms of overall economic growth, building up the defence industry, maximizing the degree of national self-sufficiency, and channelling resources into specified export activities (Bićanić 1973: 18–19). We need not read into this any very high defree of effective integration of policy. But Vladimir Pertot has perceived a clear continuity with the traditional Austro–Hungarian policy of import substitution, and pin-pointed this as a major obstacle to the expansion of exports (Pertot 1971: 2 and 3). Equally interesting is the way that Bićanić ties in this autarkic, state-capitalist approach with Serbian political domination.

> Self-congratulation on the one side and disappointment on the other were to be at the root of many tensions in the future between those who considered it their sacred mission to consolidate their war gains and build up a self-contained (autarchic) National State, and those [i.e. the Slovenes and Croats] who felt more or less clearly that the development of the country's economy required larger markets and a wider extension of economic forces than the Yugoslav frontiers permitted. The former developed a sense of economic xenophobia, originating in an inferiority complex about underdevelopment and an insecurity caused by fear of competition. The latter considered themselves able to meet foreign competition on an equal footing in specialized fields of production, as had been the case before 1914, and they favoured an open economy which would trade with

foreign countries on a wide scale. This struggle between the two con-
ceptions continued through the inter-war period and even after the
socialist revolution. Not until the mid-sixties did it become clear to
the majority of people that even if the area of Yugoslavia were ten
times larger and her income per head four times bigger this would
still not provide a basis for a successful autarchic policy.

(Bićanić 1973: 2–3)

The Balance of Trade and the Balance of Payments between the Wars

As we can see from Table 1.1, the overall Balance of Trade pattern for
Yugoslavia 1922–39 was one of occasional large deficits being cancelled
out by frequent small surpluses. Over the period 1926–39 the terms of
trade moved strongly against Yugoslavia, with the index of prices of
her principal exports falling by a total of 22 per cent, and that of her
most important imports by only 7 per cent (Cobeljić 1959: 88), and in
this context the Balance of Trade surpluses of the 1930s look quite
creditable, even if they did reflect economic stagnation in the domestic
economy. In fact, the external situation was not as favourable as the
aggregate figures suggest. In the general milieu of neo-mercantilism
which dominated the thinking of European governments after the onset
of the Great Depression, all the Balkan states turned to bilateral clearing agreements as a way of maintaining trade without recourse to foreign
currency. In particular, bilateral trade with Germany grew rapidly, and
Yugoslavia was no exception to this trend. But the Nazi government,
showing an admirable understanding of the value of maximizing domestic
absorption, was content to let the Balkan states run up surpluses on these
accounts, surpluses which, of course, the latter could not cash in
(Momtchiloff 1944). Thus part of Yugoslavia's trading surplus in the
1930s was, in fact, illusory. The same pattern would, of course, repeat
itself in relation to bilateral trade with Comecon after the war.

When we look at the Balance of Payments we find that the position
was still less favourable (see Table 1.2). As exports fell after 1924 and
the burden of interest payments and dividends grew (it averaged over
15 per cent of the value of exports 1926–9 – Račić 1955: 173), the current
account moved into substantial deficit in 1927–8. It moved back into
the black in 1929, as exports recovered somewhat. But as international
foodstuff prices continued to fall, and with the decrease in the value of
emigrant remittances after 1929, the Balance of Payments on current
account went back into serious deficit in 1930–1. Even after the trading
situation was stabilized from 1931 onwards, deficit remained the rule
rather than the exception. There had been a lot of borrowing abroad on
short term for industrial investment purposes during the 1920s, but this
all stopped after the collapse of the Vienna stock market in 1931, and

Table 1.1 The Yugoslav Balance of Trade 1922–39, in millions of dinars

	Exports	*Imports*	*Balance*
1922	3,691	6,441	−2,750
1923	8,349	8,310	−261
1924	9,539	8,222	+1,317
1925	8,905	8,753	+152
1926	7,818	7,632	+186
1927	6,400	7,286	−886
1928	6,445	7,835	−1,391
1929	7,922	7,545	327
1930	6,780	6,960	−180
1931	4,801	4,800	+1
1932	3,056	2,860	+196
1933	3,378	2,883	+495
1934	3,878	3,573	+305
1935	4,030	3,700	+331
1936	4,376	4,077	+299
1937	6,272	5,234	+1,038
1938	5,047	4,975	+72
1939	5,521	4,757	+764

Source: Mirković 1968: 374

in that year the ratio of debt service to exports reached 36 per cent. In early 1932 Yugoslavia found itself obliged to contract new short-term loans in order to repay the earlier ones. Debt service rapidly came to present insurmountable problems, and in April of the same year Belgrade declared a unilateral moratorium on the bulk of debt service transfers. In 1936 the royal government came to an arrangement with creditors which permitted the resumption of regular debt service on a reduced basis. In addition Yugoslavia was able to buy up substantial volumes of its own obligations at depressed prices during the middle 1930s. Perhaps most important, the sharp devaluations of the creditor countries' currencies over the same period produced an automatic and very substantial cut in effective debt-service commitments. By 1937 Yugoslavia's total foreign debt stood at $388m, with annual debt service representing a much more manageable 16 per cent of annual export earnings (Nötel 1986: 252–64). But debt-service payments were never fully regularized in the period up to the outbreak of war.

The Communists and the New Yugoslavia

The Partisans would certainly never have defeated the Germans on their own, and it was, indeed, the Red Army which liberated Belgrade in 1944. But Soviet troops did not stay on Yugoslav territory, and in 1945 the Partisans held the laurels of victory and complete control over the

Table 1.2 The Yugoslav Balance of Payments 1926-36, in millions

	Capital balance	Capital movements Long-term	Capital movements Short-term	Current balance	Goods	Services	Interest and dividends	Gold	Errors and omissions
1926	8.9	5.2	3.7	−8.0	−13.1	21.1	−15.9	−0.1	0.9
1927	20.2	25.3	−5.1	−23.2	−31.6	28.5	−20.0	−0.1	−3.0
1928	26.3	19.2	7.1	−27.2	−38.3	31.6	−20.5	n.a.	−0.9
1929	−8.2	14.5	−22.7	12.7	−9.4	44.5	−22.3	−0.1	4.5
1930	17.2	−16.4	33.6	−17.2	−9.3	15.2	−23.3	0.2	n.a.
1931	18.1	33.8	−15.7	−18.1	−11.1	15.4	−22.6	0.2	n.a.
1932	7.5	–	7.5	−7.5	−1.2	4.2	−10.5	–	n.a.
1933	−1.2	–	−1.2	1.2	1.8	3.5	−4.1	–	n.a.
1934	3.4	–	3.4	−3.4	−2.7	3.6	−5.6	1.3	n.a.
1935	4.5	11.4	−6.9	−2.2	4.0	8.7	−13.6	−1.3	2.3
1936	−2.9	−1.2	−1.7	2.9	5.0	8.5	−10.5	−0.1	n.a.

Source: Nötel 1986: 188, 221 and 242

Yugoslav lands. Thus the pattern of communization in Yugoslavia had little in common with the experience of the 'people's democracies' in other parts of Eastern Europe, where the large-scale presence of Soviet troops was the main factor in the establishment of communist regimes, often against a background of minimal popular support. The Yugoslav pattern, by contrast, was based on communist leadership of a successful anti-fascist resistance movement and in this it closely resembled the way in which communists came to power in Albania and, a little later, in China.

But this fundamental difference between Yugoslavia and the Soviet bloc proper had little impact on policy formation in the first years after the end of the war. Proud to be counted an ally of the great Stalin, the Yugoslav leaders proceeded to try to construct, at breakneck speed, an image of the Soviet Union in Yugoslavia. This was the period, in the words of George Hoffman and Fred Neal, of the 'hard-boiled dictatorship'. A powerful secret police organization – UDBA – was created, and it proceeded to repress and dragoon the population in the best tradition of the Soviet KGB. On the economic side the great bulk of industry was nationalized, and a Soviet-style hierarchy of central planning, running from the Federal Planning Commission, down through an array of sectoral industrial ministries to the actual enterprise level, established. In agriculture, the first move, incorporated into a law of August 1945, was to implement further redistribution of land. The holdings of Germans, Italians, 'collaborators', banks, private companies and churches were confiscated, and an upper limit of 25–45 hectares placed on private ownership of land. The agricultural reform of the 1920s had, however, already created a fairly egalitarian structure in Yugoslav agriculture, and the 1945 measure affected only 11 per cent of the land held privately, with land being apportioned to 70,000 landless families, mostly the families of Partisan veterans. Later in the same year a measure was promulgated which cancelled all peasant debts (Hoffman and Neal 1962: 90). But while these measures essentially extrapolated the measures of the pre-war government, plans were already afoot to establish a system of Soviet-style collective farms in Yugoslavia, with a Basic Law on Cooperatives being passed in July 1946.

Following the Soviet model also meant constructing a Soviet-type state, with a Soviet-type territorial structure based on the ethnic principle. This did create problems, inasmuch as nationality in Yugoslavia is far less neatly defind by language than it is in the Soviet Union. Slovenia, Croatia and Serbia would clearly have their national republics, but after that things became rather more complicated. In the far south of the country lay Macedonia, an area considered Serbian – at least by the Serbs – before the war, but hotly disputed by the Bulgarians, who considered, with some justification, that the linguistic variant spoken in the region was closer to Bulgarian than to Serbo-Croat. Tito's solution to this

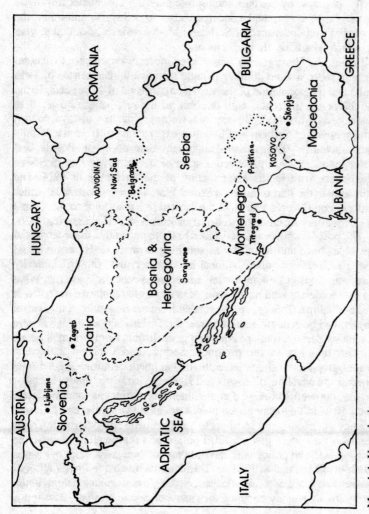

Map 1.1 Yugoslavia

problem was to create a Macedonian republic, and to preside over the codification of an official Macedonian language – recognizably a cousin of Bulgarian, but sufficiently distinct to make the key political point. In 1967 the Serbian Orthodox Church of Macedonia attained autocephalous status.

Montenegro also presented something of a problem. That tiny mountain state had originally been built up by refugees from the Turkish occupation of Serbia, and again the pre-war Yugoslav regime had considered their descendants as simply Serbs. The Communists, swayed partly, perhaps, by the outstanding role played by Montenegrins in the Partisan movement, and concerned also, possibly, to minimize the territorial preponderance of Serbia within Yugoslavia, decided to give the Black Mountain its own republic.

Bosnia and Hercegovina was an even more awkward case to handle, for here there was no dominant single nationality. The census of 1948 found that the population of that province consisted of 44 per cent Serbs, and 24 per cent Croats, with the bulk of the rest being registered as 'undeclared Muslims'. Bosnia and Hercegovina had always been a battleground for Serbian and Croatian expansionism, from the Middle Ages onwards. The Austro-Hungarian annexation of Bosnia and Hercegovina in 1908 produced a wave of irredentist feeling in Serbia which bore fruit in the assassination of the Archduke in 1914, and ultimately in the start of the First World War. The worst Ustaše atrocities of the Second World War, and the most active resistance to the Ustaše by Serbian organizations, occurred in Bosnia and Hercegovina.

The post-war government decided to try to put paid to these territorial squabbles once and for all by establishing Bosnia and Hercegovina as a separate republic, multi-national in character, but with no ethnically based sub-divisions on the Soviet 'autonomous republic' patterns. What the Tito leadership did not do straightaway was to regularize the position of the Muslims. This group, descended from the Bogomils of mediaeval Bosnia, had been dominant throughout the Turkish period, though always remaining Serbo-Croat-speaking and quite distinct from the small ethnic Turkish minority in the province. Serbian and Croatian nationalist historiographers of the nineteenth and twentieth centuries argued over whether the Muslims of Bosnia and Hercegovina were 'really' Serbs or Croats, but were united in denying them any distinct nationality status. The post-war Yugoslav government went along with this, and followed a policy of encouraging Muslims to 'declare themselves' Serbs or Croats (later on they were given a third option of simply calling themselves Yugoslavs). The policy was certainly not an oppressive one, but it was rather artificial, and in 1961 the Bosnian Muslims were finally allowed to take their place as a fully-fledged, Serbo-Croat-speaking nation, under the internally slightly contradictory name of *Ethnic Muslims (Muslimani po etničkoj pripadnosti)*. This move confirmed the multi-national character of Bosnia and Hercegovina, while ultimately establishing the Ethnic Muslims as the dominant group, with some 40 per cent of the total population of the republic at the 1981 census.

But the most awkward problems were presented by the minorities within the Serbian and Croatian heartlands. It was decided to create autonomous provinces, on the Soviet model, in the Vojvodina and Kosovo areas within Serbia. The establishment of AP Vojvodina proved an effective vehicle for accommodating the large Hungarian minority in that region, but the story has been less happy in the case of Kosovo. The most impoverished part of Yugoslavia, with a large Albanian majority and an embattled Serbian minority, it continues to be, for historical reasons, a major focus of Serbian national identity. It has proved difficult, however, to demonstrate to the Albanians of Kosovo why they, the third most numerous nationality of the Federation, should not have their own national republic, like every other major Yugoslav nationality. The whole issue has been complicated by strategic considerations, with a less than friendly Albania just over the frontier. The problem of Kosovo has remained, on both political and economic planes, one of the most intractable of post-war Yugoslav history right up to the present day.

Finally, there were the Serbian minorities within Croatia. The Habsburgs had settled Serbs along the frontier with the Turkish Empire on a 'land for military service' basis, and as of the immediate post-war period around 15 per cent of the population of the Croatian republic were Serbs, largely concentrated along the old military frontier. *Prečani* Serbs, i.e. Serbs whose ancestors had migrated from Serbia proper northwards into Habsburg lands to get away from the advancing Turks, played a prominent role in the newly independent Serbia of the nineteenth century, providing the young state with many of its administrators. During the Second World War we find Serbs from Croatia, radicalized by the excesses of the *Ustaše*, playing an outstanding role in the Partisans, and the same group remained heavily over-represented in the police during the post-war period. The Serbs from Croatia are, then, an important and influential, if not particularly numerous, group. That they were not accorded any special territorial status after the war may again reflect a concern to do as much as possible to prevent Serbia and Serbians from bulking too large on the map of post-war Yugoslavia.

The Soviet model of development

Tito and his compatriots took the USSR as their exemplar in more than just institutional terms. Stalin's Soviet Union stood as a unique embodiment of experience of socialist construction, an experience which Stalin, in his arrogation of the mantle of Marx and Lenin, had sought to raise to the level of a Marxist–Leninist classic. In particular, the practice of centralized, command planning had been developed as a socialist vehicle for the implementation of socialist developmental goals. To a degree, indeed, the interaction between planning and development strategy took on a life of its own in the Soviet case, taking the economy in directions quite unforeseen by the central planners. But let us start by trying to pin-point the factors which conditioned the initial emergence of classic, Soviet-type central planning around 1930.

It was the First Five-Year Plan, approved in 1929, which provided the initial impetus. After wide-ranging debates through the 1920s on the best possible approach to industrialization (see Gregory and Stuart 1986: ch. 4) Stalin decided to go for a high-growth, high-investment option. Because in the political conditions of the time it was not possible for the Soviet Union to borrow abroad, high investment ratios had to mean high domestic savings ratios. The first requirement of such a strategy, therefore, was a sufficiently tight degree of central control of wages to permit the imposition of an 'unnaturally' high accumulation rate. But in a predominantly rural society, such as the Soviet Union was at that time, the problem of accumulation took on a more specific form. With the great bulk of agriculture still organized in small, private peasant farms, the Soviet government had but imperfect control over the terms of trade between agriculture and the towns. The growth strategy debaters of the 1920s had clearly recognized the importance of the issue of resource flows between agriculture and industry, and Stalin followed his political opponent, Evgenii Preobrazhenskii, in considering that industrialization would be possible only on the basis of some 'pumping-over' of resources from agriculture, of some 'primitive socialist accumulation' at the expense of the peasantry.

The experience of the 1920s indicated that the price mechanism would not be powerful enough to effect this pumping-over. When the Soviet authorities tried to cut procurement prices, in order to push the terms of trade in their favour, they found themselves faced with a sharply reduced level of supply to the market, as peasants switched into auto-consumption or ancillary non-agricultural activities, hoarded grain or simply reduced sowings (Nove 1969: ch. 6). Stalin made the momentous decision at the end of 1929 to impose a system of collective farms on the peasantry, in order to make it possible for the centre to control agricultural resource flows, as they could with industry. Because the great mass of the peasantry were opposed to collectivization, it could only be implemented on the basis of generalized, often brutal coercion. Without the quasi-military principle of command, there would surely never have been a Soviet collectivization.

Stalin did not intend Soviet industrialization to be totally autarkic. The period of the early five-year plans was characterized by large-scale import of technology, involving substantial imports of equipment. But with capital imports as such ruled out, and as the collapse of world agricultural commodity markets in 1929 coupled with the disruption of collectivization curtailed the scope for earning hard currency through traditional exports, the Soviet Union would clearly only be able to maintain an investment drive if it produced a large proportion of the necessary investment goods itself. Hence Stalin's priority was to develop the machine-building industry, but to do this he had first to improve the production of steel, iron ore, and coal. Thus the heavy industrial orientation which we have come to think of as the very epitome of Stalinist development strategy is something which flowed inevitably from the combination of basic decisions on growth rates, investment ratios, etc., and the international economic environment of the time. The tense international political atmosphere of the 1930s served only to strengthen the heavy industrial orientation as a basis for building up the sinews of war.

But to turn a predominantly agrarian country into a heavy-industrial power-house in a matter of decades requires colossal and abrupt shifts in resource allocation patterns. We have seen such shifts take place in other countries without the need for five-year plans, as market demand generated a price structure which created the necessary incentives for structural change. But in the countries of the capitalist West these shifts have generally unfolded over a rather longer time period than Stalin thought was available for the Soviet Union. However effective the market mechanism as an allocator of resources, a market-based process of fundamental structural change is likely to be heavily lagged, particularly in a society where traditionalist socio-economic forms are still strong. Soviet collectivization served, *inter alia*, the purpose of destroying those traditional forms. More generally, the power of centralized command made it possible for the Soviet authorities to redirect resources to massive new developments, like the Urals–Kuzbass coal-metallurgical combine, with quite remarkable speed.

But the new Soviet industry also had to be administered from day to day, and it is on this dimension that Soviet central planning developed its most familiar characteristics. Plans were to be implemented through instructions running down from the centre to the producing enterprises, via the intermediate industrial-ministerial level. But in what terms were those instructions to be couched? The simplest way, and the way that made most sense in terms of the sectoral growth priorities of the plan as a whole, was to try, as much as possible, to give every ministry and every enterprise, even every worker, an output target.

These output targets served as the operational focus of Soviet planning for growth. As well as being relatively easy for the central planners to calculate and administer, they served admirably as a vehicle for *taut*

15

planning, whereby extreme pressure was applied to obtain maximum performance in key sectors. For enterprise managers with little economics or business training (they usually came from a straight engineering background) output targets were easy to understand. For the ordinary worker too, such targets provided a powerful basis for socializing individual efforts into the grand, aggregate output targets which made up the sectoral, and ultimately the national plan.

How do we reconcile the high-investment development strategy with the realities of a society in which capital was scarce, the more so that it could not readily be borrowed abroad, and unskilled labour abundant? The fact is that Soviet development strategy in practice showed a striking capacity to adjust to the resource endowment pattern of the time. For all the emphasis on giant 'leading projects', capital–labour ratios in Soviet industry were substantially modified through the continued use of highly labour-intensive techniques in ancillary activities, producing a very clearly delineated dual technology pattern. While the Soviet planners fully intended a massive transfer of labour from country to town, the transfer that actually took place in the 1930s grossly exceeded the plan. Thus the impressive growth achievements of the Soviet economy in the period 1928–55 present a classic example of 'extensive growth', where high rates of output growth can be imputed largely to rapid growth of inputs. Meanwhile the high level of overall centralization ensured that the system could economize on the types of skilled manpower which were, indeed, in very scarce supply, particularly managerial cadres.

While we lay particular stress on the extensive mobilization of labour resources, we can make exactly the same point in relation to natural resources. The Soviet Union, during its period of early industrialization, was able to count on abundant reserves of all the main industrial raw materials. While some deposits, like those in the Urals and the Kuzbass, required massive initial capital investments, they offered, once on stream, low and stable marginal costs of extraction. Thus the Soviet Union was able to pursue its policy of broadly-based *resource mobilization* here as elsewhere. Its unique endowment with primary resources, particularly energy resources, meant that it faced none of the Balance of Payments bottlenecks which so frequently stymie the industrialization efforts of less developed countries (Dyker 1985: ch. 1).

The split with Stalin

This, then, was the model which the Yugoslav leadership intended to follow in its attempts to industrialize and modernize their economy. It was, indeed, a model which they were determined to follow, *whether the Russians liked it or not*. For Moscow took a distinctly cool view of Tito's highly ambitious first five-year plan, viewing it at best as excessively taut, at worst as 'megalomaniac and utopian' (Hoffman and Neal 1962: 119). In negotiations to set up joint Yugoslav–Soviet companies, the Soviet side seemed primarily interested in developing primary extraction in Yugoslavia. Vladimir Dedijer, Tito's friend and biographer, credits the chief of the Soviet delegation to talks on joint industrial projects with the remark; 'What do you need heavy industry for? In the Urals we have everything you need.' (Dedijer 1953: 278).Dedijer concluded that 'the Soviet Union intended to subjugate Yugoslavia economically, to prevent Yugoslavia's industrialization and to delay the further socialist development in our country' (Dedijer 1953: 289).

We need not necessarily go all the way with Dedijer's assessment of Soviet attitudes. While the Yugoslav side complained justifiably that joint venture arrangements tended to favour the Soviet side unreasonably, the USSR and her allies did make capital transfers to Yugoslavia, in the period from 1945 up to the break, of $11.3 m. To place that in perspective, however, let us note that the Yugoslav deficit on Balance of Trade for 1947 alone was over $100m (Gnjatović 1985: 78–9). Under an agreement of 1947 the Soviet Union committed itself to lending Yugoslavia a total of $135 m for industrial development purposes (Hoffman and Neal 1962: 118). The political drama of the following year ensured that this initiative never got off the ground. Whether, under more favourable circumstances,it would have gone through according to the agreement, and how strong, accordingly, was Moscow's real initial commitment to Yugoslav industrialization, must remain an imponderable.

It is, in the light of all this, nothing short of bizarre that when Stalin excommunicated Yugoslavia from the Soviet 'commonwealth' in June 1948 the indictment centred largely on the Belgrade leadership's ideological deviations. The Yugoslav Communist Party was not a proper, Leninist vanguard party, it attached too much importance to mass organizations, i.e., in terms of Stalin's idiosyncratic dialectic, it was not democratic enough. Following on from this, the Yugoslav Communists had shown insufficient commitment to the class struggle, and in particular had failed to pursue agricultural collectivization with sufficient vigour.

It is not possible to take these charges seriously. On collectivization, for example, it is true that Tito and his compatriots had followed a cautious policy. The fact remains that, by 1948, they were further advanced with collectivization than most of the People's Democracies. On the class war issue in more general terms, the hard-boiled dictatorship surely left nothing to be desired in terms of repressive totalitarianism. So where did the roots of the disagreement lie? If we go back to 1945, we find the first major case of friction – significantly on a completely non-ideological, non-economic issue. The Yugoslav communists were

17

anxious to press the claim of their country to Trieste. Stalin did not give them full support on this, in line with his interpretation of the 'spheres of influence' deal he had done with Churchill in 1944 (see Hoffman and Neal 1962: 76–7). As a result, the Yugoslavs were forced to accept a compromise which left the actual city of Trieste to Italy. In May 1945 Tito attacked Soviet policy on this matter in a speech in Ljubljana, and the Soviet government in turn complained sharply about the Yugoslav attitude in a formal note to the Belgrade government.

Other foreign policy disagreements followed. Tito was keen to form some kind of a Balkan federation, involving Yugoslavia, Bulgaria, Albania and possibly Romania. Stalin was initially well disposed towards this idea, but by early 1948 he had changed his mind, probably because he began to see that any such federation would inevitably be dominated by the prestigious and militarily powerful Yugoslav communists. About the same time Stalin also censured Tito for his active support of the Greek communists in the Greek civil war – the Stalin–Churchill deal had, of course, left Greece as an area of predominant British influence.

It was, therefore, in the old-fashioned area of foreign policy that the Yugoslav leadership consistently upset the Russians, and this helps to explain the true nature of the Stalin–Tito split. 'The trouble was that the Yugoslav leaders were unable to see the difference between Soviet and Anglo-American foreign policy' (Hoffman and Neal 1962: 133, paraphrasing Stalin). More generally, the trouble with the Yugoslav communists, in the eyes of the Soviet dictator, was that they kept having ideas of their own, and doing things off their own bat. That was certainly not surprising, given that they had their own power base, and a large measure of popular support amongst the Yugoslav population. Going back to economic policy, we must underline again that in their attempts to begin the process of socialist construction, the Belgrade leadership seemed almost to be trying to outdo the Soviets themselves in terms of the classic characteristics of Soviet development strategy. *And when Moscow tried to moderate these policies Tito and his compatriots insisted on having their own way.* One looks in vain for the seeds of decentralization and self-management in those early post-war years. The great crime of the Yugoslavs, in Stalin's eyes, ultimately lay not in ideological deviance, but in an obstinate presistence in doing their own thing, even if that thing did, in fact, represent slavish imitation of what the Soviets had done before.

Chapter two

The Origins of Yugoslav Market Socialism

Excommunication and crisis

The initial reaction of the Yugoslav leadership to their expulsion from the Cominform was one of deep shock and disappointment. However much they may have chafed at Soviet tutelage during the period 1945–48, they had never questioned Stalin's leadership of the world communist movement. Their first instinct, when the crisis started to develop in 1948, was to try to make amends. Just as the temperature of the correspondence with Moscow was rising, the Yugoslav government rushed through further nationalization measures and a new grain tax. These measures seem clearly to have been aimed at impressing the Soviets with the Yugoslav desire to be orthodox. But the Cominform resolution of June 1948 which set the seal on Yugoslavia's excommunication dismissed these measures as being leftist and adventurist (Hoffman and Neal 1962: 135) – the Yugoslavs clearly could not win.

But they kept trying. In July 1948 we find them giving the Soviet Union 100 per cent support at the Danube River Conference. In January 1949 they applied for membership in the newly formed Comecon – the Soviet bloc's economic cooperation organization. The request was, of course, turned down (Hoffman and Neal 1962: 142). Finally, a new collectivization drive was launched in 1949 which did great damage to Yugoslav agriculture and brought the Yugoslav peasantry to the brink of insurrection.

We may search for some early indications of the momentous changes that were to follow in the Yugoslav responses to Stalin's charges. In particular, we may note that the embryo of the notion of 'different roads to socialism', of the need to adjust the Soviet model to local conditions, was present in Yugoslav thinking as early as 1948. But the notion had taken absolutely no concrete form at that time, and we can only agree with Hoffman and Neal when they declare that:

the excommunication of Yugoslavia has been compared to Martin Luther's defiance of Rome; but the analogy is faulty. Luther deliberately proclaimed himself a heretic when he nailed his theses to the cathedral door . . . The Yugoslavs, on the other hand, denied heresy; they had no desire really to challenge the authority of the Kremlin.

(Hoffman and Neal 1962: 140)

The beginnings of reappraisal

But by late 1949 things were beginning to change. Faced by these repeated rebuffs from the Soviet side, the Yugoslav leadership understandably began to wonder whether it could really be all their fault. Because they were Marxists they felt the need to systematize these thoughts, and to build an interpretation of the Stalin–Tito split which would fit with their understanding of the methodology of historical materialism. In the first instance this took the form of a critique of Stalinism in the Soviet Union.

How had Stalin gone wrong? First, most obviously and most painfully for the Yugoslav leadership, he had refused to recognize equality between socialist states, and thus implicitly the right of those states to seek their own path to socialist development. That right, Yugoslav ideologues like Milovan Djilas, Edvard Kardelj and Moše Pijade now argued, was an integral part of Leninism, and by denying it Stalin was himself guilty of revisionism. Beyond that, Stalin stood accused of hi-jacking the Soviet revolution in the interests of a 'new class' of bureaucrats, of using the principles of centralization and command to establish a dictatorship over the proletariat, rather than a dictatorship of the proletariat. There is an obvious parallel here with the kind of critical approach first developed by Trotsky in *The Revolution Betrayed*. The Yugoslav leaders themselves have, however, been anxious to reject that parallel (see Kardelj 1960: 108–9).

It is worth emphasizing that the developing Yugoslav critique of the Soviet system of 1949–52 was couched in very general, essentially political terms. Thinkers like Djilas and Kardelj were concerned with grander themes than the sorts of micro-economic deficiencies which make Soviet-type economies so weak in relation to, for example, quality control and cost efficiency. In any case, there was no basis, in the early 1950s, for laying any special stress on these weaknesses. In the course of the Fourth Five-Year Plan, 1946–50, the Soviet economy had made a spectacular recovery from the appalling destruction of the war-time period, reporting growth rates as impressive as those recorded at the height of the pre-war industrialization drive. It was not until the late 1950s, when Khrushchev, in the wake of his destalinization campaign, started to question the real content of Soviet economic performance, that the more specific, micro-economic approach came to dominate critical accounts, both Eastern and Western. Only then, or a little later, when a general downward trend in growth rates became apparent, did the issue of *economic reform* come to dominate policy discussion throughout the Comecon area. Only then, with the gradual re-emergence of a publishing economics profession in the USSR, did it become possible to mount a systematic critique of the Soviet economic system.

The reinterpretation of the Yugoslav experience of central planning

Not surprisingly, therefore, the reappraisal of the role of Soviet-type planning concentrated mainly on the Yugoslav experience. As Croatian Party leader and agricultural specialist Vladimir Bakarić so succinctly put it, in describing his own personal reappraisal:

> I have already mentioned my acceptance of Stalin's views. Not [in this case] of his theoretical ideas . . . , but of his practical assessments. If Stalin was happy with the situation [in Soviet agriculture], why not we also? For me this was just a matter of figures, but for the Soviet Union it was a matter of bread. If Stalin thought that there was enough bread, or that enough bread could be provided, there was no reason to doubt him. When I moved over onto the question of our own peasant work cooperatives, this whole line of reasoning was quickly nullified. The critique of practical experience, it has to be admitted, went faster than our theoretical critique.
>
> (Bakarić 1960: 9–10)

But it was in the realm of industry that the experience of centralization was most chastening for the Yugoslav leaders. Let us start by putting some flesh on this image of Soviet-style centralization:

> The Plan [i.e. the first five-year plan] fixed extraordinarily detailed quantitative production targets for 1951 for about 600 groups of commodities for the country as a whole and for each of the six republics. The glass industry, for example, had targets for ordinary glass, optical glass, safety glass for autos, fire-proof glass, glass containers for medical use, and glass for electric bulbs. Targets were set for the output of a wide range of consumer goods, including soap, sets of furniture, boxes of matches, pairs of stockings, pairs of shoes with leather soles, and pairs of rubber footwear for peasants. The quantity of goods and the number of passengers to be carried, in 1951, by each mode of transport were enumerated. The number of telegrams to be sent and the number of telephone calls to be placed were estimated, as were the number of restaurants, the number of meals they would serve, and the estimated number of days which the estimated number of tourists would spend

at the estimated number of hotels. For agriculture, the 1951 target for each agricultural commodity was specified, as was the number of fruit trees (divided by type: olive, plum, apple, etc.), areas of vineyards, number of each kind of livestock, amount of poultry, millions of eggs which hens would lay, milk yield per cow, kilograms of wool per sheep etc., etc.

(Waterson 1962: 10)

A number of things about this picture are immediately striking. Firstly, it reflects a strong element of institutional unreality. Let us look more closely at those agricultural targets. At the height of the Yugoslav collectivization drive, in 1950, more than 80 per cent of the agricultural land of the country remained in private hands. Certainly the private peasants were subjected to Soviet-style compulsory procurements during this period, but to call this 'planning', even in the rough and ready sense of Soviet experience, would be pure fantasy.

While it is very difficult to make direct comparisons, the impression is that the industrial planning system erected by Tito's lieutenants in the immediate post-war period may have been if anything rather more centralized than its Soviet model, at least in intention. This would fit in with the general picture of a Yugoslav leadership consistently trying to be more Soviet than the Soviets themselves. It does, however, raise some fundamental questions in relation to the mundane issue of administration of the plan. As we saw, there is a perfectly sound argument to the effect that centralization of planning in principle permits economy of scarce managerial cadres. But if taken to extremes, the principle defeats its own object. Thus:

there were over 215 federal and republican ministers issuing orders for enterprises to carry out. The Federal Planning Commission had a staff of about 700 organised into four sections, one of the largest of which was concerned with controlling the execution of the economic plans. This inspection staff operated more or less independently of the large staff on the Federal Control Commission, which also checked administrative efficiency. There were also control commissions in each of the six republics, and in each district and commune. . . The number of administrative personnel in enterprises expanded greatly. Each enterprise was required to prepare daily reports of its production, raw materials and fuel consumption, the number of workers employed etc.

(Waterson 1962: 14)

The really extraordinary thing about this pattern is the degree to which it runs counter to Yugoslav traditions of administration and attitudes to administration. Here is a new country, most of the disparate parts of which are but recently emerged from imperialist subjugation, in which the only substantial indigenous tradition of administration comes from the ruritarian authoritarianism of old Serbia. Here, the most advanced as well as the most backward regions are imbued with negative or adaptive attitudes towards central authority, attitudes which have only been strengthened by the tragedies of the country's first quarter century. Could any country have been *less* well suited, from the socio-political point of view, to a system of centralized planning?

We should not, then, be surprised at the data in Table 2.1, which show the extent to which the achievements of the period 1947–51 fell short of the targets of the five-year plan.

Table 2.1 The five-year plan for 1947–51, targets and achievements (index numbers for 1951, 1939 = 100, unless otherwise stated)

	Plan	Actual
National income	c.200	116*
Industrial production	c.500	166
Agricultural output	c.152	−34
Retail trade turnover	180	
Total investment 1947–51		
(bn dinars at 1947 prices)	278.3	229*
*Estimate		

Source: Waterston 1962: 92–5: *Jugoslavia 1945–64* 1965:83, 97 and 142

The official Yugoslav line is that this model of 'administrative planning' played its part in setting up the foundation of Yugoslav economic development, but quickly started to become obsolete as the planners sought to build on that foundation. Borivoje Jelić develops the ideas of Boris Kidrič (Kidrič 1951: 26–7), one of the fathers of Yugoslav market socialism, in the following terms:

> Thanks to this system we were able to raise the rate of accumulation to a level which would be an unattainable dream for many undeveloped countries, to channel resources into industrialization and create an initial base for industrial development, to open up a process of positive change in the demographic structure of the population and in the economic structure of a backward agrarian land. If, in this context, spectacular results were not achieved over the brief period of 4–5 years. . . , the spectacular results which were achieved in the later phase were to a great extent made possible by precisely these initial changes and results.
>
> (Jelić 1962: 120)

This is all good, orthodox Marxism – nothing is accidental in history, and quantitative change is forever laying the basis for qualitative transformation. Every period has its meaning and its role to play as a handmaiden to the succeeding period. Every phase, therefore, contains the seeds of its own destruction. Jelić goes on:

> But such a system certainly contains the roots of the development of a bureaucratic system, it carries the origins of that development within itself. The longer the system is employed, the more it tends to weaken the role of democratic institutions of management: the longer it continues to operate after its justification in terms of material and social conditions has gone, the greater the chance that the administrative-centralised system of planning and management will gradually turn into bureaucratic power. . . The result may be the creation of a bureaucratic monopoly in social relations, of obstacles to social development, stifling of initiative, and the destruction of that free creativity which is a necessary element of any progress. . . The basic problem is to use the system as long as it operates positively, and to replace it with an appropriate system once material and social conditions no longer justify its existence.
>
> (Jelić 1962: 123–4)

But for all the elegance of Jelić's argument, it comes dangerously close to a false historicism. The main legacy of the five-year plan to the succeeding period was a string of uncompleted 'priority' investment projects. Did this provide a springboard for growth in the 1950s? Well, even if it did not, and we must suspend final judgement on that matter, we cannot really blame Yugoslav central planning. Rather we should look in the first place at the effects of the Cominform economic blockade of Yugoslavia imposed in 1948, and not lifted until 1954. In addition to cutting off most of Yugoslavia's initially planned foreign trade for the five-year period and dislocating projected equipment deliveries, the blockade deprived Yugoslavia of the expected capital transfers from the Soviet Union and her allies which lay at the foundation of Yugoslavia's ambitious investment targets for 1947–51. UNRRA relief and US food aid apart, large-scale capital transfers from the West did not start until the USA, Britain and France allocated $425.8m of tripartite aid to Yugoslavia for the 1951–4 period (Gnjatović 1985: 79). Thus the massive shortfall on planned aggregate investment shown in Table 2.1 was completely unavoidable, and cannot possibly be laid at the door of ineffectual central planning. Nor, therefore, can the specific investment failures of the five-year plan period. It is simply not possible to attribute the material legacy of the immediate post-war period of development to the forms of economic administration being used at the time.

But the main weakness of Jelić's argument becomes apparent when we analyse more closely the notion that central planning was a good idea for a very limited period of time, and then had to give way, under the pressure of historical regularities, to something qualitatively quite different. If central planning could apparently produce good results in the Soviet Union for a period of some thirty years, why did it start to run out of steam in Yugoslavia after only three of four? Given that the slow-down in the Soviet case is clearly attributable to exhaustion of the sources of extensive growth, and given that those sources were still very much present in Yugoslavia in the early 1950s, particularly in the form of rural labour reserves, why should the diseconomies of central planning have come to impinge so seriously so soon? We can only agree with Deborah Milenkovitch when she argues that:

> Although something of this sort [i.e. the extensive/intense development argument] may be a plausible explanation for East Europe in the sixties, its relevance to Yugoslavia in the fifties is not immediately apparent. Certainly Yugoslavia in 1950 was a very underdeveloped country. It is not clear why Yugoslavia would have 'outgrown' the advantages of a centralized economy so early, and so much earlier than other countries at broadly similar levels of development. . . There is no denying the severe economic situation by 1952, but the nature of the disaster is not clearly related to the economic system as such and it is not immediately obvious the a change from centralization to decentralization was the answer.

> (Milenkovitch 1971: 75–6)

None of this, of course, is to argue that there were not good reasons for Yugoslavia to abandon central planning. We have already emphasized the difficulties created by the interaction between traditional Yugoslav political culture and any form of central administration. We can add a more technical economic dimension to the argument by looking at the question of Yugoslavia's economic relations with the outside world. Richly endowed with underemployed peasants and metal ores, Yugoslavia around 1950, as now, was a country poor in energy materials. It was also a small country, constrained, if only by economies of scale arguments, to trade a substantial proportion of its National Income. We have already seen, in our brief resumé of economic developments between the wars, how dominant were the currents of international trade and finance in determining the course of Yugoslav economic development. We need only add that Soviet-type planning, with its overriding emphasis on physical planning and insensitivity to price factors, has proven peculiarly unsuited to the planning of foreign trade, as any Hungarian or Polish economist will confirm.

If we take the political culture and external trade dimensions together, we surely have a sufficient basis for arguing that central planning was, indeed, unsuitable in Yugoslav conditions. But this is not a historically relativist argument. These factors are permanent features of the Yugoslav scene. Far from providing an argument for the abandonment of central planning in Yugoslavia, they presented a powerful case for not adopting central planning in the first place. There is a strong element of political apologia in treatments which contend that the transition to and from central planning in Yugoslavia was part of a law-given process. The fact is that the reappraisal was largely politically motivated. All the developments of the period 1950–3 illustrate a fundamental characteristic of the Yugoslav scene, namely the primacy of politics over economics, to which we shall return repeatedly.

Reappraisal takes wing

It is Djilas, comrade-in-arms to Tito, but soon to turn into the first great Yugoslav dissident, who claims much of the credit for formulating the idea of an alternative socialist model, based on decentralization and workers' self-management.

The idea of self-management was conceived by Kardelj and me, with some help from our comrade Kidrič. Soon after the outbreak of the quarrel with Stalin, in 1949, as far as I remember, I began to reread Marx's *Capital*, this time with much greater care, to see if I could find the answer to the riddle of why, to put it in simplistic terms, Stalinism was bad and Yugoslavia was good. I discovered many new ideas and, most interesting of all, ideas about a future society in which the immediate producers, through free association, would themselves make the decisions regarding production and distribution – would, in effect, run their own lives and their own future.

The country was in the stranglehold of the bureaucracy, and the party leaders were in the grip of rage and horror over the incorrigibly arbitrary nature of the party machine they had set up and that kept them in power. One day – it must have been in the spring of 1950 – it occurred to me that we Yugoslav Communists were now in a position to start creating Marx's free association of producers. The factories would be left in their hands, with the sole proviso that they should pay a tax for military and other state needs 'still remaining essential'. With all this, I felt a twinge or reservation: is not this a way for us Communists, I asked myself, to shift the responsibility for failures and difficulties in the economy on to the shoulders of the working class. . . ? I soon explained my idea to Kardelj and Kidrič while we sat in a car parked in front of the villa where I lived. They felt no such reservations, and I was able all too easily to convince them of the indisputable harmony between my ideas and Marx's teaching. Without leaving the car, we thrashed it out for a litttle more than half an hour. Kardelj thought it was a good idea, but one that should not be put into effect for another five or six years, and Kidrič agreed with him. A couple of days later, however, Kidrič telephoned me to say that we were ready to go ahead at once with the first steps. In his impulsive way he began to elaborate and expound on the whole conception. A little later, a meeting was held in Kardelj's cabinet office with the trade-union leaders. . . . Kardelj suggested that my proposals for management should be associated with the workers' councils, first of all in a way that would give them more rights and greater responsibilities. Debates on issues of principle and on the statutory aspects soon began, preparations that went on for some four or five months. Tito, busy with other duties and absent from Belgrade, took no part in this and knew nothing of the proposal to introduce a workers' council bill in the parliament until he was informed by Kardelj and me. . . . His first reaction was: our workers are not ready for that yet! But Kardelj and I, convinced that this was an important step, pressed him hard. . . . The most important part of our case was that this would be the beginning of democracy, something that socialism had not yet achieved; further, it could be plainly seen by the world and the international workers' movement as a radical departure from Stalinism. Tito paced up and down, as though completely wrapped in his own thoughts. Suddenly he stopped and exclaimed: 'Factories belonging to the workers – something that has never yet been achieved!' With these words the theories worked out by Kardelj and myself seemed to shed their complications, and seemed, too, to find better prospects of being workable. A few months later, Tito explained the Workers' Self-Management Bill to the National Assembly.

(Djilas 1969: 157–8)

But if it was Djilas and Kardelj who first spelled out the political bases of a self-managing society, it was Kidrič, the then chief of the planning commission, who first developed a model of operational decentralized socialism. The most important features of his model can be defined in terms of two key principles – 'socialist commodity production' and the 'average rate of accumulation and funds' *(prosečna stopa akumulacije i fondova)*. The first of these is largely self-explanatory. The output target, the fundamental nexus of plan implementation in a Soviet-type system, should give way once again to the market principle as far as day-to-day production decisions were concerned. Thus the pattern of assortment of output of each enterprise should be determined on the basis of market demand, subject to a centrally determined minimal capacity utilization level. The latter constraint was clearly conceived as a 'slack' target, in contrast to the typically 'taut' targets generated by the Soviet system, which would ensure that the economy as a whole kept to a given, minimal growth trend.

The average rate of accumulation and funds is a more complex concept. Its essence and purpose is clear enough, viz.– 'nothing other than the basic allocation of National Income between consumption. . . , expanded reproduction [i.e. investment] and various social funds' (Kidrič 1951: 14–19). What this meant at the enterprise level was that the centre should determine a normed level of wages fund, sufficient to produce at the planned minimum capacity level, and an average ratio of expenditure on investment and collective consumption, i.e. of 'accumulation and funds' to the wages fund. This formula in turn produced a basic formula for price-fixing, a formula which was intended, however, to leave maximum freedom to the planners in individual cases. The gross income which these arrangements left to the enterprise would then be taxed, not on the basis of universal bands, but rather through specific rates of accumulation and funds determined individually for each enterprise, though stable over time. The general principle here was that the net income ultimately left at the disposal of each enterprise for purposes of incentive payments, enterprise-level investment, etc., should be as far as possible equalized.

There were a number of inherent weaknesses in Kidrič's scheme (see Milenkovitch 1971: 87–9). Most importantly, his fiscal proposals were effectively impossible to administer, as the Yugoslav planners quickly discovered when they tried to use them as a basis for the 1952 plan:

> The results were absurd and. . . arbitrary . . . No account was taken of the capital cooperating with labour in different enterprises; on the contrary, often very capital intensive branches were charged lower rates of accumulation because much of the new investment yielded very low returns on capital or even losses. The first set of rates in the 1952 plan, for instance, charged an accumulation rate of 110 per cent on agricultural machinery production, 3,200 per cent on the production of ordinary nails at Jesenice, and about 700 per cent on nail production elsewhere. For this reason the results of enterprises depended largely on whether they had to pay high or low accumulation rates, and most enterprises kept asking for lower rates.
>
> (Sirc 1979: 18)

But Kidrič's specific fiscal devices were soon overtaken by events as the impetus of reform gathered pace through 1952 and 1953. More generally,

> although Kidrič's scheme was a major break with the Marxist heritage and the past practice, and although he envisioned expanding the role of the market, he remained basically a *central* planner . . . He emphasized the transitory character of commodity production in socialism and recognized only limited freedom for the enterprise. He

objected to proposals to extend the market and to increase the independence of the firm.

(Milenkovitch 1971: 89)

But we should not thereby underestimate the ongoing importance of Kidrič's ideas in the evolution of the Yugoslav system. His rather cumbersome system of norms and taxes for the enterprise were basically calculated to ensure that the centre would retain direct control over the investment profile of the economy as a whole.

> Influence over the structure of new investment determines relations between production capacities, and by virtue of that makes it possible to influence directions of development and the future structure of the economy. Thus influence on the structure of investment is *one of the basic characteristics of a planned economy and one of its most powerful instruments* (emphasis added)

(Jelić 1962: 146)

That principle would remain paramount in Yugoslav planning practice for many years after Kidrič's death in 1953.

We saw that Kidrič was among the foremost of those who sought historicist rationalization of the period of central planning in Yugoslavia. Strikingly, he interpreted the reestablishment of commodity relations in the same way. While the state ownership of the means of production of the stage of administrative planning represented and advance on the private ownership of capitalism, the socialized ownership of socialist commodity production meant further progress in terms of the methodology of historical materialism. But socialist commodity production could not, Kidrič argued, form any direct basis for transition to the ultimate stage of 'full communism', characterized by liberation from scarcity and the withering-away of the state. Even within the strictly socialist stage of development, itself a transitional phase, then, Kidrič's market socialism would only be a sub-phase. The subsequent development of Yugoslav thought and practice to a great extent abandoned the traditional Marxian periodization of 'progress', and by the middle 1950s the package of self-management and market mechanism was firmly established as defining the Yugoslav system for the foreseeable future. But the historical relativism and political voluntarism which come through so strongly in the work of Boris Kidrič, technocrat though he was, echo one of the most fundamental and persistent leitmotifs of post-war Yugoslav development.

The institutionalization of market socialism with global planning

The law establishing workers' councils was passed on July 2, 1950.

Substantial measures of operational decentralization 1952–3 re-established a considerable degree of enterprise autonomy and reinstated the market as the principal nexus of economic activity. But by 1954–5 the authorities, fearing a loss of macro-economic control and worried about inflationary trends, had clawed back some of the powers they had earlier given up. Let us now glance at the profile of the new economic system as it looked by the time it had settled down in the middle 1950s. Taking as a starting point the re-establishment of the market mechanism, what instruments of control did the central authorities retain in their own hands, which did they delegate to republican and local governments, and how much power was effectively invested in the workers' councils at enterprise level? Let us start by looking at the federal government.

The Planning Commission, transformed into a *Federal Planning Institute*, continued to elaborate plans, initially just on an annual basis. They produced projections of the breakdown of National Income into consumption, savings/investment, collective consumption, etc., parallel estimates for output, by main sector and for aggregate production of consumer goods, capital goods, construction output, etc., plus a corresponding breakdown of aggregate investment. Kidrič's minimum capacity utilization requirement, which had been in force in 1952–3, at least in principle, was dropped. While production targets were worked out for some specific commodities, they were not made obligatory. This, then, was the general framework of 'planning by global proportions'.

But it was no system of pure indicative planning, no mere exercise in 'generalized market research'. On the contrary, the purpose of the plan was to map out the broad implications of strategic goals on growth rates, Balance of Trade, etc., so as to provide a basis for the implementation of those goals. Perhaps the most important specific instrument, as in most market economies, was *fiscal policy*.

The fussy and unmanageable proposals of Kidrič for enterprise taxation were quickly abandoned, and by the end of 1953 Yugoslav enterprises were facing a fairly familiar fiscal regime. The old wages fund tax was abolished and replaced by taxes on enterprise income, defined net of wage payments (*dobit*), and a sales tax. In addition, enterprises would have to pay a fixed rate of interest on their capital assets, plus any interest due with respect to borrowing for investment in fixed or working capital. Finally, rental payments were charged to organizations benefiting from unique natural advantages or endowments.

But these provisions soon came under pressure as workers' councils took advantage of the scope for raising wages, irrespective of trends in productivity. Early attempts to introduce penalty tax rates for excessive wage increases were largely ineffectual, and in 1957 the whole system was revamped. The most important change of principle was in the accounting base of the system. The old category of *dobit*, not very different from the capitalist concept of profit, was dropped. From now on enterprise taxation would be based on the concept of *dohodak*, or net income, which netted out costs of material inputs, etc., but not wage payments. This effectively meant that 'profits' tax now taxed wages as well as profits. The enterprise was constrained to place specific tranches of after-tax net income into enterprise funds for wages, investment, housing, etc. – no more than 50 per cent was to go to the wages fund. In the following year the restrictions on the allocation of net income were abolished. At the same time, however, the authorities introduced a progressive tax on distributions (Hoffman and Neal 1962: 255–6; Milenkovitch 1971: 105–6).

Of course none of these modifications represented any kind of return to the micro-economic pretensions of Kidrič's fiscal system. They were essentially pragmatic measures aimed at keeping control over the general macro-economic situation and strengthening the link between productivity and wages. Nor was this the last time that the Yugoslav authorities would address themselves to those problems. Through all the changes of the 1950s one factor remained constant – the very high proportion of Yugoslav National Income accounted for by enterprise taxation. In 1959 this proportion stood at around 33 per cent (Fleming and Sertić 1962: 213, quoted in Milenkovitch 1971: 105).

Monetary policy

During the period of central planning in Yugoslavia the banking system performed a basically passive, accounting role for socialist-sector organizations, as in the classical Soviet system. Only enterprises were allowed to have bank accounts, and all dealings between the private sector and the socialist sector were in cash. The same went for intra-private sector transactions, including those between private consumers and private peasants. Irregularities in consumer goods supply from the state sector and seasonality on agricultural produce markets meant that the demand for cash was a volatile element. The cash plan, through which the authorities sought to control the amount of currency in circulation, was the key element in monetary policy. In its relations with state enterprises the National Bank performed the role of commercial as well as central bank, keeping the bulk of short-term lending under its direct control (Dimitrijević and Macesich 1973: 14–17).

At the beginning of the period of initial decentralization the Yugoslav authorities did, in fact, pursue a policy of further centralization of the banking system, and by 1954 the National Bank was the only bank in existence. The trend was reversed in 1955, however, with the creation of a specialized Foreign Trade Bank and a network of local banks. This was followed by the creation of Investment and Agricultural Banks. One of the most striking characteristics of the banking system as it developed through the 1950s was its markedly regional character. All the new banks created except for explicitly federal ones operated exclusively in the territory of its founding authority (Dimitrijević and Macesich 1973: 25–8).

The period 1953–4 marked a fundamental change in the Yugoslav financial system in that monetary policy now took on a much more active character for the socialist sector. The dichotomy between monetary policy for private and socialist sectors did, however, persist to the extent that enterprise money continued to be heavily 'earmarked' in the sense that particular monies had to be kept in specific funds – a current account, an investment account, etc., and could not be transferred between accounts. Thus

> the role of money was fundamentally changed and became very similar to that in a market economy, although earmarking diluted the 'moneyness' of the money supply and made the effects of its changes erratic and variable.
>
> (Dimitrijević and Macesich 1973: 32)

But if funds were to be earmarked at enterprise level, they also had to be earmarked at the level of the National Bank.

> The credit system in this period. . . was based on the selective credit regulation. This was different from the usual system of quantitative regulation of the supply of credits in a market economy, *and many components of it originated in the system of credit planning in the period of central planning* [emphasis added] . . . No general-purpose credit existed. Each credit was granted for a specific purpose . . .
>
> (Dimitrijević and Macesich 1973: 32–3)

Thus in an area of economic policy-making which we tend to think of as *ipso facto* aggregate, macro-economic in character, we find, in the Yugoslav case, a very powerful element of micro-economic selectivity, an element which was bound to make credit regulation a much more complex and uncertain business than it would otherwise have been. The selective principle, and all that it implies, has, indeed, remained one of the outstanding features of the Yugoslav monetary system up to the present day.

Prices

It was not the intention of the founding fathers of Yugoslav market socialism to use price control as a major policy instrument. But as we saw, the establishment of the workers' council system produced predictable inflationary pressures which the existing array of controls seemed in danger of failing to contain. Parallel, then, with the restrictive tax dispositions discussed earlier, the authorities started in 1954 to introduce price ceilings for basic materials. By 1955 half the total value of industrial raw materials and semi-finisheds came under this regime (Montias 1959: quoted in Milenkovitch 1971: 108). Subsequently a Federal Price Office (*ured za cene*) was created. Under the Price Office regime, any price increase for the great majority of product groups had to be reported and sanctioned. While the Price Office did not wield price-fixing powers as such, it could propose emergency action to control specific elements of price pressure – but with the final decision lying with the government. This approach was further systematized in 1958, when a law was passed which forbade enterprises to use money coming from price increases deemed by the Price Office to be unjustified to increase wages. But they could keep the money if they used it for investment purposes (Hoffman and Neal 1962: 253–4). Thus the authorities sought, through price controls, to strengthen the disincentive to distributions already incorporated into the fiscal system in 1957.

The general trend throughout the period 1954–65 was for the extent of price control to expand steadily, though certainly not systematically. By the early 1960s the prices of nearly all commodities were subject to some kind of price control. And while public justification for price control was often couched in terms of control of monpolistic tendencies, the reality was much more of pragmatic response to macro-economic pressures. It is odd that in this archetypal market socialist economy monetary policy – perhaps the most obvious macro-economic instrument – was used so much for micro-economic policy purposes, while prices, which form the basis for resource allocation in most theoretical models of market socialism, seemed almost to be diverted from their true purpose by macro-economic weaknesses elsewhere in the system – but of this more in the next chapter.

Investment finance

We saw that the fiscal arrangements of the 1950s were calculated, among other things, to transfer a very large proportion of enterprise net income to the state. Substantial budgetary revenues were, of course, spent on defence and communal consumption, but in 1954 fixed capital investment absorbed some 45 per cent of total budgetary income. Compulsory depreciation provisions were also used as a major vehicle for the diversion of enterprise resources to central investment priorities (Sirc 1979: 31). State investment finance in 1954 accounted for nearly 75 per cent of total investment, and federal funds alone for over 50 per cent (Cobeljić 1959: 144; Hoffman and Neal 1962: 250). The main channel for federal investment finance was the *General Investment Fund*. Inherited from the period of central planning, the fund was, from the mid-1950s, administered by the Investment Bank.

Between 1954 and 1957 a substantial proportion of state investment finance in Yugoslavia was in principle allocated on the basis of *investment auctions*, whereby funds were allocated to the enterprises offering the highest rate of interest. This reflected a desire on the part of at least some Yugoslav policy-makers to combine the institutions of state socialism in the investment field with parametric planning instruments. In reality, the allocation of funds was influenced by a variety of factors – strategic development goals, regional development considerations, etc. – not to mention pure political horse-trading. This reality was to a degree recognized and institutionalized in 1957, with the abandonment of the investment auctions and the pretence of 'neutrality' in the investment finance system.

But while the impetus towards the development of market-based allocation criteria fizzled out in the late 1950s, there was at the same time a definite trend towards reduction in the share of the central authorities in total investment finance. Thus by 1957 the Federation was accounting for less than 35 per cent of the total, compared to over 50 per cent in 1954 (Hoffman and Neal 1962: 250). We should not exaggerate the importance of this trend. The Investment Bank's practice of requiring substantial obligatory levels of borrower participation in the financing of projects supported by the General Investment Fund made it possible for the bank to 'spread' its effective control over a very wide area of the investment front. Around 1960 the bank probably had effective control over two-thirds to four-fifths of the total volume of fixed capital formation being implemented in Yugoslavia (Waterston 1962: 78). In any case, the shift in the formal share of the central authorities in investment finance had little impact on the amount of investment funds staying at the enterprise level. It was, in fact, principally the local governmental (commune) level which benefited. This change parallels the increasing regionalization of the banking system in the 1950s.

Foreign trade

During the period of administrative planning foreign trade was conducted on classical Soviet lines. Decisions on what to import and export were taken on the basis of development priorities and the availability of goods considered surplus to those priorities. All of this went on without reference to a domestic price system that was in any case arbitrary in the extreme. To keep enterprises' books right, any differential between the foreign and domestic prices of goods exported and imported was automatically received from or paid into a Equalization Fund (*Egalizacioni Fond*).

From 1952 the price mechanism began to be reintroduced into the foreign trade system. The basis for the new arrangements was a rate of exchange of 300 dinars to the dollar. (The old rate, which had, of course, played no active role under central planning, was 50 dinars to the dollar.) Enterprises were now permitted to make exporting and importing decisions freely on the basis of this exchange rate, tempered as it was by a complex system of 'coefficients'. This effectively amounted to a system of multiple exchange rates. Administrative elements in the system included the limited use of import and export quotas, and even outright bans. The exporter was initially compelled to sell 55 per cent of his foreign exchange earnings to the National Bank at the official rate, but this proportion was progressively raised until it reached 100 per cent in 1955. By the middle 1950s, then, the amount and composition of imports was again largely under the direct control of the central authorities.

The trend back towards a more *dirigiste* system was also evident at the purely organizational level. Initially all enterprises had been allowed to participate in foreign trade, but in 1955 the authorities moved to create a much more selective structure. A Chamber (*komora*) of Foreign Trade was created, with the remit of regulating and overseeing external trade activity. From now on exporting would be restricted to enterprises named on a foreign trade register maintained by the Chamber (Hoffman and Neal 1962: 259). This legislation effectively created a privileged elite amongst Yugoslav enterprises, and a fruitful source of tension within the body politico-economic of Yugoslavia in the years to follow.

Republican and local governments

As we saw, the new Yugoslavia adopted a federal structure right from the start, though there was little genuinely federal content in the 'brotherhood and unity' policy of the hard-boiled dictatorship. Once decentralization had got under way in the early 1950s, on the other hand, it inevitably involved regional political authorities as well as production units. At this stage, however, the policy was to emphasize the local commune level rather more than the republican level. Possibly viewed as being potentially less divisive in ethnic terms than the republic, the commune, average population less than 20,000 in 1958, was also seen as a major vehicle for the development of self-management, of direct democracy at the community, as distinct from the production unit level.

Between 1954 and 1957 the share of the republics in total state investment finance fell from 12 per cent to 7.7 per cent, while that of local governments increased from 11.5 to 20.8 per cent (Hoffman and Neal 1962: 250). The finance for this, and for other commune activities, came in the first place from a predetermined share of federal profits and wages taxation. In addition, the communes were allowed, within limits, to levy extra taxes on their own initiative. The trend throughout the 1950s was for the fiscal power of the communes to increase, and a law of 1959 institutionalized a substantial degree of financial autonomy for local governments.

Communes were also entrusted with a number of key roles in relation to enterprises situated on their territory. They were empowered to set up new plants, and to suspend, temporarily, self-management in problematic enterprises. In addition, the commune was always represented on the commission choosing a new director for an enterprise within its jurisdiction.

Socio-political and conveyer-belt bodies

Chief among these was, of course, the League of Communists. The change in title from Party to League in 1952 was intended to symbolize the abandonment of the Leninist concept of leading role, the final debolshevization of the Yugoslav Communist Party. Indeed the rapid shift in the direction of market socialism meant that the Communist Party *had* to change its approach, whether it found that congenial or not. In a Soviet-type economy the leading role comes down in practice to the trouble-shooting function. Party apparatus professionals in the Soviet Union provide much of the lubrication which keeps the wheels of the centrally planned system turning, using their political skill and influence to sort out supply problems as the arise, hauling laggard enterprises over the coals, etc. In other words, the Soviet apparatus man operates as a substitute – of varying effectiveness – for the market. Once the Yugoslav leadership had decided to reintroduce the market mechanism that role was bound to become redundant.

The process of debolshevization, certainly, was not a smooth one. Ordinary communists found it difficult to adjust to the new 'educational' role of the party. Djilas was by the end of 1954 calling for the formation of a second 'loyal opposition' socialist party. He was imprisoned for his pains, and the affair deepened the demoralization that was already creeping into party ranks. Tito responded to this crisis of spirit by calling, in the spring of 1956, for a renewed activization of the role of the League of Communists. The following two years witnessed a movement back to Leninist principles, with the reformation of professional party groups throughout industry and government departments. Inevitably, however, these groups started to interfere directly in business matters in a way that was simply incompatible with the new system. By 1958 they also stood accused of using their power as a basis for exacting material privileges from the system – in just the way that one would expect from a 'new class'. It did not come as a surprise, then, when a Circular Letter from the Executive Committee of the League of Communists of February 1958 issued a sharp condemnation of these tendencies, and reaffirmed that the role of rank and file communist should from now on be an essentially educational one (Hoffman and Neal 1962: 176–203). While exactly what that should mean in practice has remained a problem in Yugoslav politics to the present day, there would be no more reversions to classical Leninism.

But this was no self-denying ordinance on the part of Tito and his associates. The changes, momentous though they were, left the position of the party leadership virtually untouched. The one-party system remained totally sacrosanct. The apex of the party, originally simply the partisan leadership from the time of the war, developed into a self-perpetuating oligarchy on precisely the Soviet pattern, a pattern that would not be disturbed by subsequent changes in the balance between federal, republican and local levels of government. Through mass organizations like the Socialist League of Working People and the Trade Unions, the League of Communists would ensure that grass-roots democracy in Yugoslavia should remain very much a guided democracy. While candidates for workers' councils, local people's committees, etc. would not have to be communists, they would have to be vetted by the League of Communists. The League saw to it that anyone who had been on the 'wrong' side during the war, who was actively involved in organized religion, or who was suspected of oppositionism as defined by the League, was excluded from public life.

But if the party apparatus could not play its traditionally Soviet trouble-shooting role in the economy, then who would have the remit of ensuring that market socialism did not develop to the detriment of the 'public interest'? At the level of strategic decision-taking the answer is obvious enough – the party leadership, as before. But the leadership needed some kind of transmission belt which was attuned to the style of a market economy. As worries about unruly workers' councils and inflationary pressures built up in 1953 and early 1954, the authorities decided to create an *Industrial Chamber (privredna komora)*. The role of the Industrial Chamber was envisaged in terms of a two-way transmission belt – it would apply pressure on enterprises to get into line with government economic policies, but would at the same time seek to represent the 'industry interest' at the governmental level. The formal powers of the Chamber were limited, though they included representation on appointing commissions for directorships of enterprises. But in 1958 membership of the Industrial Chamber was made obligatory for all enterprises, and as the decade progressed the Chamber took on an increasingly regulatory role, like its sister organization, the Foreign Trade Chamber.

Giving . . . the chambers a 'social character' – that is, making them representative not only of enterprises but also of government and assigning them regulatory powers is illustrative of the Yugoslav concept of having what would otherwise be governmental functions performed outside the formal framework of government. Thus it would be possible to cite the new position of the chambers as a continuation of decentralization, while, in fact, insofar as it further delimited the power of individual workers' councils, it was really a form of greater centralization.

(Hoffman and Neal 1962: 244)

The enterprise and the workers' council

The picture we have drawn of the instruments of planning and state intervention gives in turn, by elimination, a fairly clear profile of the range of enterprise autonomy. We have pin-pointed a rather high incidence of central control over basic financial parameters – prices, tax rates, rates of investment – and this incidence grew as the 1950s progressed. The really fundamental change of c.1953 was the re-establishment of *basic freedom of contract*, with the abolition of output targets. Through all the subsequent ups and downs of Yugoslav market socialism that was one feature which would never be seriously called into question. Thus however hemmed in by financial parameters Yugoslav management was in the 1950s, it knew that it had to make its own deals.

But what do we mean by Yugoslav management? Do we mean directors, workers' councils, or both? The law of 1950 on self-management established that all enterprises should elect a workers' council (*radnički savjet*) of 15 to 200 members, depending on the size of the workforce. In small plants with fewer than 30 workers the entire workforce should sit on the council, while all enterprises should hold occasional mass meetings of the whole working collective to discuss the work of the workers' council. Subordinate workers' councils were subsequently introduced at shop and plant level for large, multi-division enterprises.

The legislation of 1950 never intended to give the workers' councils an active role in day-to-day management. They were given the right, subject to the constraints of the environment, to decide on basic strategic issues, like the balance between distributions and plough-backs, the direction of new investment, etc. But executive managerial authority was to be wielded, in the first instance, by the director (an ex-officio member of the workers' council) and his professional managerial team, under the supervision of a *management board (upravni odbor)*, elected, in turn, by the workers' council.

Exactly how this configuration worked out in practice is something we must leave for the next chapter. But it is worth pointing to a few key features at this stage. Firstly, let us remember that directors were not chosen by the workers' council, but by a commission made up of representatives from the council, the trade union organization, from the commune, and after 1954 the Industrial Chamber also. Initially the right of the workers' council to dismiss the director was untrammelled, but after a rash of sackings in the early years of the system an arrangement was introduced which imposed the same checks and balances on the process of dismissal as on that of appointment, with commune and Industrial Chamber again playing a key role. Thus the system was not conceived as a system of direct democracy as such, and its evolution through the 1950s tended to strengthen the position of the director, and of the sitting members of the organs of self-management. In 1958 the term of office for members of workers' councils and management committees was increased from one to two years.

We can see from the foregoing that the workers' council system, as it operated in the 1950s, was certainly not a sham. Within the constraints of the limited freedom of operation conceded to the enterprise, the workers' council was able to exert significant pressure on the general economic environment – significant enough to compel the government to take measures specifically aimed at curbing cost-inflationary pressures. At the intra-enterprise level, we again find the authorities taking steps, at an early stage, to redress somewhat the balance of power between self-management organs and professional management in favour of the latter. Whatever its true content in terms of participatory democracy, self-management was certainly a good deal more than just window-dressing.

The reform in agriculture

As we saw in Chapter 1, the break with the Soviet Union had initially sparked off renewed attempts by the Yugoslav communists to impose a Soviet-style collectivization in agriculture, and comprehensive reappraisal of the whole approach to the countryside came a good deal later than it had with respect to industry. It was not until March 1953 that the abandonment of collectivization was officially announced. Of course the collectivization campaign had never got very far in Yugoslavia, but there was a good deal of brutality in its later stages, and this inflicted lasting damage on the psyche of the Yugoslav peasantry, leaving them insecure and distrustful. Nevertheless the recognition, increasingly explicit through 1953–4, that private peasant agriculture would remain the predominant form within the sector was of epoch-making importance.

But the authorities did not simply abandon agricultural policy-making in 1953. On the contrary, they sought, from the beginning, to ensure that the private agricultural sector would fit in with *their* plans for the overall development of Yugoslav economy and society. First of all, in

May 1953, a law was promulgated which laid down one last redistribution of agricultural land. The new redistribution was highly egalitarian, specifying a maximum individual holding of 10 hectares, a limit which stayed in force until 1988.

The motivation behind this last of the classic land reforms in Yugoslavia may have been a mixture of the socio-economic and the political. Nothing much had happened on the urban/industrial development front 1945–53 to provide a safety-valve for rural overpopulation, and the mass exodus of Yugoslavs to find work abroad was still in the future. As the peasants left the collective farms, taking their own land with them, a genuine problem arose of what to do about the formerly landless or near-landless peasants who were now again threatened with indigence. The land reform of 1953 did ensure that the great majority of individual peasants had a minimally adequate subsistence basis, and that the surviving collective farms would also have operational holdings. Nevertheless the quantitative impact of the reform was marginal. As little as 3.7 per cent of total arable land was redistributed, and very little land was transferred from private to collective sector (Hoffman and Neal 1962: 276–7). The fact is that the average holding in Yugoslavia was already so small that the most egalitarian measures could have little further impact.

But there was also a somewhat ambivalent political side to the 1953 agricultural reform. Tito may not have followed Stalin all the way in using the kulak ('fist' – rich peasant) myth as an excuse for a military assault on the countryside, but he was anxious to make it clear to the Yugoslav peasantry that the development of capitalist agriculture would not be permitted. And while that might seem like a fair setting-out of the 'rules of the game' as they would operate under the planning by global proportions system, the impact on the minds of the peasantry, already scarred by the experience of collectivization *manqué*, was rather different. They tended to see the 1953 measures, not as the final act in a historic land reform process, but as an expression of arbitrary power, with the implicit threat that that power might be exercised again. The scenario of yet another redistribution might seem a rather unreal one, since there was so little left to redistribute, but the feeling of helpless insecurity on the part of the peasantry was exacerbated by other policy measures.

Certainly rates of tax on farm income were progressively reduced from 1954. Perhaps more important, that year saw the introduction of a cadastral system of assessing farm income. Thus farmers would now be taxed on the basis of what they *ought* to manage to produce on their land, rather than what they actually produced. This created an incentive for the efficient peasant and a threat to the inefficient. But systematic tax discrimination against the peasantry was not removed, and to that extent the ghost of 'primitive socialist accumulation' at the expense of the countryside was never laid. In 1958 the private peasantry was paying a total of 50.3bn dinars in income tax and communal tax, amounting to 11 per cent of total income, as compared to 28.2bn dinars in 1955 (Hoffman and Neal 1962: 290).

The picture is thrown into sharper relief when we look at prices. There was a definite improvement in agricultural procurement prices from the very low level of the early 1950s, with the average index increasing from 122 in 1953 to 196 in 1961 (*Jugoslavija 1945–64*, 1965: 231). But the state maintained direct control over a number of key agricultural prices, and the *General Agricultural Cooperatives*, which were set up as a link between the socialized sector and private agriculture, were given a monopoly of grain procurement, and therefore effective control over the price of grain.

The peasants were also faced with serious constraints with respect to the purchase of equipment. They were not allowed to buy new tractors or other large pieces of machinery, nor could they procure credits directly from the banking system. That did not mean that they could not obtain these things – rather the system was set up so that they could only obtain them through the General Agricultural Cooperatives. In this way, the authorities hoped to use the Cooperatives as a bridgehead of socialism in the countryside, a basis for developing an integrated association of socialized and private sectors, but with the socialized sector in the leading role. The peasantry also found themselves in reluctant tutelage to the commune, which was given the right to prescribe land improvement and maintenance provisions for private agriculture within their jurisdiction, with the ultimate sanction, in case of non-compliance, of confiscation of land.

None of this is to deny that the state of private agriculture improved greatly in Yugoslavia during the 1950s. Average cash income doubled in real terms over the decade, as did aggregate agricultural output, and the contrast with the corresponding period of Soviet development, when output stagnated and peasants starved to death, could not be more total. But Yugoslav peasants did find themselves condemned to second-class citizen status in economic terms, and this status was reflected also in the political sphere. Under the 1953 constitution private peasants not actively cooperating with the cooperative sector went unrepresented in the lower house of the *Skupština* (Parliament), the Council of Producers. In practice the great majority of the peasantry sought to minimize their contacts with the General Agricultural Cooperatives, preferring to maximize their independence, even at the price of intensifying the discrimination they suffered.

Chapter three

The Great Leap Forward: Industrialization and Extensive Development 1953–65

The pattern of development under planning by global proportions

Table 3.1 highlights the remarkable growth achievement of the Yugoslav economy in the 1950s and early 1960s. Between 1953 and 1961 National Income nearly doubled, and industrial output rose by more than two-and-a-half times. Agriculture fell away rather after the bumper year of 1959, but was certainly firmly established on a new plateau by the early 1960s. Yugoslavia's growth record for the 1950s was, indeed, one of the most impressive in the world for that period.

What were the sources of that growth? Let us start by looking at *investment trends*. Table 3.2 shows how the ratio of gross fixed investment to National Income was maintained at a remarkably high level throughout the 1950s – bearing in mind the low level of National Income per capita at the time, and the heavy burden of defence expenditure in a period when relations with the Soviet bloc were still tense. It then rose even further to over 30 per cent in the early 1960s. To put this into perspective, the gross investment ratio has rarely risen above 20 per cent in post-war Britain, while in high-growth West Germany it averaged just over 25 per cent 1965–75 (Dyker 1983: 186).

Dragana Gnjatović has highlighted the tremendous importance of foreign capital in financing this unusually high rate of fixed capital formation. She identifies aggregate capital import with the Balance of Trade on goods and services, not including remittances from Yugoslavs working abroad (i.e. those remittances are counted as foreign rather than domestic savings). She then derives a series for domestic saving by subtracting the capital import figures from the gross investment figures. We have to exercise a little care in interpreting these series. They should not be taken to imply that without capital import the level of fixed capital formation in Yugoslavia would have been lower by exactly the amount of the capital actually imported. In practice, had foreign capital not been available, a domestic belt-tightening exercise might well have raised the domestic savings ratio and maintained the investment

Table 3.1 Yugoslav rates of growth 1948–64 (based on data in constant prices of 1960)

	National Income	Industrial Output	Agricultural Output
1948	20.2	23.9	16.2
1949	8.4	10.5	2.6
1950	−10.3	0.6	−35.6
1951	9.5	−1.3	45.2
1952	−15.8	−0.9	−50.0
1953	17.9	9.4	44.8
1954	3.8	14.6	−14.9
1955	13.9	14.0	23.7
1956	−4.2	9.6	−24.2
1957	22.8	17.2	44.1
1958	3.0	11.9	−13.3
1959	16.5	11.7	31.2
1960	6.3	13.8	−12.8
1961	5.5	6.9	−2.0
1962	4.2	7.2	0.5
1963	12.2	15.6	6.7
1964	13.0	16.2	7.4
1948–52	2.3	6.2	−3.3
1953–6	7.5	11.9	5.8
1957–61	10.6	12.3	7.7
1962–4	9.8	13.0	4.9

Note: National Income, Yugoslav definition, is, more or less, NNP minus 'unproductive services'. The industrial and agricultural output series in the table are also calculated on the basis of the National Income methodology.
Source: *Jugoslavija 1945–1964* 1965: 80

ratio at something nearer its actual level in the presence of capital imports. Thus Gnjatović's figures do not prove that the Yugoslav investment effort of the 1950s and early 1960s would have been impossible without capital import. But they do show in a very striking way what the implications for the balance of savings and consumption would have been, had foreign capital not been available.

Labour supply

Despite the terrible losses of the war-time period, the total population of Yugoslavia in 1953 was 3 million greater than it had been in 1931. Between those two census years the agricultural population had fallen, in relative terms, from 77 per cent to 61 per cent of the total population, but had hardly fallen at all in absolute numbers (Hoffman and Neal 1962: 324). A study done by the Economics Institute of Serbia around this time estimated that on average, in Serbia proper, there was only 151 days' work per annum for each able-bodied peasant. That meant that of 2.3m active rural dwellers 1m could have been taken away without affecting

Table 3.2 The contribution of imported capital to Yugoslav economic development 1948–64 (in percentages, calculated on the basis of data in constant prices of 1966)

	Ratio of gross fixed investment to Gross Social Product	Ratio of capital import to Gross Social Product	Ratio of capital import to gross fixed investment	Ratio of domestic savings to Gross Social Product
1948	26.4	4.1	15.6	22.2
1949	27.2	14.3	52.8	12.8
1950	26.3	19.1	78.7	7.2
1951	24.1	29.9	124.3	−5.8
1952	26.3	14.3	45.3	12.0
1953	26.8	26.5	98.6	0.4
1954	28.3	9.5	33.7	18.5
1955	24.0	7.7	32.3	16.2
1956	25.1	5.3	21.0	19.8
1957	24.3	7.1	29.2	17.2
1958	27.3	6.2	22.9	21.1
1959	26.7	5.6	21.1	21.1
1960	30.1	5.9	19.6	24.2
1961	31.7	6.8	21.5	24.8
1962	32.3	5.8	17.8	26.6
1963	31.3	5.6	17.8	25.7
1964	32.1	5.4	16.9	26.7
1948–52	26.0	16.5	63.5	9.5
1953–60	26.7	8.5	31.9	18.2
1961–4	31.9	5.9	18.4	26.0
1953–64	29.0	7.4	25.4	21.6

Note: Gross Social Product is, approximately, GNP, minus 'unproductive services'.
Source: Gnjatović 1985: 48.

production (Mihailović 1977: 107). Thus as of the early 1950s the agricultural over-population problem inherited from the pre-war period had hardly been touched. This reflected the failure of the first five-year plan to absorb significant volumes of labour into new, urban-based activities, as the agricultural population fell by less than 300,000 between 1948 and 1953 (*Jugoslavija 1945–1964* 1965: 46). That in turn reflected not only the modest growth achievements of the period of administrative planning, but also the heavily capital-intensive profile of the investment programme of the five-year plan.

The pattern during the 1950s was quite different. Between 1953 and 1961 the total agricultural population fell by over 1.1m, and the active agricultural population by 670,000. Over the same period the active population in mining, industry and construction increased from 830,000 to 1.46m. The active population in industry taken by itself almost doubled, from 513,000 to 993,000 (*Jugoslavia 1945–1964* 1965: 46). Thus the decade of the 1950s in Yugoslavia appears, *prima facie*, to present a classic example of *extensive development*, with high rates of growth of National Income deriving mainly from a powerful dynamic in industrial and related sectors, and that dynamic fueled primarily by sharp increases in the volume of inputs. While the industrial labour force doubled, the maintenance of an unusually high investment ratio made it possible for the industrial capital stock to grow, in terms of replacement cost values, by nearly 70 per cent 1953–60, an annual rate of 7.8 per cent (Vinski 1965: 16 and 19). Foreign aid and loans facilitated the maintenance of that investment ratio, but were also crucial with respect to specific input flows. The $650m worth of US food aid given to Yugoslavia 1950–9 (Hoffman and Neal 1962: 351) not only helped Yugoslavia to survive the dark days of the early 1950s, but also enabled it to run a deficit on agricultural Balance of Trade 1953–9 averaging $40m annually (Gnjatović 1985: 54). Thus in a period of uncertain policy orientation and uncertain performance in agriculture, the Yugoslav authorities had little need to worry about food supplies to the growing towns. Turning to production inputs, it is striking that throughout the period 1953–61 investment goods and semi-finisheds made up some 75 per cent of total Yugoslav imports (*Jugoslavija 1945–64* 1965: 207). To a great extent, then, foreign aid and loans were used directly to finance the import of production inputs.

The pattern of extensive development is highlighted if we look at productivity trends. Industrial productivity grew at an annual rate of just 3.7 per cent 1953–61 (*Jugoslavija 1945–64* 1965: 144). That is a respectable, but not a dramatic rate of growth, especially if we take into account the amount of new technology which large-scale imports of equipment must have been bringing in to the Yugoslav economy (investment goods taken by themselves accounted for 22 per cent of total imports 1953–61 – *Yugoslavija 1945–64* 1965: 207). A comparison with Abram Bergson's figures for rates of growth of industrial productivity 1955–70 in major industrial countries (Bergson 1978: 168) reveals an interesting pattern. Yugoslavia during her period of extensive growth reported a figure for industrial productivity growth rather superior to those reported for the US (2.1 per cent) and the UK (2.9 per cent) over the 1955–70 period. But those were slow-growing economies, exhibiting rates of growth of National Income of only around 3 per cent at that time. When we turn to the high-growth economies of France, West Germany and Italy, we find rates of growth of industrial productivity of, respectively, 4.6, 4.6 and 5.4 per cent – well above the Yugoslav average for 1953–61. Most interestingly, Bergson quotes a figure of 4.2 per cent for the Soviet Union for the period 1955–70. This is clearly comparable to the Yugoslav figure. Any attempt to derive industrial productivity growth figures for the USSR during the crucial period of the 1930s is bedevilled by the index number problem and difficulties with the actual data base. But a straight average of the available alternative estimates likewise produces a figure of about 4 per cent. Thus a comparison of (highly impressive) output growth figures with (less impressive) productivity growth figures suggest that the underlying pattern of extensive growth in Yugoslavia in the initial period of industrialization was very similar to that experienced in the Soviet Union over a rather longer period of time.

When we turn to capital productivity, the pattern is rather different. According to Bergson's calculations the rate of growth of capital productivity in the Soviet Union was negative throughout the crucial phase 1928–40 and for the longer period 1928–58, irrespective of what price base you use (Bergson 1978: 122). In Yugoslavia, by contrast, the average COR (capital-output ratio) fell steadily from 1952 to 1959, and then remained fairly stable up into the early 1960s (Blagojević 1968: 22, *Statistički Godišnjak Jugoslavije 1975 (SGJ)* 81–2). To a degree, certainly, this impressive statistic may have reflected the very specific conditions of the time. There was a definite easing-off in the rate of growth of investment activity in Yugoslavia after 1954, which may have helped it to avoid some of the problems of investment 'over-heating' which have always been such a marked characteristic of the Soviet scene (see Dyker 1983: chs 2–4). It is striking that the Yugoslav construction industry did not regain the level of output reached in 1949 until 1960 (*Jugoslavija 1945–64* 1965: 80). Perhaps more important, the First Five-Year Plan, failure though it was, had bequeathed to Yugoslavia many grand projects which were only finally brought on stream in the middle 1950s. This gave the capital productivity figures a one-off boost around that time. Finally, there is some evidence that the official statistics may present a somewhat embellished view of the actual situation. Sirc argues that

> the figures may conceal many follies of the 1950s: some useless investment would have been written off by 1960, the rest was valued at 1962 prices instead of at the original very high production costs. . . . Sometimes even world prices were used instead of the much higher domestic prices.
>
> (Sirc 1979: 56)

For all that, however, we must give Yugoslav planning by global proportions credit for producing significantly better results in terms of capital productivity than we would have expected on the basis of the Soviet experience of extensive development.

It is worth making one last point of comparison between the phases of extensive development in Yugoslavia and the Soviet Union. In both cases plans for output growth were fulfilled despite very substantial shortfalls on plans for productivity growth. In the Soviet Union, the First Five-Year Plan envisaged non-agricultural employment reaching

15,764,000 by 1932–3. In the event, it reached 22,804,000, with employment in large-scale industry and construction rising to almost twice its planned level (Nove 1969: 195). In Yugoslavia the increase in employment in the socialized sector for 1957–61 was planned at 602,000 (*Društveni Plan . . .* 1957: 54). In the out-turn the figure reached 1,026,000 (*Jugoslavija 1945–64* 1965: 58).

We should not overstress the element of *failure to fulfil the plan* in this connection. Over-plan absorption of new labour in the Soviet case represents a classic case of the adjustment of unreal or inappropriate planning decisions to actual conditions. In particular, it permitted the adjustment of a highly capital-intensive strategy for basic industry to the reality that *labour* not capital, was the abundant factor. The very weaknesses of central planning did, indeed, encourage the *de facto* development of a dual technology profile, as managers, under tremendous pressure to fulfil plans and unable to trust the central supply apparatus to provide small components and other 'fiddly little things', sought to mount their own components manufacture capacity on a cottage-industry basis. More generally, in the face of an overriding priority on the fulfilment of short-term plans, *month by month*, they tended to engage extra labour *just in case* (see Dyker 1985: ch. 1).

The Yugoslav case is rather different. The abandonment of target planning and reinstitution of the market mechanism around 1953 meant that the specific systemic pressure which forces Soviet managers to build up and maintain substantial degrees of over-manning was not present in the Yugoslav economy as it passed through the initial stages of industrialization. But there were other pressures – pressures to build 'political factories' in the poorer regions, with the express purpose of absorbing as much labour as possible, pressures to give every major regional centre its 'share' of basic industries like steel-making, so that a given volume of aggregate investment expenditure tended to generate more jobs than would have been the case with single, integrated plans. In Yugoslavia, as in the Soviet Union, this pattern was ultimately problematic but the problems were for the future rather than the present – as long as 'new' labour was abundant and cheap. Rural overpopulation in both cases meant that the marginal productivity of labour in agriculture was near-zero. That in turn meant that the shadow-price of transferring labour into the towns was just the cost of providing accommodation and facilities for them in their new location. Such costs were substantial, and in 1960 housing and urban amenity construction was taking 21.5 per cent of total investment expenditures in Yugoslavia, compared to just 7.5 per cent in 1952 and 11.5 per cent in 1956 (Hoffman and Neal 1962: 372). The trend would, however, have been much more dramatic had it not been for the emergence in Yugoslavia of a major new social category – the 'worker-peasant' – living in the family home in the country, but working in the town. By the early 1960s there were probably around 900,000 of these (Hamilton 1968: 54). It is not an exaggeration to say that Yugoslav industrialization, as it developed in the 1950s, would have been inconceivable without the worker-peasant.

Planned or not, then, the extensive absorption of new labour into urban-industrial activity provided key inputs into the Yugoslav 'Great Leap Forward'. At the same time it did create sociological difficulties which survived the policy changes of the 1960s to take their place among the most recalcitrant of Yugoslavia's problem areas. Hoffman and Neal wrote in the early 1960s that '. . . the condition of existing living quarters is deteriorating rapidly . . . Crowded living conditions have often made for low morale and in some cases even posed a hazard to health.' (Hoffman and Neal 1962: 485–6). Kosta Mihailović, doyen of Yugoslav regional specialists, writes:

> The massive penetration of labour from the countryside has numerous sociological and economic implications. Hand-in-hand with urbanisation, a process which affects country as well as town, there unfolds a process of ruralisation of all social strata in the towns. Sometimes these two parallel processes meet in the same individuals, as with the worker-peasants, an enormous category which makes up about 40 per cent of the total industrial work force . . . It is difficult to maintain work discipline among these workers during the busy times in agriculture . . . The massive shift in population from the countryside brings with it a primitive way of thinking and peasant psychology. Perhaps the most dangerous attribute of this psychology is the tendency to go always for short-term gains, while more long-term and indirect concerns are ignored or despised. This breeds a parasitic attitude towards social property and a general neglect of the broader social interests which indirectly also serve private interests. Closely tied in with this is a relatively undeveloped capacity for abstract thought, and a distrust of the knowledge and experience of others. This in turn conditions a distrust of science, the general fund of generalised, distilled experience and knowledge. . . Having abandoned the moral norms and rigorous social controls of traditional society, the new arrival in the city has the feeling that everything is permitted . . . One could talk at length about the desire for rapid social affirmation, about conformism, careerism, education for the sake of obtaining diplomas rather than real knowledge. Of particular importance is the acquisitiveness and passion for material consumption of the new arrival from the countryside, historically deprived of all and everything.
> (Mihailović 1977: 30–1 and 113)

But the rapidity of urbanization and semi-urbanization had profound implications for agriculture as well. The peasant-worker came typically from a small holding, and a study from the mid-1960s found that in homesteads with less than 1 hectare of land it was common for all the farm work to be done by the woman (Prokić 1966: 48–9). The menfolk on larger farms tended to remain much more agriculture-oriented, obviously raising the issue of rationalization of private agricultural holdings. But the land-maximum, and the prohibition on the sale of agricultural land, meant that such rationalization was in practice impossible. This represented the beginning of the problem of abandoned arable land which continues to plague Yugoslavia to the present day.

The Balance of Payments problem

We have seen that import of capital was a systematic element in Yugoslav growth strategy in the 1950s and early 1960s. *Ergo*, it was inevitable that Yugoslavia should run a deficit on Balance of Trade in goods and services. But in practice deficits were always much bigger than envisaged. In 1955 the deficit was planned to fall by about one-third, but actually rose by 70 per cent, as can be seen from Table 3.3. The 1957–61 plan foresaw a gradual reduction in the deficit to about 60 million dollars annually. In the outcome, the deficit in 1961 was almost five times that figure, and more than twice what it had been in 1956. None of this raised any problems until US aid dried up in the early 1960s, but it does raise issues as to how exactly the Yugoslav leadership formulated its ideas about the role of foreign capital during this crucial period.

In introducing the new foreign trade system in an article published in 1952, politician and self-management theorist Milentije Popović acknowledged that there was a serious Balance of Payments problem, currently being covered by foreign aid, but then went on to argue that

> there is no danger of penetration by foreign capital, for the simple reason that there is no capital in our country, because we have working collectives, and the economic system as a whole cannot accommodate foreign capital . . . If there is a problem with the Balance of Payments, society will protect it through the system of coefficients.
>
> (Popović 1964: 51–2)

Thus he seems to have taken the view that aid was not foreign capital as such, and was in any case a purely temporary expedient, pending removal of the Balance of Payments deficit through the use of policy instruments. Svetozar Vukmanović-Tempo, speaking a couple of years later in his capacity as economic policy overlord, gave a more systematic assessment of the role of foreign capital:

> A deficit on Balance of Payments is an inevitable result whenever a backward country makes a conscious effort to accelerate economic

49

Table 3.3 The Balance of Payments 1947–65, in millions of dollars

	1947	1948	1949	1950	1951	1952	1953	1954	1955	1956	1957	1958	1959	1960	1961	1962	1963	1964	1965
Current account																			
Trade balance	−106	−55	−140	−125	−248	−143	−245	−121	−205	−167	−272	−236	−217	−269	−347	−199	−278	−435	−200
Exports	173	323	193	162	186	249	183	246	265	329	401	463	487	476	582	701	780	907	1120
Imports	279	378	333	287	434	393	418	367	470	495	673	699	704	845	929	900	1078	1342	1320
Balance of services	−2	4	13	78	11	11	16	8	18	44	44	53	48	51	60	82	134	162	185
Transport (net)	−1	9	17	12	19	21	1	18	−26	33	15	47	43	48	56	67	81	96	118
Travel (net)	–	–	2	1	–	–	2	2	4	4	4	4	6	6	8	22	44	56	63
Interest (net)	…	…	−2	−3	−5	−5	−9	−9	−8	−8	−6	−8	−10	−18	−17	−21	−34	−48	−60
Other services (net)	−1	−5	−4	−4	−3	−6	−8	−3	−4	15	10	10	9	15	13	14	43	58	64
Balance of goods and services	−108	−51	−127	−118	−237	−132	−244	−113	−187	−123	−249	−183	−169	−218	−287	−11	−144	−273	−15
Transfers (net)	126	78	42	37	217	123	164	163	153	159	218	173	175	80	69	122	147	33	37
Reparations	35	52	16	15	35	–	2	–	10	20	52	40	33	24	11	14	3	3	3
Economic aid	63	6	6	9	152	102	137	90	104	72	5	4	16	10	23	11	2	16	27
US govt. holdings of dinars	–	–	–	–	–	–	–	48	11	33	112	78	85	14	−1	53	84	−33	−43
Private transfers	28	20	20	13	30	21	25	25	29	34	49	51	41	32	36	44	58	47	50
Balance of current transactions	18	27	−85	−81	−20	−9	−80	50	−34	36	−31	−10	6	−138	−218	5	3	−240	22
Capital account																			
Errors and omissions	−14	−11	6	−8	−2	1	−1	−6	3	4	−2	27	−15	−8	−1	21	−24	−16	−111
Net new credits	−3	−59	73	91	24	9	82	−43	33	−39	29	−14	2	141	221	−28	31	258	87
Long-term (net)	−33	−36	2	47	25	15	23	5	−4	41	2	3	−9	6	6	61	44	117	121
Short-term (net)	30	−23	75	44	−1	−6	59	−48	37	−80	27	−17	11	135	84	−89	−7	141	−34
Change in reserves	−1	43	6	−2	−2	−1	−1	−1	−2	2	4	−3	7	5	−2	2	−10	−2	2

Note: I have followed Gnjatović in entering reparations, economic aid, etc. under current account rather than capital account. It should be noted, however, that this does not correspond to IMF reporting practice. When considering the current account balance from the policy point of view we should obviously concentrate on the balance of goods and services.

Source: Gnjatović 1985: 78

development. It thus appears as a function and a condition of such development. True, [in the Yugoslav case] specific unforeseen difficulties affected this process of development, so that the deficit was bigger than it would have been under normal circumstances. But the vigorous process of strengthening our production forces has meant, at the same time, the creation of conditions for the gradual removal of the deficit. At our present stage of development we have already to a great extent created the material base for increasing exports, reducing imports and gradually cutting the deficit.

(Vukmanović-Tempo 1964: 193)

Thus while Vukmanović has a clear perception in 1954 of the role of foreign capital in economic development, he maintains the line that Balance of Payments deficit is very much a short-term phenomenon, of little importance on the level of long-term, strategic policy-making. The experience of the middle 1950s certainly seems to have had some impact on his thinking. Thus in 1957 he reasoned that:

The basic problem in our economic relations with the USA is that our economy is still not managing to sell enough goods on the American market to pay for the goods we buy on that market. This deficit . . . has been covered up to now by the aid we have received from them, and in the future it will be covered by the credits on favourable terms approved by the USA for us. These credits are a very big help to our economy, but they would be an even bigger help if they were made on a medium-term rather than an annual basis. That would allow us to use them to develop those sectors of the economy which would allow us to increase our exports to the United States.

(Vukmanović-Tempo 1964: 394)

By 1957, then, Vukmanović was taking a more realistic view of how long it would take to turn foreign capital into exports. But he still seemed to be assuming that there would be something *automatic* about the process. And he appeared to be holding to the Popović line that short-term foreign aid for Balance of Payments support purposes is irrelevant to long-term investment matters. But of course *any* form of Balance of Payments support increases the potential for investment as it increases absorption, and the increased potential can be channelled into export-oriented sectors as easily as any other – or not as the case may be.

Popović and Vukmanović were, of course, in the first place men of action, and we should not, perhaps, expect too much analytical precision in their presentations of the Balance of Payments/foreign capital issue. But did they receive any help in this matter from the Yugoslav economists active in the 1950s and 1960s? In fact the most striking characteristic of much of the scholarly debate of the time, distinguished

51

though it was, lay in the absence of any reference to the international dimension at all (Milenkovitch 1971: 129–41). Thus Aleksandar Bajt and Branko Horvat, in their path-breaking articles on the optimal rate of investment, concentrated wholly on the problem of diminishing returns to successive increases in the rate of investment, as cuts in consumption produce disincentive effects and excessive strain on the investment front disorganizes the economy. They simply ignored the issue of the optimal balance of domestic and foreign finance for investment.

On a more micro-economic level we find orthodox Marxist economists like Nikola Cobeljić and Radmila Stojanović arguing in favour of the traditionally Soviet–Marxist notion of the necessary primacy of the producer goods sector of industry in any long-term development plan. They based their arguments on the proposition that you cannot maintain a high rate of investment if you do not place priority on increasing production capacity in the investment goods industries. In the first place that means the machine-building industry; going one step further back, it means the machine-tool industry. Now under specific assumptions, and if we are talking about limited periods of time, these propositions can be accepted as flowing directly from the most simple Input-Output analysis. But they are based on the assumption of a closed economy, and as soon as we introduce the dimension of foreign trade they collapse completely.

There were, certainly, economists around in Yugoslavia at that time who said just that. Jakov Sirotković, for example, argued that the dimension of foreign trade was of key importance in any consideration of optimal development patterns. But the dominant tendency amongst Yugoslav politicians and economists alike in the period of to 1965 was to either fudge or ignore the problem of what role foreign capital *should* play in the economic development of their country.

One more point remains to be made before we leave the Balance of Payments. While there cannot be the slightest doubt that the deficit was primarily structural in character, the extent of deficit was almost certainly exacerbated by purely operational factors. The system of foreign trade planning introduced in 1952–3 turned out to be extremely clumsy in practice, and the complex of coefficients provided fertile ground for administrative inefficiency. Thus, for example, products in joint supply were sometimes subject to totally different treatment, presumably because they came under different general classifications. In 1956 the effective rate of exchange for live poultry was 304.94 dinars to the dollar. As a result of this, the export of poultry was depressed to only a quarter of its pre-war level, and Yugoslavia's comparative advantage in poultry nullified. Meanwhile exports of eggs and chicken feathers continued to be encouraged, with effective rates of exchange of, respectively, 605.4 dinars to the dollar and 406.25 dinars to the dollar (Dyker 1974: 337).

But the perniciousness of the system went deeper than such obvious *non sequiturs*:

> These multiple rates of foreign exchange . . . led to a situation where nobody could figure out what the effect of the exchange of goods on international markets was, i.e. whether and when the Yugoslav economy gained or lost through its transactions . . . They were decided on by the Federal Government, whose decisions were often subject to the influence of large enterprises and influential political persons or the intervention of socio-political bodies.
>
> (Bićanić 1973: 161)

Thus however inevitable the deficits of the 1950s were, they were certainly not *minimized*. At the same time Bićanić's pithy assessment illustrates and underlines another of the recurrent characteristics of Yugoslav reality. Where symptoms of operational inefficiency appear, political lobbying and special pleading are rarely far beneath the surface.

Workers' self-management in practice

Our preliminary discussion got as far as establishing that the worker's councils, though very much *imposed* on the Yugoslav people, did have a real impact on the Yugoslav socio-economic system in the 1950s, if only at the level of engendering cost-inflationary pressures. Clearly then, the setting-up of the councils gave the workers some genuine 'trade-union' rights, something unheard of in other communist countries prior to the emergence of Solidarity in Poland. But those rights were limited to the extent that the workers' councils were not permitted to federate into national organizations – bear in mind that the Trade Unions themselves operated very much as transmission belts for the League of Communists.

Rather more striking is the extent to which the institutions of self-management did *not* develop into vehicles for genuine participatory democracy. Research from the 1960s indicates that decision-making in a typical Yugoslav enterprise of that period was dominated by professional management, and that the workers were aware that that was the case. At the commune level the picture was even more sharply drawn, with little participation and little interest in participation. Indeed major public opinion surveys from the early and middle 1960s found that participation in management *per se* was not generally rated highly as a feature of Yugoslav society, and that the man in the street was more likely to emphasize 'freedom and democracy' and equality. Most startling of all, those surveys found that workers' council meetings, etc. were only a minor source of information to workers – they obtained most of their news from the media, as in other countries! (Dyker 1977: 83–6)

But that is not the end of the story on self-management. While it was generally recognized that *samuopravljanje* did not work in a genuinely participatory sense, it was also genuinely felt that it *ought to be made to work*, at least at the enterprise level. Thus the mass of the people did believe in the system, in the sense that they thought it was worth trying to give it a more meaningful content. And because the notion of self-management did fit in which many elements in the traditional political culture of the Yugoslav peoples, it was easily absorbed into the mass consciousness.

> Under the rubric of self-management, the doctrine of socialist democracy . . . became so secularized that it lost most of its character as an ideological 'action programme' and was absorbed into a new Yugoslav political culture.
>
> (Johnson 1972: 249)

Beyond that, perhaps the most important thing about the workers' council system was the way that it provided a fairly open influence structure at enterprise level, and a variety of avenues for ambitious and able people to push up to positions of responsibility. Thus while the Partisan old boys' club kept a firm grip on all the key political positions in the country, the institutions of self-management provided some safety valve for young aspirations, some scope for meritocracy in the business sector. This was a clever compromise on the part of the leadership, but it was also an uneasy one. As we shall see in a later chapter, it eventually became an untenable one.

The problem of investment efficiency

We saw that in aggregate terms the record on the effectiveness of fixed capital formation through the period of planning by global proportions was not bad at all. But at the same time the Yugoslav authorities remained fundamentally dissatisfied with the investment planning set-up throughout the 1950s, yet unable to make up their minds on the precise mixture of plan and market required. This dissatisfaction did, indeed, form one of the main elements in the strictly economic background to the reforms of 1961–5. So just how good or bad was Yugoslav investment planning in the phase of planning by global proportions?

We must start by emphasizing the constraints that the Yugoslav investment planners were working under in the 1950s and early 1960s. Something had to be done with the mess inherited from the period of central planning, and the Key Investment Programme, not completed until 1956, inevitably projected the structural characteristics of the earlier period into the middle 1950s. Thus the share of total investment going to manufacturing and mining, which peaked at 61 per cent in 1952, was still as high as 45 per cent in 1955 (*Jugoslavija 1945–64* 1965: 282).

Second, they inherited a problem of regional imbalance which, as we can see from Table 3.4, worsened slightly over the period of administrative planning. The Yugoslav authorities felt obliged to channel resources into the poor regions, irrespective of return, if only for political reasons. As Table 3.4 shows, the impact of these policies on regional differentials in the period up to 1962 was negligible. Over the following two years, however, a significant improvement was recorded. This kick in the early mid-1960s probably had a good deal to do with the unique circumstances of the reconstruction after the Skopje earthquake of 1962. Be that as it may, we should probably conclude that in the context of very high growth rates in the more developed regions the poorer areas did well to narrow the gap a little by 1964 – particularly since their above-average birth rates put them at a permanent disadvantage in terms of per capita income growth. To that extent the decision to transfer substantial tranches of resources to the south irrespective of whether they could have yielded a better return in the north and west was shown to be justified.

Table 3.4 National Income per head of population by region.
Yugoslav average = 100, based on data in constant prices of 1960

	1947	1952	1962	1964
Yugoslavia	100	100	100	100
Bosnia & Hercegovina	86	88	73	71
Montenegro	71	64	66	73
Croatia	107	117	121	120
Macedonia	62	59	57	69
Slovenia	175	188	198	195
Serbia proper	95	87	90	90
Vojvodina	110	89	103	105
Kosovo	52	50	34	37

Source: Jugoslavija 1945–64. 1965: 89

But that is not to say that those resources could not have been more efficiently used *within the south itself*. Even in this period of state capitalism (at least as far as investment was concerned) the forces of local nationalism were already beginning to impinge heavily on locational patterns:

The Annual Plan, 1953, scheduled an integrated steelworks for construction in Macedonia to provide the heavy industrial basis for a 'take-off' there in metal-fabricating industries. Delays in constructing the plant were lengthy (more than five years before the site was cleared) chiefly because technological and economic problems of producing iron and sheet steel from the only local resources, low-grade phosphoric ores from West Macedonia and semi-coke from Kosovo lignite, were formidable. Undoubtedly Skopje is the best location for assembly and distribution in south-eastern Yugoslavia, but it is an economic location only within this area; costs of expanding steel production in Bosnia would have been far lower. These considerations were subordinated to the need of utilizing resources and providing employment locally in the one republic without a steel industry, to lengthen the life of Bosnian ore resources and to make more effective use of spare transport capacity on railways in south-eastern Yugoslavia rather than overburden already congested lines in Bosnia. Cost-benefit analysis was thus invoked to justify what was basically a political decision.

(Hamilton 1968: 243–4)

There was, of course, absolutely nothing wrong, in terms of the extensive growth strategy, with building capacities in the less developed regions with the express purpose of creating employment. But building something as capital-intensive as a steelworks is obviously not the best way to mobilize these resources. The Skopje steelworks is only the most extreme example of a general tendency in this period to go for a markedly capital-intensive factor mix in precisely the areas with the biggest labour reserves.

But why, one might ask, should local politicians be so anxious to develop industrial profiles clearly second-best from the point of view of the development prospects of their regions? The Skopje case illustrates the extent to which political structures in the less developed parts of Yugoslavia have been affected by *investment good fetishism*, the tendency to envisage economic development in terms of spectacular, prestige projects, and to view these projects, consciously or otherwise, as ends in themselves. To a degree we can trace this back to the Stalinist heritage, the notion of the necessary primacy, in development terms, of heavy industry – we saw how that 'law' was developed by distinguished Yugoslav thinkers in the 1950s. But if we look around the world, particularly at its less developed parts, we can find plenty of examples of investment good fetishism from areas little affected by the Soviet–Marxist tradition. The fact is that unsophisticated people tend to view what they do not have, namely development, in terms of its most striking outward symbols, whether motor cars, skyscrapers or massive industrial projects. Investment good fetishism is, indeed, in some senses simply a special case of Mihailović's 'ruralization of the city' syndrome. But the specific element of Marxist heritage must have strengthened the tendency, and must have made it more difficult for Belgrade to resist.

Yugoslavia's investment planning problems in the 1950s were, certainly, not restricted to that of the regions. The experience with investment auctions, for instance, highlighted technical deficiencies as well as strategic dilemmas in the programming of fixed capital formation.

Although the plans from which they originated contained integrated inter-sector and inter-industry balances, the competitions themselves, partly due to their variable character and to the voluminous analyses that they generated, were often treated in isolation, with important consequences. The time between initiation of competitions and the activation of plants varied greatly, frequently causing temporary bottlenecks in supply. Co-ordination in executing interlinked projects which were being analysed in different competitions was very poor. A three year delay (1960–2), for example, in deciding the development and location of electric power stations and transmission lines, because of insufficient response by investors or poor documentation of projects, caused serious power shortages in processing industries developed in Montenegro and Macedonia under competitions similarly dated 1959 . . . More serious, however, has been insufficient co-ordination on the spatial level. The Bank's [i.e. the Investment Bank] experts in deciding upon proposals in three separate competitions, for example, allocated grants for developing slaughtering facilities and meat-canning capacities in area 'A', greater livestock rearing in area 'B' and cattle-feed factories in area 'C'.

(Hamilton 1968: 248–9)

Once again, however, we find that technical shortcomings shade into socio-political complications and systemic problems. Political authorities in the more developed regions were by no means free of the sin of localism, and we find the development of the chemicals industry, for example, fragmented down to republican, and even to commune level for this reason (Gerl 1968). The tradition of earmarking funds probably intensified rather than alleviated the problem. Thus:

The decentralized funds were strictly confined within the boundaries of administrative units in the territorial (republic, district, etc.) or functional sense (housing, agriculture, schools, etc.). This made them highly dependent on corresponding political officials, territorial or departmental. The splitting of investment and other funds on administrative lines into so many hundreds of funds, and on functional lines into so many thousand separate funds, approached more closely the individual enterprises, but did not secure a proper functioning of effective investment policies.

The constant fear that their investment funds would be blocked or expropriated by the central government for its own purposes encouraged the agencies and enterprises administering them to allocate funds to the first project they could think of.

This was called the system of decentralized investment.

(Bićanić 1973: 125–6)

There were also structural problems at the level of Yugoslavia as a whole. The share of mining and manufacturing in total investment started to rise again after 1958, and by the early 1960s was once more running at nearly 40 per cent (*Jugoslavija 1945–64* 1965: 182): throughout the period 1953–65 heavy industrial sectors reported higher growth rates than light industrial, and of those only ferrous metallurgy showed a significant slackening-off after 1956. More specifically, the very rapid development of the engineering industry (the output of the metal industry quintupled 1952–64, while that of the electrical industry increased by 1200 per cent – *Jugoslavija 1945–64* 1965: 144) created serious intersectoral strains and stresses.

> It became clear that the home market was too small to absorb the output of the engineering industry, especially as the demand for one-off equipment decreased and the industry was not ready to switch over to serial production. Exporting was difficult because of competition and the inefficiency of Yugoslav engineering. Finally, there were disproportions between different stages of the engineering industry itself too.
>
> (Sirc 1979: 35)

Thus the traditionally Soviet, nay Stalinist, emphasis on heavy industry and machine building lived on in Yugoslavia after the completion of the Key Investment Programme, and there can be no doubt that the reasons for this were in some sense ideological. But we have to exercise a little caution here. Whatever imbalances its development in the 1950s engendered, engineering must be allowed pride of place amongst industrial sectors as an engine of extensive development. It is normally fairly highly labour-intensive, but affords considerable scope for the employment of a dual technology approach, as Soviet experience has illustrated (see Dyker 1985: ch. 1). In addition, it provides an excellent *training ground* for the new proletariat, an ideal context for on-the-job training in basic industrial skills.

Our critique of the investment planning record in the period of planning by global proportions must, then, be set firmly in historical and developmental context, and we can, indeed, develop this theme at a higher level of generalization. It is not really proper to criticize Yugoslav engineering in the 1950s for failing to generate substantial streams of exports, since the Balance of Payments was not a serious constraint at that time, and the Yugoslav authorities knew that very well. And when we talk of bottlenecks and tensions, are we not simply back with the mechanics of taut planning, as practised very successfully in the Soviet Union during its early period of development? Clearly Yugoslav investment planning in the period 1953–65 could have been more efficient, notwithstanding its undoubtedly impressive aggregate results. Equally clearly we can only hope to place the experience of investment planning during this period in full context if we place it within the framework of an overall assessment of planning by global proportions as a growth model and a growth strategy. It is to that task that we now turn.

Market socialism and growth maximization

The main thing that strikes one about the course of Yugoslav industrialization in the 1950s and 1960s is how very similar it is to the corresponding period of Soviet development. Growth is predominantly of the extensive variety, with massive mobilization of underemployed labour resources and an unusually high rate of investment serving as the main mobilizatory impetus. The contrast in agricultural policies might seem at first sight to represent a major difference between the two cases, but on closer examination we discover (a) that Soviet collectivization, because it did such terrible damage, both materially and morally, to Soviet agriculture, contributed little to 'primitive socialist accumulation' in the crucial early period of industrialization (Ellman 1979: 92–8); (b) that Yugoslav agricultural price policies through the 1950s and early 1960s ensured that there was a substantial degree of 'pumping-over' of resources from agriculture to the urban/industrial sectors. The Economics Institute of Serbia has estimated, taking 1966 prices as 'normal', that over the period 1952–66 $5bn were pumped over from agriculture. This represents some 8 per cent of total Gross Social Product over that period (Mihailović 1977: 74). When we add in the 7 per cent supplement to Gross Social Product which foreign capital provided over the same period, according to Gnjatović's calculations, we can begin to understand why urban living standards in Yugoslavia never fell under the strain of industrialization in the way they did in the Soviet Union during the 1930s. Official Yugoslav statistics show stagnation in the index of real incomes in the socialized sector 1952–6, followed by steady growth through the rest of the period.

But it is not only in terms of development *strategy* that the Yugoslav experience of planning by global proportions shows a surprising similarity to the Soviet model. In relation to *tactics* too, the echoes are numerous and insistent. As we saw in relation to investment patterns, it is difficult to make sense of the period of extensive development without reference to the notion of *taut planning*. In the Soviet case, it may certainly be argued, the key vehicle for the implementation of the principle of tautness was the ubiquitous output target. Now there can be no doubt that when output targets were abolished in Yugoslavia in the early 1950s they stayed abolished. There is no evidence that gross output ever 'crept back in through the window' in Yugoslavia, that formal output targets were simply replaced by informal, as has tended to happen during successive waves of reform in the Soviet Union. Yet patterns of production achievement at enterprise level were, again, very similar in both cases. Remarkable quantitative results were frequently recorded, but often at the cost of some neglect of the quality dimension. This certainly did not reach the ludicrous proportions in Yugoslavia that it sometimes has in the Soviet Union (see Dyker 1985: ch. 2), and we may be inclined to feel that it is unreasonable to expect any developing country to reach international standards in manufacturing within the first couple of decades of industrial development. But one of the most striking features of the period 1956–65 was an average annual rate of growth of inventories of nearly 10 per cent (Sirc 1979: 76–7), and Tito said in 1962 that 'last year our warehouses were full up with enormous quantities of unsaleable goods. These are of bad quality and cannot be sold, but they are counted as National Income' (quoted in Sirc 1979: 74). This was, of course, recognized as a thoroughly unsatisfactory state of affairs, and it forms part of the background to the reforms of the 1960s which we will be discussing in the next chapter. Its importance in the present context is that it proves how during the period of planning by global proportions Yugoslav enterprises, in principle under the discipline of the market, the obligation to sell, seemed inclined to pursue Soviet-style short-term growth maximization, and seemed able to get away with it. Why so?

Let us first examine the dimension of *entrepreneurial motivation*. Bearing in mind that the dominant socio-political ethos in Yugoslavia in this period was still very much one of growthmanship, and of a peculiarly Marxist type of growthmanship which laid great emphasis on the physical output which seemed best to personify the physical labour process, we should perhaps not be surprised to find enterprise management in general more disposed to go for growth than to bother about fine calculations of efficiency and profitability. But the predilection may have been greatly strengthened by the specific sociological input into the managerial situation provided by the workers' council. We have seen that the effective power of the councils, limited though it was, did extend as far as basic decisions on wages. Now the annals of industrial sociology teach us that industrial workers normally assess their *own* production achievement in terms of output – and indeed find it difficult to cope with a situation in which high achievement in those terms is not matched by correspondingly high earnings (see Industrial Relations Counsellors Inc, 1972: 203 and 210–11). We may surmise that in the Yugoslav case the workers, anxious to maximize their own incomes, may have seen short-term maximization of enterprise output as their most direct route to that result.

Why were they not pulled up short in this behaviour by the discipline of the socialist market? In the first place, because investment finance was largely provided from on high, so that the crucial trade-off between plough-backs and distributions was systematically fudged. Second, because the pattern of provision of working capital was in practice little different from that of fixed capital. For all its fussy earmarking of credits, monetary policy was essentially passive, and the supply of money grew at an average annual rate of over 20 per cent 1954–65 (Sirc 1979: 76–7). Price control ensured that this did not boil over into serious inflation, but at the *microeconomic* level passive monetary policy meant that the market nexus, the imperative to sell *in order to meet a payroll* which normally lies at the heart of any market economy, was seriously weakened, as enterprises were allowed to run up overdrafts at will. No wonder the warehouses began to bulge.

But we are, perhaps, in some danger of overstressing the similarities between Yugoslav and Soviet patterns. The element of foreign capital in the Yugoslav case, the total absence of it in the Soviet case, and the contrasting patterns in urban wages, are enough by themselves to mark out the uniqueness of the two cases. However much Yugoslav invest-ment policy in the 1950s and early 1960s may have sought linkage ef-fects through a degree of tautness, the Yugoslav investment scene never exhibited the fever pitch of overstretch which the Soviet investment scene was suffering from by the mid-1950s. And in arguing that planning by global proportions plus self-management proved a sturdy vehicle of short-term growth maximization we are not disputing that the Yugoslavs were doing things, at the level of the enterprise, in a very unsoviet way. Rather we are simply demonstrating that centralized, Soviet-style planning is not the only possible vehicle for socialist, extensive development, that market-based systems may be as relevant to that stage as to the later intensive development stage.

None of this qualifies our earlier conclusion that the Yugoslav leaders introduced market socialism with little regard to its likely economy impact. But with the benefit of hindsight we can see that the system of planning by global proportions was in practice as explicitly and effec-tively oriented to growth priorities as any other system of socialist planning.

By that very token, however, and just as in the Soviet Union, the very success of the mobilization for extensive growth contained within it the seeds of its own reversal. By the 1960s the most developed parts of northern and western Yugoslavia, especially Slovenia, had exhausted their immediate reserves of spare labour, and were beginning to face conditions of labour shortage. By 1970, indeed, Slovenia was facing the prospect of 30,000 unfilled vacancies for skilled workers, and was setting in motion a programme to tempt back the c.60,000 Slovenian workers then employed in Austria and West Germany (*'Repatrijacija . . .'* 1970). Northwards immigration by people from the underdeveloped south provided some alleviation, but was limited by the dimension of ethnic tension. With productivity now the key variable for those north-western regions, the weaknesses of the investment planning approaches of the 1950s became increasingly apparent, the rationale for political factories increasingly compromised. Meanwhile the ever-increasing rate of absorption of imported industrial inputs was placing increasing strain on the Balance of Payments, while the crude growth priorities of planning by global proportions held out no *prospect* for establishing the kind of quality and technology parameters which might help Yugoslavia to conquer world markets. In 1961 the current account deficit reached $250m, its highest level to date. This is where the international political dimension comes in, for that was the very year in which the US Congress decided that no more economic aid should be given to Yugoslavia. Worse was to follow as another big deficit in 1964 left Yugoslavia unable to meet its external financial commitments. This was the first of Yugoslavia's post-war debt-service crises. It was not a particularly grave crisis, in that it related largely to the maturation of short-term trading credits – the total debt in 1964 was only just over $800m. But it forced Yugoslavia, not for the last time, to go to the IMF for help. The help was forthcoming, but only on condition that Yugoslavia liberalize her trading regime. Thus as the Yugoslav economy matured, and as the world became a harder place to survive in, the need for a further stage of institutional reappraisal became pressingly apparent, with the IMF doing some of the pressing.

Chapter four

Systemic Reform in the 1960s and 1970s: the Sovereignty of Associated Labour

The reforms of the early 1960s

Concern about the efficiency of investment and investment finance surfaced in legislative terms in 1961, as the central authorities set about dismantling the essentially monolithic banking system inherited from the period of administrative planning. As of that year the central government was still in direct control of as much as 37 per cent of total investment funds – a percentage point or two up on the corresponding figure for 1957. The transfer in 1961 of short-term credit operations from the National Bank to the local communal banks set up in 1955 had no direct implications for investment finance, though as we saw, the distinction between overdrafts and investment loans had never been a clear one under planning by global proportions. Of more fundamental importance was the creation in the same year of a network of republic-level banks programmed to take over primary responsibility for investment finance. By 1963 the share of the central government in total investment finance had fallen to 22.5 per cent, and at the end of that year the General Investment Fund, the main instrument of state socialism under planning by global proportions, was abolished. Its assets were redistributed amongst the three specialized banks – the Investment Bank, the Agricultural Bank and the Foreign Trade Bank. By the end of 1963 there were 232 separate banks operating in Yugoslavia, in addition to the National Bank. All of them apart from the Post Office Savings Bank and the federal banks, operated on a strictly regional basis, confined to the territory of the political authority which had set it up (Dimitrijević and Macesich 1973: 26 and 28).

But these changes seemed to serve only to highlight the weaknesses of the Yugoslav banking sector. The territorial principle left local and republic-level banks at the mercy of their political patrons, and the general quality of investment finance decision-making still left much to be desired. Not surprisingly, then, the sweeping economic reform of 1965 again focused strongly on the banking/investment finance area, introducing three main innovations. Firstly, the sharp distinction (of principle) between short- and long-term credit was initially relaxed, and subsequently abolished, leaving banks to take the business that seemed most profitable to them. Secondly, the credit system was deterritorialized. Banks would now be allowed to open branches anywhere in Yugoslavia. This move was clearly aimed at weakening the tutelage of regional political authorities over the system. Thirdly, industrial and trading interests were given formal rights of representation at the level of bank management. The 1965 legislation created a system of bank assemblies, which were to determine the general lines of credit policy and which were made up of delegates from the 'founders' of the bank, i.e. organizations which had provided a share of its basic capital. Those could be enterprises or local authorities (Dirlam and Plummer 1973: 178–9) Clearly this dimension of the legislation raised as many problems as it solved. It meant that the political establishment retained a strong foothold in banking counsels, and it introduced the danger that a bank's lending policies might unduly favour the interests of founders. But the idea was clear enough – to get the views of business leaders more strongly across to the banks, so that lending operations might be prosecuted on a more business-like basis. And whatever the ambiguities and uncertainties of the banking reform, one thing was left beyond question. The central authorities had ceased to play a major direct role in the provision of investment finance. In 1966 the Federation accounted for just over 6 per cent of the total (Dirlam and Plummer 1973: 195), with most of that being accounted for by the Federal Fund for the Less Developed Regions, which had been created in 1964.

But the thrust of policy on investment finance was not restricted to the banking system, and its relations with the business sector. Tax changes instituted in 1965, including the abolition of the tax on enterprise net income and a reduction in the level of the charge on enterprise fixed assets (*kamata*), were aimed precisely at raising the capacity of the enterprise to finance its own investment through plough-backs. (The *kamata* was finally abolished altogether in 1971, and replaced by a compulsory rate of contribution to the Federal Fund for the Less Developed Regions.) Between 1964 and 1966 the share of business enterprises and other autonomous organizations in total investment finance rose from 32.4 per cent to 45.5 per cent (Dirlam and Plummer 1973: 195).

The other main area affected by the reforms of the early 1960s was foreign trade. In 1961 the clumsy coefficient system was replaced by a more conventional array of import duties and export subsidies, with an average level much lower than the old coefficients, but based on a new, more realistic exchange rate of 750 dinars to the dollar. Some 75 per cent of imports were, however, still to be subject to direct control through a comprehensive licensing system, which also covered certain exports. The role of exchange control as such was greatly reduced, but enterprises continued under the obligation to sell most of their foreign exchange earnings to the National Bank. Thus the 1961 measures represented a rationalization rather than a fundamental reform. But a year later, in 1962, Yugoslavia acceded to GATT, which meant commitment to a programme of phased abolition for direct controls. The 1965 reform cut the average level of import duties by half and predicated the abolition of export subsidies, while devaluing the dinar further to a rate of 1,250 dinars to the dollar (12.5 dinars to the dollar in term of the 'new' dinar introduced at the same time). The 1965 measures represented a clear recognition of the need to bring the domestic price system more into line with world prices and to open up the Yugoslav economy to international currents and pressures, so as to increase its participation in the 'international division of labour'. But in truth it represented more of a statement of intent than a clearly delineated policy measure. Export premia were never in fact abolished, and indeed survive to the present day. The same is true for direct controls on imports. The level of import protection, having remained stable through 1966, then rose by more than 50 per cent in the succeeding 18 months. Of course by the mid-1960s, normal trading flows had been re-established with the countries of the Soviet bloc. (In 1964 about one-third of total Yugoslav trade was with Comecon.) The bulk of this trade was carried on on the basis of bilateral clearing agreements, as was a proportion of Yugoslavia's trade with the Third World. Thus a substantial part of total Yugoslav trade turnover remained in any case largely insulated from price parameters.

As we saw in Chapter 2, the Law on Prices of 1962 had codified the price controls which had developed piecemeal during the 1960s, and instituted the principle that price increases had to obtain the approval of the Price Office. On the eve of the 1965 reform just 20 per cent of sales of industrial goods were at wholly free prices. In March of that year, worried about mounting cost-inflationary pressures, the authorities imposed a general price freeze. Then in July 1965 a comprehensive reform of the whole pricing structure was instituted. The price reform went hand in hand with the foreign trade reform. Prices of imported goods had to be raised to take account of the devaluation of the dinar. More generally, prices of raw materials and transport services were increased relative to those of manufactures, in pursuance of the theme of bringing the domestic price structure more into line with world prices (Dirlam and Plummer 1973: 90). But the reform did also seek to introduce more flexibility into the price system, and there was a general unfreezing of prices through 1967 and 1968. As of 1969 56 per cent of sales of manufactures were going through at uncontrolled prices, though that year did witness the re-imposition of controls on prices of services and imported goods.

The last major dimension of the reforms of the 1960s related to the central institution of Yugoslav market socialism – self-management. The fiscal reforms already discussed clearly increased the potential clout of self-management organs in the business sector, because they increased the scope for independent action on the part of the enterprise itself. But reform policy on *samoupravljanje* went further than that. Originally developed exclusively through *workers'* councils, self-management was now programmed for extension through a broad area of social activity. Education, health, welfare, cultural activities, were handed over to autonomous organizations, run on a self-managing basis involving representation by employees and citizens, and financed from earmarked tax revenues which had previously gone to the local government. These developments marked the entry onto the Yugoslav stage of the 'para-state' organization – a new and important theme to which we shall return.

The reforms of the early 1960s were clearly aimed at solving the problem of transition from extensive to intensive development which we pin-pointed at the end of the last chapter. But while pragmatic elements were to the forefront, ideology too left a deep imprint on the legislation which created, for the first time, a system which we could describe as 'full-booded market socialism'. Of course the investment finance scene had to be rationalized, but the origins of the peculiar recipe for a symbiosis of self-managing business and self-managing banking must be sought largely in the political sphere. Again, the impetus towards extension of self-management came in the main from a sense of pursuing the origianl *political* decisions of the early 1950s to their logical conclusion, rather than from any concern about the *efficiency* of management. The changes on the foreign trade side were, certainly, in the main a reaction to changing circumstances, and a reflection of heightening awareness of the importance of international exchange, spurred on by the need to accommodate IMF views. Significantly, however, this was precisely the area of the reforms which had least impact.

The crisis of the late 1960s and early 1970s: socialist finance capital and socialist self-management

It was not long before the worst fears of those who had felt uneasy about the banking and finance reform were realized. Enterprise managements, no doubt under strong pressure from workers' councils, tended to use their increased disposable income to increase wages rather than invest-ment – average real personal incomes grew by 24 per cent 1965–7, while National Income grew by just 11 per cent. But rather than make corresponding downwards adjustments to investment levels, enterprises simply turned to the banks for finance to maintain investment at previous levels. The banks had plenty of money to lend, partly because savings of the population held in the banking system increased by nearly two-and-a-half times in nominal terms 1965–7. The result was that enterprise indebtedness grew dramatically, and by the late 1960s the bulk of enterprise net income was going on debt service. In 1968 the proportion of total investment financed by enterprises and other autonomous organizations was just 37 per cent, 8.5 percentage points lower than it had been in 1966 (Dirlam and Plummer 1973: 195). The following year it dropped by another couple of percentage points. By the middle of 1969 more than half the enterprises in Yugoslavia were unable to meet their financial commitments, and the situation worsened steadily as the new decade began. Total unpaid bills grew in value by 300 per cent July 1970–July 1971, and by the beginning of 1972 the non-business sector (*neprivreda*) owed business enterprises 7.5bn dinars – some 3.4 per cent of National Income in that year. The wave of strikes in 1971 and 1972 was precipitated largely by unpaid wages, as managements struggled to meet their outside financial commitments. By September 1975 business enterprises held unpaid bills totalling 273bn dinars, but themselves owed a total of 262bn dinars to the banks (Sirc 1979: 154–5). Organizations which looked financially strong on paper increasingly found that dangerously large proportions of their total assets were in the form of overdue bills.

In at least one crucial respect, then, the financial reform seemed to have failed. Enterprises were by the late 1960s financing a rather smaller proportion of investment from plough-backs than they had been in 1961. The pre-1965 pattern whereby total gross investment financed from enterprise own funds was consistently less than total depreciation allowances was broken for only one year – 1966. After that the old pattern set in again, and in 1967 the shortfall for the business sector as a whole represented 37 per cent of total net investment (Bakarić 1971). These trends in enterprise finance became the focal point for a whole complex of economic and political issues which rapidly assumed the dimensions of a politico-economic crisis. Let us try to distinguish the main systemic elements in that crisis.

First of all, the whole status of the system of self-management was in jeopardy. A reform which had set out to make workers' sovereignty more meaningful by giving it more financial clout had ended up, it seemed, by delivering the proletariat into the hands of the bankers. Veteran politician Vladimir Bakarić portrayed the issue in terms of a classic battle for surplus value, arguing that the position of the worker *vis-à-vis* his creditors was increasingly approaching that of hired labour, and suggesting that this was now the main contradiction – he used the word in its technical Hegelian/Marxian sense – in Yugoslav society (Bakarić, 1971).

Of course the situation was in reality much more complex than that. The workers had been guilty of irresponsibility in raising wages the way they did in 1966 and 1967 – average *nominal* personal incomes grew by nearly 60 per cent over those two years. Econometric analysis shows conclusively that cost-inflationary pressures provided the main impetus behind the increase in the inflation rate from an average of seven per cent 1960–4 to one of 17 per cent 1969–74 (Popov and Jovičić 1971). As the aggregate level of economic activity fluctuated, prices tended to rise in periods of deceleration, when labour productivity was stagnating, and stabilize in periods of acceleration, when labour productivity was rising (Horvat 1969: 8 and 10). This shows clearly the presence of a basic inflationary factor operating independently of the level of aggregate demand, but which could be cancelled out by productivity increases, and points the finger firmly at the wage element. Bakarić was, however, quite right to emphasize that the 'pumping-over' of funds from the business sector to the banking sector in the late 1960s and early 1970s could only exacerbate cost-inflationary pressures, as workers strove to protect their income levels in the face of the growing burden of debt service.

There was, on the other hand, more to debt service problems than the purely financial dimension. Real rates of interest in this period of accelerating inflation were, after all, consistently negative. One must suppose that, had the funds borrowed been profitably invested, the enterprises involved would have found little difficulty in maintaining debt service flows. Yet in 1970 total losses in the business sector amounted to over 6bn dinars – around 4.5 per cent of National Income in that year. Some of these losses may, certainly, have been directly attributable to anomalies of price control. Prices of basic drugs, for instance, were not changed between 1952 and 1973. To the extent that losses did reflect inefficiencies in resource allocation, furthermore, we must seek their ultimate origin in the pre-reform structure of the Yugoslav economy. But here is the key question. Given that the reforms of the early 1960s had been targeted precisely at the establishment of an investment allocation mechanism more sensitive to the requirements of efficient structural adjustment, why had their impact been so marginal in precisely this respect? Why did the Yugoslav economy enter the 1970s with an average level of industrial capacity utilization of barely 70 per cent (in individual cases as little as 15 per cent)? Why did the specific problem of overexpansion of the metal and electrical industries which we pin-pointed in the last chapter remain unresolved, with capacity in those sectors less than 50 per cent loaded?

One reason was certainly the chronically poor level of Yugoslav project assessment, exacerbated by the odd rule whereby funds for design work could only be released after projects had been approved in principle. Yugoslav journalists who visited the World Bank in 1972 found that the bank threw out 85 per cent of the projects proposed by the Yugoslav side because of poor costing or grossly over-optimistic assessment of prospects for sales on the world market. On one project estimated costs were cut by the bank from $10m to $1m. But, as always, there is more to this lurid picture of technical inefficiency than meets the eye. One of the most striking examples of bad project choice from this period is the Mratinje hydro-electric project in Montenegro. The application for a loan for the Mratinje from the Yugoslav Investment Bank, heir to the General Investment Fund, was accepted on the basis of estimated capital costs of 400m dinars. In the event it cost 1.1bn dinars. The reason for this, according to the general director of the Investment Bank, had nothing to do with the technical side of the project, but was quite simply that 'the applicant had intentionally left out some elements in the original estimate in order to win the loan against stiff competition' (Čemović 1969). Attempts in the late 1960s to take advantage of favourable world market conditions by developing the aluminium industry foundered on the total inability of the authorities in the republics of Croatia, Bosnia and Hercegovina and Montenegro to agree on any kind of an integrated investment programme. By 1971–2 the international price of aluminium had collapsed, and the opportunity was lost. The situation was similar with petrochemicals, with Serbia and Croatia both determined to build up their 'own' industries. Calling in 1970 for a return to sanity, the general director of the Jugovinal enterprise said that

> some will sneer at this kind of argument and talk of a relapse into strong-arm policies. But I consider that, just like every household, so every enterprise, every republic, and every state must have a unified economic policy. By the same token I believe that we cannot permit anarchy – we cannot allow a situation where everyone builds just what he wants, *even when the sources of finance and the deals involved are dubious.* (Emphasis added)
>
> (Žulj 1970)

But surely, one may ask, the problem of 'duplicating capacities' should solve itself in a market economy? Surely banks will not lend for unprofitable projects, and if mistakes are made, surely they will ultimately be rectified by liquidation and re-allocation of capital assets? These questions do, in fact, merely serve to highlight the essence of the investment problem in Yugoslavia after 1965. The reform had *failed* to establish the market principle in the sphere of fixed capital formation, and large-scale projects, bad ones and good ones alike, were in the post-reform period decided on by côteries of politicians, bankers and (sometimes) managers. That the process of decision-taking was *pluralized* is indupitable. That it became significantly more sensitive to cost-efficiency considerations is at least controversial. And as the figures cited on excess capacity indicate, the reform likewise failed to introduce into the economy any automatic mechanism for the *ex post* correction of errors of investment policy. At the time of the 1965 reform Yugoslav economists talked of the need to liquidate, or at least reorganize, up to one-third of the total number of business enterprises in Yugoslavia. Yet in 1969, out of a total number of 8,955 enterprises unable to meet their financial obligations, only 109 went into liquidation. The fact is that no *procedure* had been set up to permit creditors to force firms into receivership. The right to place an erring enterprise under 'compulsory management', and ultimately to liquidate it, rested solely with the local commune government, dominated by the local party organization. How that kind of arrangement tended to work out in practice can be illustrated by the reaction of the Zagreb city authorities to the regulation, introduced in 1969, that enterprises could pay only 80 per cent of wages if they were in default on their tax obligations. Such a regime would have meant 100,000 workers in the Croatian capital on short pay over the summer of that year. But the *Party Municipal Committee* decided that all wages should be payed in full.

It would, certainly, be quite wrong to suggest that the politicians never had any positive ideas about industrial structure. On the contrary, one of the dominant policy themes from 1965 up to the early 1970s was that of *industrial integration*. This was seen as a vital part of the package which sought to deepen Yugoslavia's involvement in the international division of labour, to exploit economies of scale, to strengthen the technological base of Yugoslav industry, and to breed 'national champions' which could lead the Yugoslav assault on world markets. More than 4,000 enterprises entered into integration agreements between 1965 and 1972, with 320 subsequently abandoning the agreements. Of the 4,000, nearly 1,400 integrated in 1965 and 1966, as the authorities waged a veritable integration campaign.

Now there can be no doubting the essential rationale of the integration idea. In practice, however, it produced disappointing results. As of 1972 the 100 biggest integrated concerns showed indifferent efficiency parameters, with capital-output ratios well above the Yugoslav average and labour-output ratios only a little lower than the Yugoslav average. Not surprisingly, their net income profile was unimpressive, while they also figured prominently in the list of major business debtors. Part of the reason for the disappointing impact of the integration campaign on business efficency was almost certainly that it had been taken too far. By 1970 13.8 per cent of firms in Yugoslavia were employing more than 1,000 people, compared to 0.7 per cent in the USA and 0.1 per cent in Japan (' "Jedinstvo". . . ' 1970). It was, after all, a *campaign*, pursued through political pressure and financial manipulation, rather than any exercise in purely indicative planning, and campaigns are perhaps not the best way to discover the natural limits of particular forms of industrial adjustment. More specifically, Yugoslav policy-makers, in their enthusiasm for large-scale production, seem to have ignored the growing importance of small, highly specialized ancillary enterprises in the advanced industrial economies, particularly in high-technology sectors.

Beyond that, an increasingly familiar pattern of policy distortion emerged in the course of implementation of the integration initiative. The great majority of integrations were limited within the boundaries of one commune, and the highest rate of subsequent disintegration was amongst cases where integration had been on a national scale, cutting across republican boundaries. Too often integration served as a cover for territorial empire-building, cross-subsidization and the fudging of efficiency problems, as stronger enterprises were pressurized to take on board the debts of weaker. More insidiously, the movement, with its odd mixture of gigantomania and feather-bedding, created a milieu inimical to the small and efficient. The director of one such organization complained in 1972 of extreme difficulties in obtaining bank finance for well-founded expansion. 'First they tell us that we are doing good business, and that priority must go to saving the weak, then they tell us that we must wait our turn' (Milić 1972).

How the piper was paid

But this simply does not add up. Political bodies cannot make arbitrary decisions to pay wages when there is no cash in the kitty, côteries of bankers and politicians cannot conspire to push through investment projects they know to be unprofitable – and survive – unless they have, in some sense, a 'licence to print money'. Certainly, some of the banks did get themselves into trouble. The Agricultural Bank (Poljobanka), for instance, overextended itself on the Dalmatian tourist belt, and had to be rescued amidst political uproar and criminal charges against the bank's directors. But the problem in this particular case was of financial recklessness, particularly in relation to foreign borrowing, rather than misdirected investment, and the Poljobanka case serves rather to underline the general immunity of Yugoslav banks, most of them under much heavier political patronage than Poljobanka, from the full consequences of their decisions. It is at the *macro* level that we must look for the roots of that tendency.

In line with the general principles of retreating from active fiscal policy and bringing forward the money and banking system as the central focus of policy implementation under full-blooded market socialism the 1965 reform had pinned high hopes on monetary policy as an instrument for the maintenance of price stability, as anti-inflationary taxes were dropped and price controls eased. The idea seemed at first sight attractively simple. Here was an economy with a fairly well developed goods market, but with no money market or stock exchange to complicate the demand for money function with speculative elements, or the money supply situation with sophisticated forms of 'near-money'. There was every chance, it seemed, with the transactions motive almost the only possible reason for holding money, that something like the quantity theory of money would hold. By using the device of varying the required relationship between total commercial bank credit and deposits of those banks with the National Bank (maximum 35 per cent), the central authorities should have been well placed to control the total supply of money, and through it the key macro-economic variables.

The reality was dramatically different. The velocity of circulation of the money stock trebled 1965–71, and continued to increase rapidly in 1972. One reason for this may have been a typically developmental one, as Yugoslav enterprises and households, new to industrial life and new to a more advanced form of market socialism, learned how to economize on money holdings. Much more important was the vigorous development of a peculiarly Yugoslav form of near-money. The volume of outstanding inter-enterprise credit grew 32 per cent in 1965, 40 per cent in 1966 and 47 per cent in 1967 (Mihailović 1969: 113). Much of this inter-enterprise credit was, of course, involuntary. It simply represented unpaid bills, with the average lead-time on payment of bills more than doubling 1965–71. Thus inter-enterprise credit as near-money is simply the other side of the coin of illiquidity, and indeed there is every indication that it developed as a direct reaction to attempts by the National Bank to impose greater monetary discipline on the system.

But of course near-money is not money, and as the build-up of the liquidity crisis showed, in the end of the day you can only settle your accounts with *money*. Table 4.1 shows that, in the period 1965–71, the Yugoslav monetary authorities did not do too badly in terms of keeping the rate of increase of money supply within projected limits. In 1972–7, however, under the pressure of the mounting liquidity crisis, the floodgates opened. In 1972 the supply of money increased by 28 per cent, and in 1973 by 36 per cent.

What were the mechanics of this explosion of money supply? Did the government and the National Bank sit down and work out a grand design for an *ex post* regularization of the near-money explosion of the late 1960s? Almost certainly not, and indeed the mechanics of the Yugoslav approach to monetary policy are such that no such grand design was necessary. The reformed Yugoslav economy had inherited the institution of selective rediscounting from the period of plannning by global proportions which meant that it was considered perfectly proper

Table 4.1 Projected and actual growth in money supply 1965–71 (annual percentage rates of growth, based on end–year figures)

	1965	1966	1967	1968	1969	1970	1971
Actual rate of growth	5	5	−2	24	12	12	12
Projected rate of growth	less than 26[1]	less than 11[1]	less than 6[1]	more than 9[1]	12	18[1]	14[1]

[1]Estimates

Source: Dimitrijević and Macesich 1973: 175

for the National Bank to increase the volume of primary money for specific micro-economic purposes. Significantly Dimitrijević, in commenting on the figures presented in our Table 4.1, states that

the higher rate of increase in the money supply for 1970 was the consequence of a substantial increase in high-powered money brought about by the National Bank as a result of two disastrous earthquakes (Bosnia and Dalmatia) and floods in several parts of the country.

He goes on to argue that

it is for this reason that 1970 should be excluded from further considerations of the efficiency of monetary policy. (Dimitrijević and Macesich 1973: 175–6, fn.)

But surely this kind of selective crediting has *everything* to do with an assessment of the efficiency of Yugoslav monetary policy! Thus in the face of increasing political and systemic pressures from 1971, it was possible for the monetary authorities to increase the supply of primary money on an *ad hoc*, essentially *unplanned* way. In so doing they were guilty, at the very least, of accommodating inflationary pressures.

It has to be said, in defence of the National Bank, that the supply of primary money was by no means the only monetary management problem in this period. The perfectly laudable principle of controlling the supply of money through the obligatory reserves ratio ran into serious difficulties, and tended to be replaced by administrative rationing of total credit. The problem with the reserves ratio approach was again an essentially political one – it penalized the poorer regions and the weaker banks too severely. The trouble with the credit rationing alternative is that

it is rather rigid and its application has many disadvantages, especially in Yugoslavia with its inadequate financial market. This is particularly valid for seasonal and differential regional needs for financing. Credit ceiling prevents banks from efficiently and effectively adjusting their policy to these needs. The fact that there are no other important sources of financing creates serious difficulties in production, trade, and the economy in general.

(Dimitrijević and Macesich 1973: 166)

To end this section we must look briefly at relations between the National Bank and the government. As in every other country, the Yugoslav central bank is, *inter alia*, the government's banker. But again peculiar Yugoslav conditions gave the relationship a special twist. Because of the absence of a bond market, government budget deficits could only be covered by emissions of primary money. Attempts in the early 1970s to use non-rediscountable government paper to cover federal commitments were not successful – not even government departments were prepared to accept them as a means of payment! (In fairness it should be said that when they tried again in the middle 1970s they were more successful.) The issue of budget deficit was greatly complicated by the existence of the so-called 'extra-budgetary balance'. This was the balance of outflows and inflows relating to the *capital* account of the central government, a hangover from the pre-1965 system, and intimately related to the hottest political potato of the late 1960s and early 1970s, state capital (see next section). Permanently in deficit from 1966, the extra-budgetary balance placed increased strain on the Yugoslav monetary system in a variety of ways. To the extent that creditors of the extra-budgetary balance were paid out of primary emissions, inflationary pressures of an orthodox Keynsian nature were created. But creditors were often not paid in the late 1960s, and that exacerbated the illiquidity problem. Finally, the interest paid by the commercial banks to the State Bank on selectively rediscounted credits was earmarked for the extra-budgetary balance. Thus the federal government had a quite specific financial interest in the institution of selective rediscounting, quite apart from any more general policy considerations.

Political trends in the early 1970s complicated these matters further with the decentralization to republic level of selective rediscounting (partially) and the extra-budgetary balance (wholly), in the wake of the confederalist constitutional amendment (see next section). As far as the extra-budgetary balance is concerned, this was seen as a step towards liquidation of 'state capital', and the extra-budgetary balances of the various republics and provinces were reportedly abolished in 1974 or soon afterwards (Stanojlović 1974). The idea in relation to selective rediscounting was gradually to shift the whole burden of selective credit policy onto the commercial banks, leaving the National Bank to concentrate on more conventional macro-economic matters (Koprivica 1973). But an exception was made right from the start for republic-level primary emissions, and these were to develop into a major vehicle of regional economic policy implementation in the late 1970s.

Thus monetary policy for market socialism proved a disappointment in Yugoslavia. The reasons for this were partly technical. The absence of a capital market, at first sight an advantage, proved through experience to be a grave disadvantage. But it was the political dimension of the problem that was of overrriding importance. The authorities continued to view monetary policy as an instrument for the implementation of specific micro-economic policies, and the policies thus implemented in the early 1970s verged on throwing good money after bad.

The crisis of the late 1960s and early 1970s: socialist finance capital and socialist nationalism

It seemed, then, that the reforms and policy initiatives of the 1960s had failed to solve the fundamental problem of how a system based on the principles of self-management and the 'leading role' of the party could generate reliable and consistent ground rules for the allocation of investment. That in itself represented a major setback for Yugoslav market socialism. But because of the unique political conditions prevailing in the country, what started off as a crisis of economic planning soon turned into a national crisis, with the very existence of Yugoslavia being called into question.

We saw in earlier chapters how inter-nationality tensions, and particularly the Serb-Croat conflict, had provided much of the thematic material for the development of politics in the early years of Yugoslavia, how they had flared into sectarian atrocities during the Second World War, how they had been repressed during the period of hard-boiled 'brotherhood and unity', and how, from the mid-1950s onwards, the authorities had increasingly followed a policy of accommodation towards regional ethnic identities, as part of the self-management package. They may well have believed that the decentralization of the banking system in the 1960s was broadly consistent with that policy line, while simultaneously increasing the mobility of capital in an essentially non-political way. If so, they were to be bitterly disappointed. Almost immediately after the promulgation of the 1965 reform murmerings were heard in Croatia about the fate of 'state capital'. The new banks, like the Yugoslav Investment Bank had, after all, inherited the capital of the old state investment funds. That capital had been raised through general taxation, to which the better-off parts of Yugoslavia had made a disproportionate contribution. Now, it was argued in Zagreb, these banks, still located in Belgrade, were using Croatian money to favour Serbian organizations, or exploit Croatian ones. It is certainly true that in 1972 more than 50 per cent of total bank assets in Yugoslavia were in the

75

hands of banks located in Serbia, and that around two-thirds of those assets were placed in other republics – not surprisingly since the four nation-wide banks were all located in Belgrade. But Croatian politicians painted a lurid picture of the big financial operators' activities in the Dalmatian tourist industry (Dalmatia is part of Croatia). They alleged a 'carve-up' of the tourist area between the big banks, and accused the latter of an assault on self-management. Directors were appointed and wage structures imposed on tourist enterprises without regard for the views of the workers' councils. Significantly, it was suggested that the tourist workers might be better off working for foreign capital.

But it was not so much with the banks as with the big foreign trade organizations that the most striking examples of sharp practice emerged. Like the banks, the big re-exporters – Genex, Inex, Astra, Proges, Intertrade and Interimpex – had been transformed by the economic reforms of the 1960s from administrative departments into commercial operators. And while it became easier during the 1960s for Yugoslav enterprises at large to participate in foreign trade, the big operators were able, *de facto*, to cling to many of their old privileges. It was easy and perfectly legal for organizations like Genex to make big profits on the sale of imported goods, since continued administrative restrictions on imports meant that there was still often no direct link between world prices and domestic prices. Going further than that, the re-exporters were able to take full advantage of price/exchange rate differences between the domestic market, the East European clearing account market, and the Western hard currency market. As early as 1968, when a re-exporter had brought a number of Yugoslav organizations to the brink of ruin by cashing in on some 'dumpings' of East European foodstuffs, an official of the *federal* government remarked that 'there is no state in the world which permits traders of this type to make the kind of superprofits that they make in Yugoslavia. These organizations are rapidly becoming the king pins of the country's economy'('Što je to . . .', 1970). But the re-exporters also stood accused of breaking the law. Retention quotas for foreign exchange were bought and sold. Most important in the present context, re-exporters would use fake cooperation agreements and other ruses to invest their superprofits – often on conditions which would have been against the law in the case of a straight loan – in sectors short of capital, but with good prospects of profitability. Frequently, of course, that meant the Dalmatian tourist industry. In one case Genex lent the Croatian agro-industrial combine Belje 4m dinars against repayment in dollars, at rate of interest of 7.5 per cent – very high for 1971, given that the loan was denominated in hard currency. In any case, the law at that time permitted loans on such conditions only when they were strictly for the purpose of developing exports. In the Belje case that was not true. Needless to say, Belje's organs of self-management had known nothng of the deal. Small wonder that by the early 1970s Croatian politicians were calling for a 'third nationalization' of the big financial concentrations.

But however shocking the details of some of Genex's ploys, we have to be careful not to over-extrapolate from individual cases. Producing balance-sheets of inter-republican economic relations did, indeed, become something of an industry at this time, and an important element in the increasingly heated exchanges between Belgrade and Zagreb. It was Ljubljana, however, which produced one of the first serious academic studies of the subject, citing data which indicated that in 1967 the net result of all financial movements – fiscal, banking, etc., was that Slovenia contributed 16.9 per cent of its National Income to the Federation (Pečar 1970). A Croatian estimate form the following year reckoned that the corresponding figure for Croatia was in the region of 30 per cent (Djodan 1971). The study published in 1972 by Serbian economist G. Grdjić took the line that Serbia had been seriously neglected from an investment point of view in the early post-war period. Even for the period 1956–68, when Serbia's rate of growth of National Income averaged 11 per cent, the republic's share of total business investment was, according to this author, rather less than its share in the total population of Yugoslavia (Grdjić 1972). The key point at issue between Grdjić and his Ljubljana and Zagreb colleagues was the impact of distortions in the price system, particularly as they affected agricultural and raw material prices, on the net position on inter-regional transfers. A 'neutral' assessment from Macedonia, published in 1973, came down guardedly on the side of those who argued that transfers due to price distortions had benefited Slovenia, Croatia and Macedonia at the expense of Serbia, Bosnia and Hercegovina and Montenegro as of the mid-1960s (Poležina 1973).

These controversies, though inconclusive, did bear a clear relationship to real economic issues. Rather less well grounded was the parallel controversy over which republic made the biggest contribution to the Yugoslav Balance of Payments. The early 1970s witnessed a growing obsession with this issue in Croatia. Finally, towards the end of 1971 two national weeklies – both published in Belgrade – released figures giving a republic-by-republic breakdown of the Balance of Payments for the first time Yugoslav history (*NIN* 14 November 1971: 15–16: *Ekonomska Politika* 15 November 1971: 19–22). The two sets of figures for 1970 differed widely, but both ageed that Serbia was substantially in the red. The major disagreement was over the position of Croatia, with *NIN* placing her in the black by a billion dinars while *Ekonomska Politika* reckoned her to be in surplus by only a few millions dinars.

The reasons for these divergences need not concern us here. The significance of the debate lies rather in the essential insubstantiality of the issue. In a normal market economy the question of where precisely exports originate from, or indeed imports are destined for, is simply not relevant to economic policy making. To the extent that it was relevant in the Yugoslav economy in this period, it was so because of the anomalous character of the foreign trade system, which automatically, and often arbitrarily, granted privileges to organizations engaged in importing and exporting against a background of dinar inconvertibility, and because, as we have just seen, distortions in the domestic price system fudged the profile of Yugoslavia's inter-regional 'Balance of Payments'. To the extent that Croatia was, indeed, the main focus of hard-currency-earning activities, she was, surely, a disproportionate beneficiary of those systemically conditioned privileges. The disproportion may have been to a considerable degree redressed by the activities of organizations like Genex, but in calling on Belgrade to recognize the special status of Croatia as pre-eminent earner of hard currency, Croatian militants seemed to be calling for a redistribution of privilege, rather than its removal.

In truth we would be wrong to seek for too much economic common sense in these debates. The fact is that by the early 1970s Croatia was in the grip of something of a nationalist fever. We can trace the origins of this fever back to the 'Declaration on the Croatian Literary Language', published in 1967 by a group of eminent Croatian writers associated with the cultural and publishing organization *Matica Hrvatska*. Now the Croatian and Serbian languages are, to a degree, distinctive in vocabulary and idiom, but no more than, say, British and American English. The *Matica Hrvatska* group took the line that the Croatian language had been suppressed by the Belgrade establishment – in much the same way that the Croatian economy was, allegedly, being exploited by that same establishment. The initial reaction of the Yugoslav political establishment was accommodating, and constitutional amendments passed in June 1971 practically turned Yugoslavia into a confederation. But these concessions only seemed to fuel the fires of militancy in Croatia, and by mid-summer, 1971, elements of explicit separatism were emerging within the nationalist upsurge in that republic. In July of that year President Tito, himself a Croat, spoke in the following terms to a closed meeting of the Croatian Communist Party Executive Bureau:

> They [the nationalists] are united in their struggle against socialism
> . . . We have to take appropriate measures. The whole movement
> is now directed against me, here and also in Serbia. I want sharp and
> decisive action. Anyone who cannot deliver that should resign his post.
> . . . I would rather use our army than allow others to interfere. The
> Party is not united, and will have to be purged of all those who are
> not on our ideological path . . . What have you done about those
> who make threatening speeches . . . or those who sing 'Comrade
> Tito, I kiss you on the brow, go and put on your Ustaša uniform

now'? They have infiltrated the University and let people into the Party
who promise us a hot autumn. The autumn will be hot for them and
I shall personally see to that. Since the Second Congress of Self-
Managers nothing worthwhile has been achieved because of
technocrats. . . In the present situation a surgical knife is needed,
and I will not hesitate to use it, since nothing can be achieved by
discussion.

(Tito 1972a)

After that, events moved fast. The Croatian Party leadership and
government was completely cleaned out December 1971–January 1972,
and the new republican leadership was quick to condemn the 'fascist–
totalitarian' tendencies which had been permitted to develop, while
emphasizing at the same time the need for serious research on the subject
of resource flows between republics (Perišin 1972). This formulation
was, indeed, a pointer to the politico–economic compromises of the
future.

The attack on technocracy, and the 'OOURization' of the Yugoslav economy

One of the odder features of Tito's key speech in Croatia in 1971 was
the way he went directly from an attack on crypto-fascist elements in
the Croatian political establishment to a broadside against technocrats.
The organic link between the two issues was certainly tenuous, but in
bracketing them Tito knew exactly what he was doing in *political* terms.
It was, in the President's view, the weakening in the the leading role
of the party which lay at the root of the malaise which had crept into
the Yugoslav system in the early 1970s, and it was now time, he felt,
to reassert that role, and to make clear that the party would not tolerate
any autonomous power foci in Yugoslavia, nationalist or technocratic,
inside or outside the League of Communists. Significantly, 1972
witnessed a sustained attack on 'liberalism' in the Serbian Party. Too
soft on law-enforcement, the media and ideology, the Serbian leadership, it was alleged, were also guilty of a patronizing attitude towards
the 'conservatism' of other republican leaderships, while at the same
time failing to come to grips with the state capital issue (Tito 1972c).
Conservative or not, those other leaderships were also subjected to a
systematic purge. The new party line was codified and embodied in the
famous 'Letter' sent out to all regional Party leaderships in September
1972.

But it was the assault on 'managerialism' which had the most direct
impact on the Yugoslav economic system. The history of this issue went
back to a constitutional amendment of 1968 which gave workers'

councils a new freedom to remodel their executive management organs as they saw fit. The years that followed witnessed rapid evolution in many Yugoslav enterprises towards a management structure which gave executives as a group a more prominent and clearly defined position. The old management committee (*upravni odbor*), made up of delegates from the workers' council, tended to be replaced by a 'business committee' (*poslovni odbor*), made up largely of professional managers. We should certainly not exaggerate the importance of this trend. The management committee had never been a very powerful organ of self-management, and the constitutional amendment did not, of course, change the position of the director. The pre-amendment law had, furthermore, always recognized the special status of the managerial group under the title of the *collegium*. Arguably the business committee system actually strengthened effective self-management by making the collegium more directly responsible to the workers' council. Perhaps the most important thing about the whole movement as the fact that *some* working collectives showed a willingness to trade the trappings of self-management for more effective, and therefore more profitable management. The constitutional amendment may not have heralded the emergence of a 'new class', but it certainly was instrumental in substantially raising the prestige of the Yugoslav executive.

Not everyone, however, was happy about these management trends. The discontent was largely articulated by the Trade Unions, very much a party organization, but with a clearly defined constituency amongst the less favoured groups of workers who could not always look to the institutions of self-management to air their grievances. By the early 1970s the Yugoslav working class as a whole found itself under pressure in a number of ways. Unemployment was rising – from a figure of under 300,000 in 1971 it had grown to nearly half-a-million by 1974, although labour shortages in particular regions, like Slovenia, and in relation to particular skills, became increasingly acute. (In 1972 22 per cent of all advertised vacancies remained unfulfilled – Nejašmić 1973). Average real incomes fell by a total of 3 per cent 1971–3(*SGJ* 1975: 299). Contemporary reporting suggested a much sharper drop in general living standards, and with liquidity difficulties delaying wage pay-outs the take-home pay situation must often have seemed dramatically worse for workers and their families.

At a time when the consumption cake was no longer growing it was perhaps not surprising that the distribution of income came increasingly to the fore as a political issue. According to a scholarly investigation, the difference between total income of the highest and lowest income groups increased only slightly, from a factor of 2.28 to one of 2.66, between 1965 and 1970 (Štahan 1972: 347). But differentials widened substantially through 1971, and while wage and salary scales within socialized enterprises remained distinctly egalitarian by international standards, media attention was increasingly directed to managerial fringe benefits as a growing source of inequality in the overall distribution of income. Meanwhile the combination of self-management and restrictions on new entry was creating differentials between groups doing the same job in different industries at a level very high by international standards (Estrin *et al.* 1988). Worker discontent was exacerbated by specific problems like housing. As of 1971 Yugoslavia was short of around 700,000 flats, and sociologists were complaining that housing policy was effectively regressive (Žuvela 1974). It is hardly surprising that by 1972, just as the political crisis reached its climax, the incidence of strikes in Yugoslavia was reaching serious proportions.

There were, then solid grounds on which Tito could rally the support of the working class behind his campaign to cut the elites down to size. Constitutional amendment 21, passed in mid-1971, embodied the principle that the primary unit in the business sector should henceforth be the smallest unit compatible with technological realities. The new basis building block of the system was christened, rather clumsily, 'basic organization of associated labour' (*osnovna organizacija udruženog rada* – OOUR). The unity of inter-connected technical processes would be maintained by permitting OOUR's to come together in 'working organizations' (*radna organizacija* – RO), with working organizations in turn having the option of federating into 'complex organizations of associated labour' (*složena organižacija udruž*enog rada – SOUR).

Perhaps the most important thing to emphasize about the implementation of amendment 21 is that, once again, it *took the form of a political campaign*. Chords it may have struck on the shop floor, but it was in every sense a revolution from above. Neither the realities of economies of scale, nor the manifold accounting problems it created, were allowed to stand in its way. Those problems were still causing severe difficulties years after the promulgation of the original legislation, viz.–

> Basic organizations of socialized labour are unable to plan their development because they lack clear criteria, a clear approach to primary distribution. They do not know what the general trading regime is going to be like, nor do they know how foreign exchange relationships will work out. The question of primary emissions of money likewise remains unclarified, as does that of relationships to capital investment, or indeed to the net income of socialized work in general. It is hardly surprising that without a clear position on these questions there can be no self-managing planning, on either the macro or micro level.
> (Rukavina-Šain and Ćirić 1975: 4)

But the party line on these issues was uncompromising. Thus one local League of Communists chief:

We cannot have OOURs with several hundred workers, especially when the creation of OOURs with far fewer workers is technologically and economically *possible* [emphasis added]. We must not permit the intrusion of anti-party attitudes in the organizational field under the excuse of the defence of technological unity. We must be adamant on the question of the further development of the number of OOURs within combines, just as we have to be adamant in demanding that divisions function better. We must not reduce self-management to a formality in the framework of Mammoth OOURs, even with the window-dressing of the 'will of the workers', and in the name of technological indivisibilities. Objectively, that cannot be self-management.

(Mijatović 1974)

There was, certainly, something a little odd, even contradictory about this old-style party campaign to strengthen self-management. It was accompanied by a stream of legislation which did, in fact place organs of self-management increasingly under the tutelage of the state. A hierarchy of self-management watchdogs (*pravobranilac samoupravljanja*) was created, stretching right down to the commune level. In 1974 a network of courts of associated labour (*sudovi udruženog rada*) was set up, charged with the job of interpreting and enforcing the new rules and regulations. The practical impact of all this seems to have been, if anything, to increase the effective authority of managers over workers – as long as the former had the backing of the politicians. Here is how one worker explained it:

The amendments, particularly the so-called workers' amendments, guarantee us workers greater rights. But what's the use of rights when we know that every word said in public has its consequences? If you tell the manager that working conditions, personal incomes, or something else connected with the workers and the work place, are not in comformity with contemporary policy lines, particularly with the idea of 'first priority to the worker', then you will get a reply like: 'if you are not satisfied go and look for a job somewhere else'. This is out of order, but after such a reply the worker, fearing for his job, holds his tongue, keeps his discontent to himself, and abandons the exercise of his rights.

(Mesarić 1973)

In 1977, with the party leadership still not satisfied that enough had been done to OOURize the economy, the *Skupština* passed a *Law on Associated Labour* (*ZUR*), which reiterated and codified the constitutional principles of 1974. But a couple of years later the centre was still complaining about formalism in the implementation of the Law (Stanoj-lović 1979).

Socialist legality and the private sector

One can perceive the same kind of ideological impetus coming through in other areas of policy-making too. As we saw, much of the discontent over distribution of income in the early 1970s had focused on fringe benefits. In a speech read to a Croatian audience in the autumn of 1972 President Tito dwelt in particular on the 'Communist millionaires' who had made their piles despite (perhaps because of?) being party members (Tito 1972b). And when Tito went on to argue that you cannot *earn* that much money, that you must be exploiting somebody, he surely struck a deep chord in the consciousness of the Yugoslav masses, still power-fully influenced by the half-peasant attitudes which Mihailović describes so well. In 1973 police powers in relation to, *inter alia*, business crime were strengthened, amidst charges that this represented a return to the pre-1965 situation. (It should be said that there is plenty of solid evidence to show that the incidence of business crime and corruption did increase sharply in the early 1970s.) The following year, a network of commis-sions was set up at commune level charged with the investigation of the origin of individual property. These commissions would work on the principle that any property not acquired through work, gift or inheritance, was subject to confiscation, *even if it had been acquired without break-ing the law*. In addition, the onus would be on the suspect to prove the legitimate origin of his property. These were clearly kangaroo courts, which gave the authorities wide scope to persecute anyone deemed to have stepped out of line. In practice they were used principally to persecute the private sector. There were a few well publicized cases of public figures being prosecuted, but by and large bureaucratic ill-gotten gains were left untouched.

The offensive against enrichment was backed up by specific measures on the private and semi-private sectors of the economy. (We leave specific discussion of the key private agricultural sector for the next chapter.) As early as July 1971 a government decree imposed a virtual ban on the import of semi-finished goods by private enterprises, and 1973 was marked by a press campaign against deteriorating working conditions, excessively (and illegally) long working hours and poor pay amongst workers in the private sector. The middle of the same year witnessed the suppression of so-called GG-enterprises (GG stands for *grupa gradjana* – group of citizens). A product of the 1965 reform, this hybrid type had permitted private entrepreneurship on the legal basis of social ownership. It had been in political trouble almost from the start, and provided an easy target for the new policy orientation. The constitutional amendments did provide for the formation of something along the same lines, and a few years later there emerged a new hybrid creature bearing the fashionably long-winded title of 'contractual organization of associated labour' (*ugovorna organizacija undruženog rada* – (UOUR). But the UOUR was kept under much stricter control than had the old GG-enterprises.

It would be simplistic and unfair to argue that the Yugoslav leadership of the mid-1970s consistently allowed economic commonsense to be overridden by ideology. In reality the situation was much more complex than that. In taking a stance on distribution of income in the early 1970s, the leadership was genuinely responding to pressures from below. By 1973 the range of regular incomes in the socialized sector had been brought back to the 1970 scale, and by 1974 it had been compressed a good deal further. But in the meantime socialized sector income had fallen from 52 per cent to just 44.5 per cent of total personal income (Vizek 1974). Policy-makers began to realize that the campaign against social differences had quite wrongly focused on regular income, just because it was the easiest variable to operate on. The result was *uravnilovka* (levelling), and in September 1974 Ivan Stambolić, president of the Business Chamber of Belgrade and a future prime minister of Serbia, declared that 'it is necessary to emphasize at the present moment that *uravnilovka* cannot be in the long-term interest of the working class. It is in the interest of that section of the population for whom socialized work is not the main source of income' (Stambolić 1974b). A month later Edvard Kardelj, the architect of the 1974 constitution and father of the concept of associated labour, publicly condemned *uravnilovka*, equating it with parasitism and irresponsibility (Kardelj 1974).

In their search for a formula that would combine incentives and fairness the party leadership had, it might therefore seem, little choice but to mount an assault on non-regular earnings. At the same time it can be argued that the explosion of these earnings in the early 1970s was largely a result of deficiencies of system design. We have already discussed the problem of the institutionalized market power of the banks and import-export corporations. We can add that private and semi-private organizations were able to make super-profits largely because they were able to fill gaps in the system, or exploit market imperfections – again often institutionalized. There may be truth in the charge that GG-enterprises were a hotbed of financial malpractice extending as far as embezzlement of socialized funds. But in the absence of clearly defined ownership rights, and of a properly constituted liquidation procedure, was this really surprising? And was it so very different from what went on in many regular socialized-sector organizations? Finally, was the problem of burgeoning business crime not essentially a by-product of over-regulation? And if so, would it be solved through the introduction of even more regulations? It is striking that as early as 1974 Ivan Stambolić was complaining of the unnecessary growth in the complexity of the social control mechanism, and calling for a fundamental rationalization of the whole social accounting system (Stambolić 1974a). Perhaps the most telling example of ineffectual over-regulation comes from the area of price policy. The early 1970s saw a gradual return to blanket price control, culminating in a series of price freezes. Meanwhile the inflation rate climbed inexorably higher and higher, even as the 'wide boys' were stepping in to exploit any anomalies in the panoply of control.

Planning by agreement and association

The new constitution of 1974, which modified and amplified the rash of constitutional amendments which the late 1960s and early 1970s had witnessed, did offer a response to these fundamental systemic problems. But it was not essentially a market socialist response. Rather the Yugoslav leadership expressed through it the conviction that the experience of the late 1960s and early 1970s had highlighted the pitfalls of an approach which relied too heavily on the market. Had the political constellation been set a little differently they might rather have pursued the line that the reforms of the 1960s, radical though they were, had failed because they had left too many areas outwith the real discipline of the market. But the approach the leadership did adopt – based on the idea of voluntary, 'self-managing' planning agreements – had perfectly good credentials, and a degree of respectability in the Western, industrial world. The transnational corporations had already discovered that, in an international environment increasingly characterized by technological volatility and extreme uncertainty on raw material prices, exchange rates, etc., relations with production partners, upstream and downstream, were best organized on the basis of a highly flexible system of renegotiable contracts. The idea was taken up by the technocratic state capitalists of the British Labour Party and embodied in the Labour Party programme of 1974. It surfaced again in the programmes of the French socialist government of the early 1980s. In its Yugoslav socialist variant the argument ran as follows:

1 The market cannot be trusted to generate an acceptable distribution of income.
2 The market cannot be trusted to provide a rational framework for investment decision-taking, particularly in the context of severe regional disparities and ethnic rivalries.
3 By introducing a comprehensive system of inter-locking planning agreements, the authorities can ensure a much higher level of

85

> *concertation –without increasing the burden of planning and regulation on the state.*

The wordiness which afflicted every aspect of the constitutional amendments is present here too, to tax our ability to remember obscure formulations and acronyms. Under the new constitution two types of planning agreement were distinguished. *Social compacts (društveni dogovor)* were of a vertical nature, linking government to business chambers and business chambers to production organizations. A model social compact on distribution of income was worked out in 1974, and in the following year a federal compact covering personal and corporate income was signed by federal and republican government, trade union and *komora* (business chamber) representatives. This federal compact aimed to consolidate the principles of remuneration according to work and same pay for the same job, and also to create a framework within which investment and development plans could be co-ordinated. It thus implied substantial limitation of effective self-management rights – but of course only on a voluntary contractual basis. Early 1975 also witnessed the signature of a Social Compact between federal government and *komora* on the implementation of the general economic and social policy line agreed for that year. It was decided at the same time that the five-year plan for the period 1976–80 should be based on 20 social compacts covering the development of key sectors of the economy.

The other main category of planning agreement distinguished was the *self-management agreement (samoupravni sporazum)*. The self-management agreement was conceived as an essentially *horizontal*, inter-enterprise contractual linkage, covering distribution of income, investment and employment matters. Similar in scope to the social compact, the role of the self-management agreement was clearly seen in terms of backing up and consolidating the process of *concertation* outlined by the pyramidal framework of the social compact.

Planning agreements, were, then, to cover investment and development matters as well as wages and differentials. How would that affect financial relations between enterprises? Would it mean that one enterprise could 'lend' money to another under the rubric of a self-management agreement, and if so how would this differ from the often unsavoury 'cooperation' deals favoured by Genex and its like in the late 1960s and early 1970s? The new idea was that investment funds could be mobilized on an inter-enterprise basis through 'association' (*udruživanje*). The terminology was carefully chosen to underline the principle that such agreements should never infringe the rights of associated labour of either party.

Finally, the legislative innovations of the mid-1970s saw the codification of a new approach to the organization of service and infrastructural enterprises. *Self-managing communities of interest (samoupravne interesne zajednice – SIZ, plural SIZ-ovi)*, originally created in 1965 to handle a limited range of social-infrastructural activities, were now to be developed as a basis which would shift the focus of the principle of self-management from the employees to the users of the services generated by the particular organization – following the same lines embodied in the principles of self-managing banking. Basic industrial-infrastructural sectors like energy and transport, in addition to education, health, employment and cultural services, would now by run by SIZ-ovi.

All of this had fundamental implications for the role of the business chamber. The 1965 reform had precipitated a crisis of role in a body which had always personified the principle of persuasion from above under planning by global proportions. The new system of planning agreements re-established the *komora* as the focal point of *concertation*, while reaffirming the principle that it should 'belong' as much to the business sector grass roots as to the governmental authorities. As one of its functionaries put it in 1975,

> The *komora* is not the 'long arm' of the state. But neither is it some kind of 'service' or 'hospital for emergency cases', but an institutional form under which the business sector can come to agreement on the development of production, on cooperation, and on the dove-tailing of particular and general interests.
>
> (Vlaho 1975)

Politics, planning agreements, and the party

It was not long before it became clear that the new approach was not working terribly well. The incomes policy dimension kept differentials down, but often at the cost of incentives and productivity (see Špiljak 1974). The rate of inflation fell sharply in 1976, but then began to creep up again, hitting a new record of 30 per cent in 1980. Self-management agreements were lightly entered into, and lightly broken. The general concept of association of investment funds soon spawned a more specific, operational form – compulsory association, whereby federation and republics raised money to finance unpopular projects – including development projects in poorer areas, which no one was prepared to finance voluntarily. These 'compulsory loans' were in practice almost indistinguishable from taxes, and did nothing to alleviate the inter-regional tensions and frustrations which had been a major root cause of the political crisis of 1971–2. Meanwhile the self-managing communities of interest were not living up to expectations. Far from acting as the faithful servants of their customers, if we can believe a barrage of complaints in the

87

Yugoslav press, they rapidly emerged as important foci of autonomous 'para-state' power, prone to over-charging for their services, ignoring the proposals of their sovereign delegates, and paying above-average salaries to their own employees. By 1979 the business sector was virtually in open insurrection against the SIZ-ovi, with mass refusals to sign proposed self-management agreements with them (Šimunić 1979). And for all the emphasis on workers' rights and OOUR-ization, the principle of self-management seemed to be faring no better at intra-enterprise level, as managerial cadres stood accused of an increasing tendency to form themselves into a 'directorium', manipulating political leaders and feeding disinformation to the workers ('Direktorijumi' 1976).

But the most disturbing aspect of the new *concertation* in practice was the way in which it was hi-jacked by monopoly interests. Now of course any system of planning agreements is bound to involve a degree of market-sharing, but in the Yugoslav case this took the form of an increasingly serious problem of regional autarky, in despite of the clause in the Constitution of 1974 which enshrined the 'unity of the Yugoslav market' as a legal principle, and threatened criminal sanctions against its violators. By the late 1970s the problem had developed to such an extent that only one-third of total turnover of goods and services in Yugoslavia involved crossing republican or provincial boundaries. Only 5.1 per cent of retail outlets in Slovenia belonged to organizations from other regions, with corresponding figures for Montenegro of 4.7 per cent, for Vojvodina of 12.8 per cent, and for impoverished Kosovo of 18.2 per cent (Vlaho, 1979e). To the extent that *udruživanje* got going as a way of making capital more mobile, it tended to do so within regional boundaries (Vlaho 1979d), thus fortifying a tendency to republicanization of finance capital that was, in all truth, strong enough in any case. And it was not just finance capital, it was *state* finance capital, or something very near it.

> It is much more profitable to hike up prices, make on imports, and collar the domestic market with the help of the state. In a certain sense it is even easier than in that biblical, pre-reform period, for now everyone has his own local state, partial towards him, with full powers, but not with full responsibility. (In the 1970s the banks) . . . became *sui generis* finance ministries of para–state political structures . . . '
>
> (Gavrović 1979b)

These remarks go beyond the issue of failure of the constitutional reforms of the 1970s, to conjure up a picture reminiscent of some of the most negative features of pre-war Yugoslavia.

Quite apart from what it did to resource allocation trends, republicanization of money and finance ensured that the fundamental problems of macro-economic monetary policy would remain unsolved. The federal authorities had some success in attacking the liquidity problem through multilateral debt-clearing operations, and by tightening up on enterprise accounting procedures, to stop enterprises counting bad debts as assets. But they were swimming against the tide. Selective re-discounting provided regional authorities with wide discretion in terms of open-ended support of favourite sons, as liquidity problems worsened again from the mid-1970s onwards. In that context it was inevitable that the inflation rate should start to rise once more, particularly in an era when external cost-inflationary pressures – mainly in the form of oil-price hikes – were particularly powerful. Using a Grainger causality test, Z. Kovačić has found that while wages provided the main inflationary impetus 1965–72, prices took over that role in the period 1973–84, though with a process of mutual interaction/adjustment visible within single quarters (Kovačić 1985). Further sharp increases in the volume of near-money in the economy in the late 1970s and early 1980s (by a total of 856 per cent 1979–84 – Rogić 1985: 163) represented both a symptom and a cause of the impotence of monetary policy. While the velocity of circulation of money fell somewhat 1974–9, it nearly doubled 1979–84 (Jovanović 1980; Rogić 1985: 163).

By the late 1970s, then, the Yugoslav economic system was looking increasingly fragmented, the centre less and less able to impose any kind of general policy orientation, the dimension of contractual planning unable to fill the resultant gap. How had this come about, following on the political initiatives of the middle 1970s, which had aimed precisely at curbing the excesses of confederalism, as institutionalized by the constitutional amendments of 1971? The answer is to be found in the manner in which the League of Communists evolved through the latter part of the 1970s. Tito had looked to the party in the crisis days of 1972–4 to reassert its leading role, and to provide a new impetus towards national unity at the political level, national *concertation* at the economic, armed with the new, very Soviet-style 'cadres policy' which layed down that candidates for all key position in a given region should be positively vetted. Such was his confidence in the party that he saw no reason to reverse the confederal provisions of the constitutional amendments as such, and these were, indeed, consolidated in the new constitution of 1974. In the event, Tito's confidence in the party turned out to be sorely misplaced. Purged of nationalists and liberals, the League of Communists proved itself, in the late 1970s, to be as powerful a vehicle of particularism – not just at the republican/provincial level, but right down to commune level – as had ever existed in Yugoslavia's history.

Yugoslavia

As one distinguished Yugoslav economist, close to the government, said to me in 1986, 'The trouble in Yugoslavia is that we have not one party, but eight'.

Chapter five

Growth Strategy and Economic Structure: the Balance of Payments and the Failure of Adjustment Policies in the 1970s

Economic performance in the 1960s and 1970s

Whatever else it did, the Yugoslav economy certainly grew rapidly over the two decades 1962–81. As Table 5.1 shows, the average annual rate of growth for National Income was consistently at, or above 5 per cent, and the rate of increase of industrial production continued to be sustained at a remarkably high level. Year-to-year fluctuations in total output trends owed more to the impact of the weather on agricultural production trends than to any instability on the industrial side. When we break the twenty-year period down into sub-periods, a clear pattern emerges. Up to 1965 the very high rates of growth of the 1950s were largely maintained, despite institutional instability. They then slackened off a little in the late 1960s, only to recover impressively in the early 1970s. Production growth rates fell off somewhat after the first oil shock, as was to be expected, but the slow-down was less than dramatic, and industrial output continued to grow at well above 5 per cent.

But perhaps the most interesting feature of these aggregate growth series is the relationship between rates of growth of industrial production and those of industrial productivity. The sub-period 1962–5 continues to exhibit the classic features of extensive development, as indeed we would expect, with just over half total growth in industrial output attributable to growth in labour productivity. In the next sub-period, and in the wake of the economic reforms, the picture changes dramatically. The increment in industrial production reported for 1966–70 came almost 100 per cent from increases in productivity, seemingly heralding a dramatic and conclusive shift from extensive to intensive growth patterns. How strange, then, to find that the acceleration of growth reported in the early 1970s was accompanied by a reversal to the old pattern of growth. For the period 1975–81 we find that labour productivity growth accounts for less than half the total increment in industrial output, marking this off as one of the most 'extensive' of all Yugoslavia's development periods, *just as growth is slackening*. From 1976 the labour productivity

Table 5.1 Yugoslav rates of growth 1962–81 (based on data in constant prices of 1972)

	National Income	Industrial Output	Industrial Labour Productivity	Agricultural Output
1962	3.2	8.6	5.9	−1.0
1963	12.0	16.2	9.3	7.4
1964	11.4	17.1	6.8	4.5
1965	1.7	7.2	4.8	−7.3
1966	7.9	3.7	6.1	18.8
1967	2.2	−0.3	0.0	−0.8
1968	3.5	5.1	7.1	−3.9
1969	9.7	9.8	6.7	6.8
1970	5.4	8.1	6.3	−6.1
1971	8.0	9.7	4.7	6.5
1972	4.2	7.1	3.4	−2.0
1973	4.9	5.4	3.0	9.2
1974	8.4	11.0	6.0	5.4
1975	3.6	6.6	1.0	−2.8
1976	3.9	3.6	1.0	6.8
1977	7.6	9.5	6.0	5.5
1978	6.8	8.7	5.0	−5.8
1979	7.1	8.7	4.0	5.6
1980	2.2	4.2	2.0	0.2
1981	1.4	4.2	2.0	2.7
1962–5	7.1	12.3	6.7	0.6
1966–70	5.7	5.3	5.2	3.1
1971–4	6.8	8.3	4.3	4.7
1975–81	4.7	6.5	3.0	1.6

Source: *Statistički Godišnjak Jugoslavije 1976*: 134–5 and 195; *Statistički Godišnjak Jugoslavije 1986*: 162–3 and 276

gap between Yugoslavia and Western Europe was actually increasing again (Zmijarević 1980).

The same picture emerges if we look at investment trends. Yugoslavia's gross fixed capital formation ratio stood at 31 per cent – a very high level for a relatively low-income country – in 1971–2, and had risen to a record level of 35 per cent by 1978–9. In 1981, with the debt-service crisis looming, it was still as high as 28 per cent (Gnjatović 1985: 65). The incremental capital-output ratio had gone up from 4.4 in 1962–5 to 5.1 for the period 1966–70 – this representing a perfectly normal reflection of the process of capital-deepening which we noted for that period – and fell again to 4.5 for 1971–4. It then rose dramatically to a level of 6.9 during the period 1975–81. Such a paradoxical combination of falling growth rates of output and even more steeply falling growth rates of productivity exactly parallels the Soviet experience of slow-down in the 1970s (see Dyker 1985: 41)

Had the reversal to extensive growth patterns set in during the mid-1970s, we might have sought an explanation for it in terms of a perfectly proper reaction to the changes in the labour supply situation brought about as the post-Oil Shock recession in Western Europe forced Yugoslav *gastarbeiter* to return to their native land. (Between 1973 and 1987 the number of Yugoslavs temporarily working abroad fell from 1.1m to 0.5m – Schrenk 1979: 251; Karakašević 1987.) In fact, it came much earlier, and it is not difficult to link these trends in growth patterns to the policy pattern we discussed in the last chapter. The whole attitude to the issue of socialist bankruptcy, the way the integration movement worked out in practice, the insistence on OOUR-ization whatever it did to efficiency parameters – all these things stood in the way of the systematic elimination of non-jobs, and ensured that new industrial developments also would be hampered from the start by feather-bedding, cross-subsidization, and the fudging of decision-taking on technology and factor proportions.

But that is, perhaps, too sweeping. For while economic development in Slovenia continued to be hampered by labour shortage throughout the early and middle 1970s, unemployment in Yugoslavia as a whole nearly doubled between 1971 and 1975 and stood at 833,000 by 1981 (SGJ 1986: 143). In truth, then, there was still substantial scope in the Yugoslavia of the 1970s for *selective* extensive development, particularly in the context of policy for the less developed regions. In Kosovo, for instance, registered unemployment was reported at 39.4 per cent of the total socialized sector workforce in 1982 ('Višak nezaposlenih . . . ', 1982). If we use as denominator total active population, including private peasants, etc., we still obtain a figure as high as c.27 per cent. Equally clearly, now that Yugoslavia could import capital only on more or less commercial terms, and with the successive hikes in energy and raw material prices which marked the 1970s, any such selective extensive development patterns would have to be strictly extensive in terms of *employment* patterns, not in terms of investment or materials utilization. We have seen already that the Yugoslav investment ratio did in fact increase significantly through the decade. We need only add that the energy intensity of industrial production in Yugoslavia actually *grew* by about 1 per cent 1973–82, while it fell by an average of some 31 per cent over the same period in the seven leading industrial countries of the world (OECD 1983: 78). As of the early 1980s Yugoslavia was using two-three times as much energy per unit of production as the industrially developed countries (*'Uslovi . . . '*, 1985: 303). Such an extension of extensive development patterns had an inevitable and fundamental impact on the *Balance of Payments*.

Table 5.2 The Balance of Payments 1966–81, in millions of dollars

	1966	1967	1968	1969	1970	1971	1972	1973	1974	1975	1976	1977	1978	1979	1980	1981
Current account																
Trade balance	−353	−455	−533	−660	−1195	−1438	−996	−1658	−3715	−3625	−2489	−4380	−4317	−7225	−6086	−4828
Exports	1223	1252	1264	1474	1679	1814	2237	2853	3805	4072	4878	5254	5671	6794	8978	10929
Imports	1576	1707	1797	2134	2874	3552	3233	4511	7520	7697	7367	9634	9988	11019	15064	15757
Balance of services	240	298	358	257	743	229	292	740	897	1014	874	1121	1029	1514	1898	1656
Transport (net)	140	145	146	171	211	226	240	323	396	430	419	568	587	731	845	1044
Travel (net)	82	95	136	168	144	141	219	589	644	702	725	750	930	1028	1505	1853
Interest (net)	−70	−74	−80	−90	−119	−140	−155	−180	−198	−275	−279	−258	−300	−633	−1084	−1710
Other services (net)	88	132	156	268	507	....	....	8	55	157	19	61	−188	388	632	469
Balance of goods and services	−113	−157	−175	−143	−452	−1209	−704	−918	−2818	−2611	−1615	−3259	−3288	−5711	−4188	−3172
Transfers (net)	74	82	80	80	104	852	1123	1403	1635	1608	1770	1730	2032	2050	1897	2422
Reparations	11	12	11	2	1	0	−1	−1	−1	−1	−2	−2	−2	−5	−5	−6
Emigrants' remittances	63	70	69	78	103	136	160	215	257	282	357	305	320	345	363	386
Remittances from Yugoslavs working abroad[1]	–	–	–	–	–	716	964	1189	1379	1327	1415	1427	1714	1710	1539	2042
Balance of current transactions	−39	−75	−95	−63	−348	−357	419	485	−1183	−1003	165	−1529	−1256	−3661	−2291	−750
Capital account																
Errors and omissions	−103	−11	−192	−30	79	−232	−287	−245	−4	18	90	97	–	−45	−468	−256
Net new credits	140	47	338	247	216	567	398	380	788	689	736	1605	1589	2279	2534	570
Long-term (net)	137	128	102	145	223	460	324	563	527	1034	1290	1377	1719	1346	814	15
Short-term (net)	3	−81	236	102	−7	107	74	−183	261	−348	−554	188	−130	933	1720	555
Change in reserves	2	39	−51	−154	53	22	−530	−620	399	296	−991	−173	−333	1427	225	436

Note: [1] Counted under 'other services' up to 1970
Source: Gnjatović 1985: 82

External economic relations in the post-reform period

If we looked only at overall current account trends through the late 1960s and early 1970s we might come away with the impression that a smooth progress towards external financial equilibrium was only halted by the First Oil Shock. Through 1966–9 deficits were uniformly small. Then after a couple of bad years in 1970 and 1971 the Balance of Payments on current account moved into substantial surplus for 1972 and 1973, only to break all records with a deficit of over $1bn in 1974. But if we look at the Balance of Trade on goods and services we find a rather different picture. The years 1972 and 1973 were years of substantial deficit, totalling, for the two years, just about the same level as for 1970 and 1971 taken together. The key to this apparent paradox is to be found in the 'Remittances from Yugoslavs working abroad' row. (Bear in mind that these were recorded under 'Other services' up to 1970.) For 1972–3 *gastarbeiter* remittances totalled well over $2.1bn, whereas for the previous two years taken together they contributed less than $1.3bn. It is this explosion of migrant worker earnings, rather than any structural trends in the Yugoslav economy, which largely explains the welcome improvement in the current account balance in the two years before the First Oil Shock.

The first two years after the First Oil Shock – 1974 and 1975 – were both very bad ones for the current account. The following year recorded a small surplus, reflecting a genuine improvement in the export situation, but 1977 again broke all records with a $1.5bn deficit on current account. The Second Oil Shock exacerbated the trend, producing a $3.7bn deficit in 1979, and leading directly to the crisis of debt service which broke in 1982. By that year the net burden of annual interest payments on the Yugoslav current account had reached $2bn.

There is a striking similarity between these Balance of Payments trends and the development trends we discussed in the last section. In the brief period in the late 1960s when the required transition to intensive development seemed to be in progress, the Balance of Payments position showed a big improvement from the crisis year of 1964. In 1966 the import bill was 78 per cent covered by export revenues, and for the period 1966–9 as a whole the corresponding figure was 72 per cent. As productivity trends worsened from the early 1970s onwards, so the underlying trend in the current account balance worsened, with 1972 and 1973 only flattering to deceive. And just as the domestic Yugoslav economy failed to respond to the new pecking order of scarcities in the middle and late 1970s, so the Yugoslav Balance of Payments during those years reflected a parallel incapacity to adjust to changing international trading patterns. (Yugoslavia's aggregate terms of trade worsened by 7 per cent 1973–5; they then recovered to the extent of 5 per cent 1975–8, only to worsen again by 6 per cent 1978–81 – SGJ 1979: 308; 1982: 307. For trade with the West taken separately the deteriorating trend was much sharper.)

We can certainly accept that Yugoslavia was doubly unlucky in that the Oil Crisis hit *gastarbeiter* remittances in addition to raising oil prices, as West European governments adopted restrictionist policies and unemployment started to rise in host countries. But this is merely to underline how badly Yugoslavia needed an effective adjustment mechanism in the 1970s, and how totally absent such a mechanism was. Yet the period was marked by much discussion of the issue of the 'right' exchange rate, and indeed the National Bank carried out successive devaluations of the dinar, meanwhile using direct controls and various forms of export stimulation to supplement exchange rate policy. Again, the 1976–80 medium-term plan included a set of key investment programmes, agreed by republics and provinces, which explicitly aimed to reorientate the structure of new investment towards more export-propulsive sectors, as well as to more effective import-substitution. We may seek the *essence* of the failure of the Yugoslav economy to adjust in those difficult times in general systemic terms: it remains nevertheless to establish what were the *mechanics* of the processes whereby the tools of adjustment available to the authorities were effectively neutralized. Before we look at exchange-rate policy, let us examine how the selective instruments at the disposal of the authorities worked in practice.

The effectiveness of administrative interference

Administrative interference in foreign trade flows is always likely to impose costs in terms of allocative efficiency. If import quotas are used to correct for an overvalued exchange rate, the beneficiaries of those quotas are likely to use the imported good in question (e.g. oil) in a wasteful manner. What we are concerned with here is the *organizational* efficiency of the mechanism of direct controls. We saw how vulnerable the old 1950s system of multiple exchange rates had been to internal inconsistency and special pleading. The post-1961 system turned out to be little improvement in this respect, and the 1960s witnessed case after case of injudicious decision-taking on licensing, involving failure to license imports crucially necessary for the fulfilment of export orders, reluctance to license the import of spare parts for imported equipment, arbitrary penalization of particular sub-sectors or enterprises, and failure to stop the large-scale import of goods already in excess supply on the home market, etc. (Dyker 1974: 337–8)

By the early 1970s the import regime had gelled into a very complicated combination of licences and quotas relating to specific categories of *goods* and, most important, quotas of *foreign exchange* for the import of more or less broadly defined categories of goods, such as consumer goods. A plan to liberalize the system gradually from 1973–5 foundered under the impact of the First Oil Crisis, and in 1975 an additional special system of licences for 139 specific categories of semi-finished and investment good and 117 categories of consumption good was introduced ('Uvoz uz dozvolu . . . ' 1975). This conglomeration inevitably produced the same pattern of inefficiency and special pleading that we had seen in previous decades. In early 1974, just as the Balance of Payments was running into real crisis, basic foodstuffs were being imported at prices higher than domestic prices, *even on the basis of an overvalued dinar*. Any movement towards the liberalization of the import regime for specific goods tended to get caught up in a web of restrictive practices, and Serbian Prime Minister Dušan Čkrebić was moved to call in 1975 for

> an end to the practice of judging the profitability of export business exclusively or largely on the basis of sectional interest and accounts, while neglecting the possible consequences of this for other OURs, and for the general market and business situation.
>
> (Čkrebić 1975)

Thus decisions on, for example, what level of car imports to permit ended up simply as trials of strength between importing organizations, eager to make a quick profit, and local producers anxious to protect a monopolistic position. As the foreign exchange position worsened in the early 1980s, new legislation increased the volume of form-filling required for import and export declarations six-fold ('Stanje duhova' 1981). In 1980 the director of the Energoinvest aluminium factory illegally took possession of crucial raw materials being held by the Yugoslav customs, on the grounds that it took too long to make formal application for release to the authorities, and that a break in supplies of the crucial materials would have resulted in a break in production of 18 months ('Naličje rizika' 1980). At a time of deepening crisis in the power supply, repairs to the Maribor power station, hit by lightning in 1980, and construction of a new gas pipeline through New Belgrade, were held up by a ludicrous mess of customs red tape ('Transformator . . . ' 1981: 'Usporeno kretanje' 1981). With the debt-service crisis only months away, the Subotica enterprise Zorka was thrown into crisis when it was forbidden to *export* more than 50,000 tons of chemical fertilizers, on the grounds that domestic agriculture should have priority supply ('Kod komšije . . . ' 1981).

The dinar and devaluation

Economic theory teaches us that a devaluation will, in the absence of serious supply inelasticities, make a proportionate improvement in the Balance of Trade of the devaluing country if the sum of the elasticities of demand for imports and exports is greater than one (the Marshall–Lerner condition). Of course if the initial deficit is very large, a proportionate improvement may not be sufficient to guarantee an absolute improvement. Adjustment for this complication makes the mathematics more involved, but for our purposes the simple Marshall–Lerner condition is an adequate approximation. The intuitive interpretation of the condition is obvious. Devaluations can only improve the Balance of Trade if they cause exports to rise and/or imports to fall in terms of total value. They make exports cheaper to the foreign customer and imports dearer to the home buyer, but these price changes will only have the desired effect on quantities bought if the demand for the commodities in question is sensitive to price. And if the demand for imports, say, is extremely inelastic, then the demand for exports will have to be that much more elastic if devaluation is to work.

Econometric investigation reveals that the price elasticity of demand for imports in Yugoslavia is extremely low, and indeed tends to zero (Dyker 1974: 333; *Znanstvene Osnove* . . . 1984: 89–90). This is not a surprising result. Raw materials, semi-finisheds and capital goods have consistently made up 80–90 per cent of total Yugoslav imports in the period since 1960, with raw materials and semi-finisheds alone accounting for 60–80 per cent. Thus on strictly *a priori* grounds we would expect the import elasticity of demand to be very low in this case, at least in the short run, since there is, for instance, little an industrial enterprise can do to reduce its unit fuel requirements in the face of a price increase, short of bringing in more energy-efficient equipment. When we add in the heavy incidence of import licensing, quotas and other forms of administrative control over imports, which has served to blunt what price sensitivity there might have been, the picture is complete.

The export situation is more complex. As a small country without a dominant share in any world market, we would expect Yugoslavia to come on to export markets primarily as a price-taker, which would imply a high degree of elasticity in the demand curve as it faces the Yugoslav exporter. The econometric evidence is not conclusive on this point, but research from the late 1960s suggested that it was certainly possible to explain the bulk of movement in Yugoslav industrial exports without recourse to price variables (Dyker 1974: 333). More recent econometric research presents a similar picture, and Mencinger and Bole, in their econometric model of the Yugoslav economy, were able to explain the bulk of movements in Yugoslav exports by the level of domestic economic activity, the level of domestic aggregate demand, and levels of stocks of finished goods (Mencinger and Bole 1980; 42; see also *Strukturne Karakteristike*. . . . 1977: 193–5). What we can say with some confidence, then, is that the price variable does not emerge as the kind of key variable that we might expect on *a priori* grounds.

Why so? A number of possible explanations spring to mind. First, the amount Yugoslavia exports is to a significant extent subject to the administrative decisions of other governments. This means not only that particular export markets may simply be cut off, as happened during the Cominform disputes, but also that a foreign importer may find that the only way he can obtain a particular product or commodity is by importing it from Yugoslavia, so that the Yugoslav exporter will be in a position, within limits, to name his price without reference to world prices. Second, a Yugoslav enterprise concerned primarily with earning hard currency (perhaps in order to import much needed equipment) may not be prepared to export to clearing agreement countries *at any price*. Third, enterprises in financial difficulties may be induced to export at a loss, simply in order to gain access to special export credit lines (Staničić 1972). The behaviour of such enterprises will clearly be little affected by the positive impact of devaluation on export profit rates. Fourth, with specific bilateral deals, as opposed to general clearing agreements, involving, say, exports, imports, and technical and scientific aid, the 'accounting prices' of the separate components of the deal may be quite unreal. Finally, there is evidence to suggest that Yugoslav exporters have increasingly tended to *think* in dollars rather than dinars (Vasić 1984). As the rate of inflation of the domestic currency gathered momentum through the 1970s, and as the authorities relaxed restrictions on the holding of foreign currency by Yugoslavs, so there developed an increasing problem of internal dinar inconvertibility (Popović 1980). Clearly, if Yugoslav exporters think in dollars, a devaluation of the dinar will have absolutely no impact on their behaviour whatsoever.

But the biggest difficulty with the results of econometric investigation of the elasticity of demand for Yugoslav exports is that we cannot be sure that we have specified the problem correctly. It can be argued, *a priori*, that in a self-managing system of the Yugoslav type, the offer curve of enterprises may not respond to the increased profitability opportunities offered by exporting in the context of a devaluation. Let us pursue the argument in terms of pure 'Illyrian' conditions. The self-managing enterprise will seek to maximize, not profits, but net earnings (wages plus profits) per worker. The way to do that, under conventional short-run assumptions where capital stock is fixed and cost curves are U-shaped, is to produce at the highest point on the average labour productivity curve. A devaluation will not affect the position of that highest point one whit. (For discussion of other aspects of the 'Illyrian paradox' see Ward 1958; Vanek 1975; Meade 1975.)

Of course this bizarre result flows very much from the specific assumptions of the simple Illyrian model, which ignores the possibility of new entry. It also depends on the assumption that exporting organizations are a breed apart, with little interest in supplying the domestic market. If we can, in practice, count on new firms coming into the market to take advantage of new opportunities for profit-making, then the paradox disappears. Under real Yugoslav conditions, however, this is precisely one of the weakest areas of the market mechanism. New enterprises can only be set up in Yugoslavia by socio-political bodies, and in the context of the regional-autarkical trends discussed in the last chapter, that effectively means an enterprise cannot be set up in a given region without the active involvement of the regional political leadership. In any case, and despite the opening-up of the foreign trade system in the 1960s, access to export markets remained, through the 1970s, the privilege, perhaps a dubious one, of a limited number of enterprises. At the end of 1975 the number of OOURs registered for participation in foreign trade was reduced from 1,444 to 810, under the rubric of a Social Compact on cadres in foreign trade, though it was subsequently increased again to 1,009 (Grubić 1976). Thus the scope for exporting organizations to respond to improved export prices by switching supplies from domestic to foreign customers was, indeed, limited. So there is nothing on the entry conditions side to invalidate the simple Illyrian theory.

A more fundamental criticism of the Illyrian approach focuses on its short-term, static nature. In a dynamic world, it may be argued, increased exporting opportunities make it possible for enterprises to invest in new plant, perhaps embodying higher technologies, thus increasing labour productivity, and increasing average net income. We can, of course, generalize this argument beyond the limits of the specific issue of devaluation. Even with a given real exchange rate new investment may offer scope for exploiting *potential* export profitability. Indeed in Yugoslav conditions, where the domestic market is relatively undemanding in terms of the technological level and styling of products, specific investments related to the assimilation of specific elements of innovation or technology transfer may be a *sine qua non* of any major breakthrough on export markets.

It is clear, however, that this has not been the pattern in Yugoslavia. Exporting has, in fact, been consistently residualized, consistently based primarily on stocks of goods left unutilized after the satisfaction of domestic demand. That is, of course, why Mencinger and Bole found it so useful to include domestic demand *and* stocks in their export function. The actual organization of exporting business by Yugoslav firms has reflected this low priority, characterized as it has been by fragmentation, low calibre in personnel, and corruption (Petrović 1974), Investment patterns have rarely reflected any specific concern with the development of exporting, and the political economy of the investment process in Yugoslavia has ensured the absence of any automatic mechanism whereby price stimuli, international or domestic, would get through to influence that process. Coming back to the short term, the high *import* content of exports, through which the export sector may have suffered seriously from insensitive administrative control over imports, can only have made it that much more difficult to respond to export price incentives. Thus any argument that lays special stress on supply inelasticity in relation to exports must ultimately be based on broadly systemic rather than narrowly theoretical grounds.

Table 5.3 The effective dinar exchange rate 1971–83 (1971 = 100)

	Nominal exchange rate	Difference between Yugoslav and world inflation rates
1971	100	100
1972	98.1	102.7
1973	99.1	103.8
1974	99.7	111.5
1975	111.5	126.3
1976	110.7	124.1
1977	112.8	127.9
1978	128.6	132.3
1979	138.1	142.1
1980	175.0	162.0
1981	203.0	205.0
1982	313.0	316.0
1983	487.5	405.1

Source: Babić and Primorac 1986: 81

Even so, the investment trends that unfolded in the couple of decades leading up to the crisis were *peculiarly* inimical to the development of exports. This brings us back to the whole question of development strategy, but it also brings us back to the exchange rate. Mate Babić has shown how adjustment of the Yugoslav exchange rate consistently lagged behind inflation throughout the 1970s (see Table 5.3). So for all the talk about using the exchange rate as an adjustment mechanism, the dinar was never really devalued in the course of that crucial decade. But Babić and Primorac take the argument further, positing that 'Yugoslavia overvalued the dinar as a matter of policy, in order to stimulate imports of machinery and equipment necessary for investment projects' (Babić and Primorac 1986: 80). Perhaps, given the evidence on the elasticities of demand for imports and exports, it would not have made a great deal of difference if the dinar had been devalued in real terms. Equally, we can argue that in conditions of permanent over-valuation of the domestic currency the main incentives to exporting would be based either on direct administrative pressure, or expectations about future exchange rates. To that extent getting the exchange rate wrong may in itself have weakened the impact of exchange rate policy (Vodopivec 1986: 31). Be that as it may, Babić and Primorac are surely right to argue that the effective strategy followed in Yugoslavia during the 1970s was one of import-led growth, that the whole structure of investment was import-intensive and inimical to exporting. Let us now look in greater detail at how that strategy and structure affected specific sectoral investment trends.

Investment and the Balance of Payments

Whatever economic problems Yugoslavia had in the 1970s, inability to perceive those problems was certainly not one of them. Throughout the post-reform period economists made common cause with a large section of the political and administrative elite in arguing that the heavy emphasis on the development of manufacturing in the 1950s had created a fundamental imbalance in the Yugoslav economy, that attempts at import substitution had in many cases a perverse impact on the Balance of Trade, because the projects involved were so dependent on foreign equipment, foreign technology and imported energy, that investment in infrastructure had been seriously neglected, and that the channelling of specific investment resources into specific export-propulsive sectors should be the main concern of planners. As we saw, it was precisely this concern which inspired the set of key investment programmes which dominated official policy-making in the investment field in the late 1970s. The programmes focused attention on energy and fuel, ferrous and non-ferrous metals, base chemicals, extraction of non-metallic minerals, machine- and ship-building, agro-industry, road transport and foreign tourism. They envisaged that 64.6 per cent of total fixed investment in the business (*privredni*) sector should go to those nominated, key sectors, compared with 53.3 per cent for the same sectors in the period 1971–5. The outcome for 1976–80 was a figure of 59.5 per cent. This suggests partial success, but when we look at what happened to specific programmes the picture is more negative. Shares of investment going to fuel, energy and primary extraction sectors certainly did increase. But the share of agro-industry fell somewhat, while those of foreign tourism and road transport fell sharply. By the early 1980s, indeed, the transport network situation had deteriorated to such an extent as to prompt the judgement that 'the state of [transport] infrastructure in Yugoslavia is now so bad that there is a danger that all the main European transport arterials will simply pass us by' (*Uslovi. . .* 1985: 235). Aggregate investment in machine-building and ship-building was programmed for a sharp decrease, but in practice it held its own (World Bank 1983: 9).

The strategy for machine-building had been to rationalize the sector, cutting overall investment, while increasing investment into specifically export-oriented sub-sectors. In practice, the perennial weaknesses of duplication and excessive scale plagued individual machine-building programmes (Vlaho 1978). In metal-working and in other sectors regional autarkical pressures seemed to grow worse. As of 1979, 62 foundries were under construction, though existing capacities were only being 72 per cent utilized, while 19 plastics factories were going up, despite just 69 per cent utilization of existing capacity. Corresponding figures for timber products were 50 and 76 per cent, for furniture 63 and 73 per cent, and for slaughter-houses 22 and 62 per cent (Vlaho 1979c). As a result of all this, the rate of industrial capacity utilization, measured in terms of the total number of hours in the year, was down to 53 per cent by 1978 (Zmijarević 1980). It subsequently improved somewhat, but was still only 62–3 per cent in 1984 (Soljić 1984). In a word, then, the key investment programmes seemed if anything to *consolidate* rather than revolutionize the existing structure of the Yugoslav economy. World Bank experts have, indeed, cast some doubt on the genuineness of the export-promotion element in the programmes.

> The investment strategy was. . . . clearly designed to strengthen the raw material base of the economy. By contrast, with the exception of the machinery and ship-building sectors, there appears to have been little attention paid to the creation of capacities explicitly for export.
>
> (World Bank 1983: 8)

We may perceive in this a certain reflection of some of the tensions which exist amongst Yugoslav economists and economic policy-makers. For just as Croatia and Serbia, Zagreb and Belgrade, have throughout Yugoslav history represented alternative, often competing poles of South Slav historical and political identity, so too we find in the realm of economic decision-taking identifiable 'western' and 'eastern' orientations. In analysing the errors of the 1950s and 1960s, Belgrade economists have tended to read the lessons of the mistaken import substitution policies of the past in terms of how to avoid these mistakes in the implementation of new and better import substitution policies. In Zagreb, by contrast, economists have tended to concentrate on the export side, arguing that considerations of economies of scale demand that Yugoslavia should develop a much more highly specialized production profile, importing more and exporting more. The strength of the Zagreb line of argument is that once a powerful export-led growth impetus is set up, the degree of 'import dependence' of a given economy ceases to matter very much, as the experience of South Korea has shown. The strength of the Belgrade approach is that it concentrates on a dimension which is susceptible to national planning in a way that exporting is not. It is all very well to try to spot 'export-propulsive' sectors, but there can never be any guarantee that the world market will vindicate the prognostication, that the risk capital invested in these sectors will be recovered.

This is, of course, an oversimplification of the complex currents of Yugoslav economic thought. But it serves to pin-point one of the most fundamental strategic problems affecting the whole question of economic restructuring. Despite the nod in the direction of predominantly export-oriented sectors like tourism, the key investment programmes of the late 1970s were clearly dominated by the eastern orientation. Yet that was perhaps not the most important feature of the key investment programmes. The impact of the programmes on capital productivity was little short of disastrous *in the most favoured sector themselves*. Incremental capital-output ratios increased sharply, by as much as 50 per cent (1976–80/1971–5) in energy and *over 500 per cent* in non-ferrous metallurgy (World Bank 1983: 44). The planned increment to electricity generation capacity 1976–80 was 7,900 MW. In practice only 5,026 MW were installed (Horvat 1984). Meanwhile imports of capital equipment increased 38 per cent in 1977, 5 per cent in 1978, and 23 per cent in 1979 (Petrašinović 1980), accounting for some 85 per cent of total equipment newly invested by the late 1970s (Zmijarević 1980). What lay behind these trends?

A variety of factors suggest themselves. First, as a result of nearly guaranteed access to investment funding, certain priority sector projects appear to have been poorly designed, initiated before supporting technical and market studies were completed, and haphazardly implemented. Second, the sheer scale of the priority projects was often larger, making for more complex management requirements and greater risks of slippage. Third, the majority of the ore bodies involved in the priority extractive metal and mineral industries were in the less developed regions with their weaker physical and institutional infrastructure. . . Fourth, there seems to have been growing competition for investment goods and finance among investors in both the priority and non-priority sectors once macroeconomic policy became expansive in 1977 and the investment boom began in earnest. This competition expressed itself in inflation, cost overruns and delay. It seems that the larger priority projects were particularly vulnerable to these cost overruns, estimated in aggregate at one-third or more of originally programmed dinar costs. The financial allocation mechanisms failed to allocate the amounts needed to permit priority projects to be completed; instead, resources continued to be stretched too thinly among a large number of projects. Thus, while in theory the brunt of adjustment was expected to fall on non-priority investment projects, the rise in ICORs in all priority sectors as well as other evidence suggests that much of the burden of adjustment fell largely on them.

(World Bank 1983: 46)

Tables 5.4 and 5.5 illustrate the extent to which the overstretch problem was actually *exacerbated* during the period of the key investment programmes.

Table 5.4 Number and total value of investment projects 1976–9

Date	Number of projects	Total value of projects (mn dinars)
31/3/76	15,712	336,826
30/9/76	20,554	413,280
31/3/77	22,546	470,762
30/9/77	28,749	596,525
31/3/78	28,926	673,501
30/9/78	31,335	841,247
31/3/79	27,969	922,200

Source: Vlaho 1979a and 1979b

Table 5.5 Size distribution of investment projects at 30 September 1978

Size	Share in total number of projects	Share in total value of projects
< 1m dinars	38.6	0.6
1–10m dinars	38.1	5.2
10–50m dinars	16.5	14.1
50–500m dinars	6.1	29.4
< 500m dinars	0.8	50.8

Source: Vlaho 1979a

The average lead time, from beginning of construction to onstreaming (*aktivizacioni period*), was 4.14 years for Yugoslavia over the period 1976–82 (*Uslovi . . .* , 1985: 128), compared to around two years in the developed industrial countries.

At first sight the most extraordinary feature of this story is the way that it resembles the investment sagas of the centrally planned economies. Big projects being pushed through on the nod, priority schedules being neutralized as non-priority sectors found ways of retrieving resources, design and construction infrastructure being stretched beyond the limit, costs over-running, lead-times over-running. . . . If we were looking at the Soviet Union or Poland in the 1970s, the picture would not be very different. And perhaps this is not so surprising after all. For the Yugoslav government tried in the late 1970s to implement radical restructuring through what was effectively a *programme of central investment priorities*. Had that programme operated against the backdrop of a market economy based on hard budget constraints, it might have produced the kind of creative tension generated in the early days of the French planning system (see Holmes and Estrin 1983). Operating as it did in practice against the backdrop of a quasi-market economy in which the whole tenor of systemic evolution through the 1970s had been towards a *softening* of budget constraints, it was bound to produce the kind of investment scene we associate with central planning as such. But there were also peculiarly Yugoslav elements in the situation, and it is to an analysis of these that we now turn.

Specific factors affecting the efficiency of the investment process

Let us start by looking at the *regional dimension*, so much stressed by the World Bank authors. Table 5.6 illustrates the problem of capital productivity in the less developed areas of Yugoslavia. Two points emphatically emerge. Firstly, the problem is concentrated in industry. Secondly, it varies in severity almost precisely inversely with levels of GNP per capita by region. Some of the disparity can be explained by differences in industrial structure between developed and underdeveloped regions, and some, possibly, by differential inflationary trends (bear in mind that the indices are constructed on the basis of data in current prices). No doubt part of the explanation for the 'net' gap is, indeed, to be found in infrastructural weaknesses in the less developed regions, but this, of course, merely poses the question: why were appropriate infrastructural investments not made? Whichever way we look at it, it is difficult to dispute the conclusion that the quality of decision-taking was the principal factor underlying these investment efficiency differentials between developed and less developed regions, that the dysfunctional, fetishistic attitude to investment appraisal we saw developing in the more backward regions in the period of planning by global proportions did, indeed, grow stronger in the 1970s ('Niso samo . . .' 1981).

We cited the case of the Mratinje hydro-electric station, built in Montenegro in the 1970s, in the last chapter. The Belgrade–Bar railway, connecting the Federal capital with the Montenegrin coast and passing through some of the most mountainous and inaccessible parts of Southern Yugoslavia, provides another classic illustration of investment good fetishism. It took 24 years to build, and by the time it was completed in 1976 its capital cost had escalated to several hundred per cent of the 1965 estimates (Stanojlović 1976). By the 1970s Yugoslav planners had accepted that the project would at best cover its running costs, and would never make any contribution to amortization of capital costs (McGlue 1979: 303). But construction continued. Once operational, the railway

Table 5.6 Indices of incremental capital-output ratios 1976–9 (based on data in current prices)

	Total business sector	Industry
Yugoslavia	100.0	100.0
Bosnia & Hercegovina	118.8	134.1
Montenegro	183.9	198.8
Croatia	93.9	87.1
Macedonia	112.3	131.6
Slovenia	92.3	77.6
Serbia proper	84.4	85.8
Kosovo	184.0	186.5
Vojvodina	106.5	115.2
Developed regions	92.3	88.0
Underdeveloped regions	127.8	143.2

Source: 'Nisu samo . . . ' 1981

created as many problems as it solved, because of the failure to build the necessary number of bridges and flyovers. Its immediate impact on the tourist industry around Bar was, for this reason, disastrous ('Pruga Beograd . . . ' 1976).

At the Sixth Congress of the League of Communists of Montenegro in 1974 it was admitted that overriding concern with finishing dubious grand projects like the Mratinje and the Belgrade–Bar line had reduced to almost nugatory proportions time and funds spent on much-needed modernization and reconstruction of existing production capacities. It is significant that these two white elephants belong to sectors – energy and transport – crying out for investments – but the *right* investments.

It would be quite misleading, however, to suggest that *poor project appraisal* has been a monopoly of the poorer regions of Yugoslavia. Nor was it a problem that emerged only under the pressure of attempts to implement the key investment programmes of 1976–80. One of the most expensive examples of sheer bad investment planning – the Omišalj oil and petro-chemical terminal on the island of Krk, in Croatia – was strictly a Croatian/Serbian/Bosnian/international affair. Originally conceived in 1973, the project was to involve the building of a pipeline from Omišalj to Novi Sad in Vojvodina and Pančevo in Serbia, with a branch going up to Gola, on the Hungarian border, whence it would link up with the Comecom pipeline.

In early 1974 an agreement covering the pipeline project was signed by the governments of Yugoslavia, Hungary and Czechoslovakia. Almost immediately fears began to be expressed that costs would escalate, and that the project might in any case lose its technical justification under post-Oil Shock conditions. But the Oil Shock may, indirectly, have strengthened the resolve of the project's backers to keep going, in that it made it easier to raise finance internationally. In January 1975, Kuwait and Libya, replete with petrodollars and anxious to do something with them, agreed to participate in the financing of the project to the extent of 50 per cent between them ('Naftovod' 1975). In 1976 the Croatian oil company, INA and Dow Chemicals of the USA agreed to share 50–50 in the initial finance for the construction of the Omišalj petrochemical complex.

Anxiety over the cost of the pipeline turned out to be justified, with estimates escalating by 60 per cent between 1974 and 1978 ('Cijena novih rokova' 1978). Originally scheduled for completion in 1976, it was not in the event opened until December 1979, and the first oil did not arrive at the Sisak refinery until February 1980. At that point it was envisaged that in its first phase of operation the pipeline should operate at some 60 per cent capacity.

The petrochemical project at Omišalj (DINA) was dogged with problems from the start. According to the original agreement of 1976, it would cost $730m, would go into operation in 1979, and would reach full capacity in 1982. The schedule was subsequently revised twice. According to the third version, as of late 1981, the plant would cost $1,212m, would begin production in 1982, and would be completed in 1985 ('Treća revizija . . .' 1981). At that point, DINA represented the biggest investment project ever undertaken in Yugoslavia. By early 1982 serious disagreements were emerging between INA and Dow, with the American company wanting to scrap Stages II and III, and concentrate on completing Stage I. The Yugoslav side, by contrast, were still committed to the full project, though INA had recorded losses totalling 8.3bn dinars in 1981 ('Iskustva . . . ' 1982). At the end of 1982 the Dow Chemical Company announced that it was pulling out of the DINA project.

We can checklist the things that went wrong with the Krk complex as follows:

1 The volatility of the world oil market during the 1970s made a nonsense of initial projections. But those projections were never systematically reworked.
2 The estimates for capital costs and lead-times were almost certainly over–optimistic on the best possible assumptions.
3 Bureaucratic delays in relation to the ratification of the INA–Dow contract made things worse. So did difficulties in getting permission to import crucial pieces of equipment (cf. earlier discussion of inefficiencies in the import control system).
4 INA's growing financial difficulties created a range of problems, most specifically a crucial shortage of imported ethylene for processing.
5 By the early 1980s Dow was also in financial difficulties, and was

getting out of international projects all round the world.
6 By the early 1980s increasing concern was being expressed about
environmental implications.

The original Omišalj–Pančevo–Gola pipeline project was certainly
poorly implemented. Yet in 1978 Yugoslav economists were reckoning
that, with all the cost escalations and delays, the pipeline would still
transport oil 50 per cent cheaper than it would go by rail ('Cijena novih
rokova', 1978). Whether that prognostication proved justified in the event
is not clear. The DINA balance sheet is more straightforward. The official
Yugoslav position in 1982 was that with costs higher than world prices
the project could not possible operate profitably, at least for the first
few years. Ominously, perhaps, the government continued to see a future
for DINA in terms of *import substitution*.

In all sorts of ways, then, the pattern of investment in Yugoslavia
in the 1970s was an inefficient one – inefficient in general rate of return
terms, inefficient in relation to the Balance of Trade. And with all the
dramas of grand projects and grand flops in industry, the weaknesses
of Yugoslav investment policy in this period are perhaps best summed
up by looking briefly at the sector which continued to occupy more people
than any other sector of the economy – agriculture.

The special problem of investment in agriculture

A key supplier of raw materials to light industry, offering very substantial scope for uncomplicated import substitution and a degree of scope
for expanding exports, particularly of speciality products, agriculture
might have seemed like one of the strongest candidates for a concerted
investment programme. Indeed agro-industry was featured in the key
investment programmes of 1976–80, though to little practical effect. What
went wrong?

As we saw at the end of Chapter 2, the Yugoslav leadership's
compromise with private agriculture in the early 1950s had been an
uneasy one, and peasants found themselves during the period of planning by global proportions discriminated against in terms of procurement
prices, freedom to dispose of and acquire land, freedom to acquire
machinery, and political representation. The small socialized agricultural
sector, which held only 13 per cent of total arable land in 1964, was,
by contrast, heavily subsidized, and this made it possible for socialized
farms to maintain high levels of investment – 76.6 per cent of total
agricultural investment in 1964 (Kamišar 1972). Reforms instituted in
1967 broke the agricultural procurement monopoly of the general
cooperatives, removed restrictions on private peasant ownership of
machinery, and opened up lines of bank credit to the private agricultural

sector. But agriculture's terms of trade nevertheless deteriorated by some 43 per cent 1965–71 (Marković 1973, ch. 5), and bank credit flows were in practice very slow to open up. With the 10-hectare limit still in force and local governments imposing prohibitive taxation on the hiring out of machinery by private individuals, it was in any case very difficult for peasants to build up an efficient machinery park. The private sector's share of total agricultural investment rose from 23.4 per cent in 1964 to 32.5 per cent in 1967, but then dropped back to 27.1 per cent in 1969 (Kamišar 1972)

Despite its privileged position, the socialized sector of agriculture failed to make any significant impact on the predominance of the private sector through the late 1960s and early 1970s. The integration movement (see Chapter 4) in socialized agriculture saw *zadruge* (cooperatives) being swallowed up into huge agricultural combines, while cooperation with the private sector went into decline. But the leadership was still anxious to further the cause of socialism in the countryside. As the notion of association came increasingly to dominate theoretical thinking on self-management from the early 1970s onwards, policy-makers saw an opportunity to use the constitutional amendments as a basis for introducing a new kind of cooperation into the villages, a system of association amongst private peasants and between them and the socialized sector which would be genuinely voluntary, and which would remove the second-class citizen tag from the private peasant once and for all. Corresponding legislation was introduced in 1973 and 1974.

But there were ominous signs, even at this early stage. While peasants were now to be allowed to organize their own cooperatives, Unions of Cooperatives would also be organized with the express purpose of creating a channel for control over the the the new cooperatives. 'Nothing is more undesirable than to leave everything to individual initiative, with insufficient social help' (Oršanić 1973). The peasants, it seems, remained as reluctant to accept social help as they had been under the previous regime, and progress with agricultural association during the middle 1970s was slow. In Macedonia, indeed, there were reports of fears on the part of the peasants that the association movement was the beginning of a new collectivization drive (Nikolić 1976). One peasant who had gone into association summed up the movement in the following terms in 1979:

> Personally I think that we approached the issue of association in agriculture in a very pompous way . . . All the talk was of methods of association, net income relations, tax and credit policy. Five years have passed since then, and everything, it seems to me has stayed just as it was in the old days, despite the passing of the law on associated labour and the law on association in agriculture. With all this association and the self-management agreements we have signed,

everything, starting from production itself and relations between the farmer and the [social sector] agricultural organisation, remains on the old basis. Social sector organisations just operate as traders and dealers.

(Kolarić 1979)

Reports from the early 1980s spoke of socialized sector organizations trying to stop peasants from crossing republican borders to seek better prices (Bašić 1981), and of extreme delays in payment for agricultural deliveries, coupled with demands for cash on delivery, or even in advance, from fertilizer producers ('Dvostruki život' 1983: 7).

But it would be unfair to suggest that the agricultural association initiative did not try to attack the problem of rural credit. In fact tax concessions were introduced in 1974 for peasants making substantial modernization investments within the framework of association. In the same year eight major Yugoslav banks agreed to open up a special line of credit at a rate of interest of 10 per cent to private agriculturalists. But in 1980 another private peasant in association described the credit situation thus:

Under the system of crediting agricultural producers in association through basic organizations of cooperants and business banks, short-term credit needs – for the purchase of seed, artificial fertilizer, various services – are in the main satisfied without great difficulties. But the situation is much less favourable with investment credits . . . Here the procedure for providing the necessary documentation is complicated and long drawn-out, and this very often demoralizes producers.

(Šublja 1980: 3)

Credit arrangements apart, private peasants continued to meet obstacles in trying to acquire equipment, and there were reports in 1982 of open discrimination against individual agriculturalists at auctions of second-hand agricultural equipment ('Licitacija' 1982).

But we should not assume that every Yugoslav leader recognized this as a bad thing. As late as 1980, for example, we find member of the Serbian government Borislav Srebrić arguing that there were too many tractors in private agriculture, that peasants bought tractors just for prestige, that tiny private plots 'have no future in agriculture based on a contemporary, socialized basis'. Top priority, he went on to aver, should be given to investment in an expanded socialist sector ('Stvar prestiža' 1980).

Now the most extraordinary thing about this statement is the stress on the small-scale profile of private agriculture holdings as an obstacle to efficient equipping patterns. For who was responsible for that profile, if not the authorities themselves? And who was responsible for the restrictions on the hiring out of equipment by private peasants to other peasants?

As the Yugoslav economy moved closer and closer to crisis, controversy over the 10-hectare limit intensified. In an article published in 1980 distinguished Ljubljana economist Jože Mencinger disposed of the arguments against lifting the limit, one by one. The possibility of a 'restoration of capitalism' is dismissed as nonsense (would Srebrić have agreed?). 'Unjustified enrichment' is extremely unlikely. There is no argument that the private sector might encroach on the socialized, since, as it is, the socialized sector does not take over land abandoned by the private sector. Rather the argument is that only by permitting peasants to build up bigger units can the problem of unused or underused land be solved. (Total cultivated area has fallen in virtually every year since 1970.) Finally, lifting the maximum would do nothing to inhibit the process of association in agriculture, since small peasants are not interested in association anyway (Mencinger 1980).

Yet for all the controversy, nothing was done, and indeed the whole question of land rights was raised to a new level of political intensity in 1982 when policemen in rural Serbia were stoned as they tried to take possession of market-garden land earmarked for a proposed industrial development. One group of Serbian peasants were preparing to go to the Constitutional Court of the republic over the same issue ('Pravo prvenstva 1982). Meanwhile reluctance on the part of the socialized sector to make full allowance for the rent due on peasant land continued to present one more major obstacle to the progress of association in agriculture.

Whether we see it as a technical obstacle to the efficient allocation of land as a key natural resource, or in more general socio-economic terms as a continued symbol of the second-class citizen status of the peasantry, we can hardly overstate the centrality of the land maximum to the condition of the Yugoslav peasantry in this crucial period. The association movement, by contrast, encompassed just 9 per cent of Yugoslavia's 3.4m private peasants in 1982, though 1.3m of them were involved in some kind of cooperation with the socialized sector ('Stari kadri' 1982). Thus the greater part of Yugoslav agriculture continued to be isolated from the main streams of the national economy, continued to labour under burdensome legal restrictions, continued to be starved of investment resources and denied the right to organize its basic capital – the land – in the most efficient way. After years of deficit, the Yugoslav balance of trade in food finally came into stable surplus in 1981. The fact that this was seen as a notable achievement underlines how totally unsatisfactory the situation with respect to an area of clear Yugoslav comparative advantage had been.

The scene is set

The overall situation as of the late 1970s and early 1980s in terms of the relationship between the domestic economy and the external balance can be summed up in the following terms:

1 The burden of investment on the economy was so heavy that it is almost inconceivable that it could have been financed, in a country still relatively poor, without significant capital imports.

2 Despite a clear recognition of the need for economic restructuring, and adoption of specific programmes to that end, the impact of this massive rate of fixed capital formation on the capital stock was largely conservative. Crass errors of decision-taking apart, it tended to shore-up the existing structure rather than to provide a basis for adjustment and restructuring. Capital productivity trends worsened, and the impact of new investment on the Balance of Trade was, if anything, negative. To a great extent good money was simply thrown after bad.

3 Putting 1 and 2 together, the high propensity to import capital of the 1970s led inexorably to an even higher propensity to import capital in the 1980s. This is the immediate background to the emergence of the foreign debt service crisis.

Chapter six

The Debt-Service Crisis of 1982

The development of the foreign exchange system in the 1970s

In 1973 the Yugoslav government took what appeared to be a major step towards full convertibility of the dinar when it implemented 1972 legislation covering the setting-up of a *foreign-exchange market*.

> This authorized a bi-weekly inter-commercial bank foreign exchange market to be organized by the Yugoslav Association of Bankers. The rates established through dealing applied to all subsequent bank to bank, or bank to customer, dealings until the next market day. Firms were entitled to trade in foreign currencies with authorized business banks at any time and to hold their own foreign currency deposit accounts. However the float was in practice 'dirty' because the National Bank intervened in the market, buying or selling to maintain the rate roughly within a 5 per cent margin of sixteen dinars per dollar.
>
> (Prout 1985: 172)

It was in July 1973 that the dinar was officially floated, though the National Bank continued thereafter to follow a positive policy on the exchange rate and to implement frequent devaluations.

There was a sense in which the setting-up of the foreign-exchange market marked a high-point in the development of pre-associationist market socialism. It also represented a degree – perhaps a culpable degree – of over-optimism on the chances of the Balance of Payments – uncharacteristically in surplus in 1972 and 1973 – staying in the black. As we saw, the current account plunged back into serious deficit in 1974, and from then on the main question for the foreign exchange market was bound to be: where is the foreign exchange to come from? The answer, a perniciously easy one in post-Oil Shock conditions, was – from foreign borrowing.

But the impact of the legislation of 1972 on macro-financial flows was more far-reaching than that. Up until then, the great bulk of Yugoslav international borrowing had been related to specific purchases. As the availability of international credit increased dramatically after 1974, Yugoslav banks came increasingly to take up foreign credits with a view to *expanding domestic credit.*'We can date from the early 1970s the development of the practice of borrowing abroad and then converting the credits into dinars and using them as a basis for dinar financing in Yugoslavia' (Čičin-Šain 1982: 264, quoted in Gnjatović 1985). It is striking in this connection to note that for all years of the crucial period 1973-8 save one, Yugoslavia borrowed on medium and long term in excess of what was needed to cover the current account deficit for that year (see Table 6.1). Quite apart from its impact on the money supply, this development made it increasingly difficult for the federal authorities to impose any kind of strategic pattern on the flow, perhaps we should say flood, of foreign borrowing. The trend was also reflected in the sharply falling proportion of total foreign debt that was guaranteed (see Table 6.3). Only the Federal authorities could guarantee loans, and as the Federation was eased out of the foreign loans game, so the weight of guaranteed loans within the total inevitably fell. Quite apart from the issue of Federal control, that inevitably worsened the conditions on which the bulk of the new credits of the 1970s were taken up. Dujšin argues that the National Bank went along with all this because it was thereby able to increase its level of hard currency reserves without having to become directly indebted abroad (Dujšin 1987: 15).

Table 6.1 Medium- and long-term debt flow/current account balance

1973	1974	1975	1976	1977	1978	1979	1980	1981
1.65	−0.62	−1.52	7.29	−1.26	−1.37	−0.45	−1.05	−0.69

Source: Ledić 1984: 55

Let us pause to place these movements into strategic context. As a developing country, Yugoslavia was surely entitled to view capital import, i.e. current account deficit, as a proper, secular feature of its macro-economic balance, however ambivalent individual Yugoslav leaders or writers may have been on this point. As the country was opened up to international capital in the 1970s, however, the whole business of capital import simply got out of hand, and the relationship between import of financial capital and specific investment plans was almost totally lost.

But there was another line of policy development, dating from 1967. In that year a law was passed permitting foreign companies to make equity investments in Yugoslav companies. Now whatever the pros and cons of getting involved with the transnational companies, private equity

Table 6.2 Structure of long- and medium-term credits by purpose (total for each year = 100)

	Non-specific financial credits	Equipment	Raw materials & semi-processeds	Food
1960	19.3	65.1	15.6	–
1961	35.1	55.3	9.6	–
1962	31.4	53.7	7.8	7.1
1963	30.2	50.9	13.0	5.9
1964	27.0	51.6	11.5	8.9
1965	25.4	50.6	8.6	15.4
1966	22.1	50.8	6.5	20.6
1967	24.9	50.8	5.6	18.7
1968	24.9	52.8	5.7	16.6
1969	24.2	57.2	5.5	13.1
1970	28.9	51.8	10.0	9.3
1971	30.3	51.8	8.4	8.1
1972	35.1	49.8	8.4	5.5
1973	38.1	48.9	5.8	5.4
1974	37.7	54.5	5.3	1.5
1975	36.4	55.8	5.3	1.9
1976	37.1	54.4	6.8	1.3
1977	35.7	56.6	6.6	0.8
1978	37.5	55.1	6.5	0.4
1979	38.5	54.5	6.5	0.2
1980	42.1	51.4	5.6	0.6
1981	42.4	49.1	7.3	0.2
1982	47.9	42.4	9.7	–
1983	51.5	36.8	11.7	–

Source: Gnjatović 1985: 98

Table 6.3 Yugoslavia's international debts, guaranteed and unguaranteed (total stock of debt for each year = 100)

	Guaranteed	Unguaranteed
1968	95.1	4.9
1969	81.2	18.8
1970	73.6	26.4
1971	58.9	41.1
1972	77.3	26.7
1973	56.9	43.1
1974	61.4	38.6
1975	50.9	49.1
1976	46.1	53.9
1977	38.7	61.3
1978	38.9	61.1
1979	31.8	68.2
1980	31.9	68.1
1981	34.1	65.9
1982	34.9	65.1

Source: Derived from Gnjatović 1985: 86

capital transfer has the advantage that (a) it is by definition project-specific; (b) it does not involve any automatic debt-service payment streams. In practice, the joint-venture legislation produced disappointing results, quantitatively and qualitatively. Foreign investors found profit-repatriation restrictions and tax regimes unfavourable, procedures for approval uncommonly complex, and the peculiarities of the self-management system difficult to get used to. Nevertheless additional legislation introduced in the 1970s actually *tightened up further* on the profit repatriation and taxation regulations (Kovačević 1982). Not surprisingly, then, there were relatively few takers. Two 1975 joint ventures involving foreign investment worth some $0.3bn had been agreed (Sirc 1979: 118). By 1980 the figure had reached $1.8bn (Gnjatović 1985: 91). The joint ventures that were agreed did, on the whole, show higher rates of profitability than other projects, though the DINA petrochemical project (see last chapter) graphically proved that foreign equity involvement was no guarantee of efficient project formulation and implementation.

The next major piece of legislation on the foreign payments system came in 1977. The Law on Foreign Exchange Operations and Credit Relations with Foreign Countries of that year sought, perhaps predictably, to impose an associationist framework on the system. A pyramid of self-managing interest groupings was created, with SIZ-ovi for External Economic Relations established at federal and republican levels, and foreign exchange interest groupings (DIZ-ovi) bringing together groups of enterprises contributing, directly or indirectly, to the generation of particular foreign exchange streams. General ideological penchants apart, the designers of the new system were seeking to solve some quite specific operational difficulties with the previous set-up. The old system of permitting exporters, and only exporters, a retention quota of foreign exchange had clearly been unfair to enterprises making a large indirect contribution to exporting, and had encouraged enterprises to seek payment for domestic transactions in foreign currency. The new legislation would, it was hoped, solve this problem through the medium of self-management agreements setting out foreign exchange shares for all organizations involved in particular pieces of export business. These agreements would also help to take a lot of the red tape out of foreign-exchange business, as DIZ-ovi became increasingly 'self-managing'.

That was not how things worked out. In practice the attempt to link importing rights more systematically to exporting performance was not successful, with the DIZ-ovi dominated by 'foreign-exchange spongers and hangers-on' (Gavrović 1979). But the fault did not lie primarily with the DIZ-ovi themselves and their constituent enterprises. The essential problem was that the whole system was hi-jacked by the republican SIZ-ovi for External Economic Relations. It was those bodies which came effectively to dominate foreign-exchange allocation under the new system – not, perhaps, surprisingly, given general trends in the Yugoslav body politico-economic of the time. And because it was so much easier for the republican SIZ-ovi to articulate import needs than export policies, the system quickly degenerated into an exercise in deficit-maximizing, as the republics vied with each other to demand the most imports and promise the least exports ('Razlog . . .' 1980). This inevitably produced a situation in which enterprises looked to political patronage rather than exporting to satisfy their hard-currency needs.

It is hard to imagine a more unfortunate perversion of well-meant legislation than the foreign-exchange set-up as it had gelled by 1979. Just at a time when, in the wake of the Second Oil Crisis, international exchange conditions were again becoming very difficult for non-oil producers, Yugoslavia went onto a system under which national stewardship of the Balance of Payments was *simply abandoned*. At the same time republicanization of the system meant an effective end to the attempt to introduce an operational foreign exchange market ('Zabluda' 1980). Beyond that, the system created all sorts of petty complications for business organizations. As the republicanization of the Balance of Payments became increasingly formalized, enterprises operating in more than one region – often the biggest and most efficient – found themselves in extreme difficulties with foreign exchange for imports if they did not export directly themselves (Gavrović 1980). This inevitably tended to reinforce regional-autarkic tendencies (Vlaho 1979f), and to *exacerbate* the problem of internal dinar inconvertibility. Provisions for export promotion turned out to be one of the most problematic areas of self-managing agreement, and when something was finally hammered out in mid-1980 it seemed like too little too late ('Usvojen sporazum . . .' 1980).

The republican SIZ-ovi were just as slow in getting agreement on the Balance of Payments 'plan' for each year. With the annual round of negotiations usually ending up as a battle between the export-oriented western regions – Slovenia and Croatia – and the rest, Yugoslavia found itself in 1980, for example, without any firm policy stance on the Balance of Payments for the first seven months of the year ('Razlog . . .' 1980). The same pattern was repeated the following year. By 1980 the whole foreign-exchange situation was coming to look increasingly bizarre. Yugoslavs travelling through the regions of their own country were coming home loaded with imported supplies of coffee and detergent, and there was a suggestion, not perhaps a wholly serious one, that excise posts should be set up at republican boundaries ('Dosledno' 1980). By 1981 local newspapers were talking explicitly about 'The Balance of Payments situation of the business sector of our commune' ('Reč ili misao' 1981).

Against a background of sky-high oil prices, rapidly escalating rates of interest on international credits, the failures of adjustment policy documented in the last chapter, and increasing competition from the NICs in many of Yugoslavia's traditional export lines (Giannitsis no date), this, then, was the organizational equipment with which Yugoslavia sought to navigate the waters of international high finance in the early 1980s.

The slippery slope

As we saw at the end of Chapter 3, Yugoslavia experienced the first of her post-war external debt-service crises as early as 1964. As Table 6.4 shows, she was back in trouble again in the early 1970s, with the ratio of hard-currency debt service to hard-currency inflow rising to above 40 per cent in 1971, and easing off only a little to 35 per cent in 1972. This was partly a reflection of the big deficits on current account of 1970 and 1971. More specifically, it reflected the way in which those deficits had been financed. It was the very sharp increase in short-term liabilities that caused the problem – if we look at the trend in amortization of long-term liabilities we see that the 1971 and 1972 figures were only a little higher than those for succeeding years. The Balance of Payments surpluses of 1972 and 1973 made it fairly easy to fund this short-term debt in the outcome, with Belgrade managing to negotiate substantial public loans on very favourable terms during those two years, and Yugoslavia's hard-currency debt service ratio was brought down to just about the crucial 25 per cent mark by 1973.

Table 6.4 Hard-currency debt-service indicators 1971–81

	1971	1972	1973	1974	1975	1976	1977	1978	1979	1980	1981
Repayments as percentage of total hard-currency inflow	37	31	21	19	20	18	20	19	24	28	23
Interest as percentage of total hard-currency inflow	5	4	4	4	4	4	4	4	6	7	10
Repayments of credits other than short-term as percentage of total hard-currency inflow	18	16	15	14	15	14	17	18	21	20	...

Source: Gnjatović 1985: 100; OECD statistics

The hard-currency debt-service ratio continued to hover at, or just under, the 25 per cent mark through the mid-1970s. But the total stock of debt continued to rise inexorably (see Table 6.5). The debt-service ratio finally moved sharply upwards in 1979, and by 1980 was back at 35 per cent. This represented partly a rise in amortization flows. But the sharpness of the increase was mainly due to the steep climb in interest payments in the late 1970s and early 1980s. Having held steady at 4 per cent of total hard-currency inflow from 1972 to 1978, the burden of interest payments then rose to 10 per cent within three years. This was very much in line with the evolution of the interest-rate structure world-wide at that time, but specific characteristics of the Yugoslavian debt portfolio meant that there was very little Belgrade could do to soften the impact.

Table 6.5 Yugoslavia's total foreign debt 1972–82 ($m)

1972	1973	1974	1975	1976	1977	1978	1979	1980	1981	1982
3,437.7	4,377.8	5,061.7	6,023.0	7,419.7	9,304.5	11,547.3	14,584.7	18,485.8	20,645.6	19,899.8

Source: Ledić 1984: 56; World Bank *World Debt Tables*

Table 6.6 Structure of credits by source (total for each year = 100)

	Public	*Private*
1968	73.0	27.0
1969	61.6	38.4
1970	56.2	43.8
1971	47.1	52.9
1972	59.1	40.9
1973	43.8	56.2
1974	46.6	53.4
1975	44.0	56.0
1976	37.0	63.0
1977	33.4	66.6
1978	35.3	64.7
1979	29.2	70.8
1980	25.0	75.0
1981	27.3	72.7
1982	20.3	79.9

Source: Gnjatović 1985: 95

Table 6.6 illustrates the emphatic shift away from public towards private sources of international credit to Yugoslavia over the period 1968–82. This parallels the shift towards unguaranteed loans we noted earlier. By the late 1970s Yugoslavia was becoming increasingly dependent on variable-interest, 'roll-over' loans from the private sector. In 1981 the average rate of interest being paid by Yugoslavia on guaranteed loans from private sources (the fastest growing element within

Table 6.7 The terms on which Yugoslavia borrowed 1973–82 (medium- and long-term guaranteed loans only)

	1972	1975	1978	1979	1980	1981	1982
Total loans (*average terms*)							
All creditors							
Interest (%)	6.7	8.5	6.8	5.8	15.1	12.6	13.8
Maturity (yrs)	12.0	15.0	15.9	16.6	8.9	11.7	11.1
Grace period (yrs)	3.5	4.2	3.5	3.2	3.3	4.1	3.9
Grant element (%)[1]	15.4	8.5	18.0	24.4	−19.5	−6.5	−16.4
Official creditors							
Interest (%)	6.3	8.9	6.8	5.8	11.6	10.9	11.1
Maturity (yrs)	13.1	16.2	15.9	16.7	11.8	13.1	16.5
Grace period (yrs)	3.7	4.0	3.5	3.2	3.7	4.3	5.8
Grant element (%)	17.8	6.7	18.0	24.5	−5.9	1.5	−7.9
Private creditors							
Interest (%)	7.3	7.5	–	8.7	17.6	18.7	14.7
Maturity (yrs)	10.4	11.9	–	8.9	6.7	7.0	9.1
Grace period (yrs)	3.2	4.9	–	1.9	2.9	3.0	3.3
Grant element (%)	12.0	13.4	–	5.0	−29.4	−34.4	−19.4
Variable interest rate loans (%age of total disbursed debt)	6.8	7.9	7.5	5.3	23.9	35.0	37.7

1 'Grant element is defined as the face value of a loan commitment less the discounted present value of the future flow of payments of principal and interest, expressed as a percentage of the face value. The discount rate used is 10 per cent, which is the conventional rate used by the OECD in assessing terms' (*World Bank Annual Report 1984:* 149)

Source: World Bank, *World Debt Tables*

total guaranteed debt over the crucial years 1980–2) was 18.7 per cent, compared to 7.3 per cent in 1972 (see Table 6.7). We must assume that conditions for non-guaranteed borrowing from private sources were even less favourable. Table 6.7 shows how conditions worsened over the crucial decade even for borrowing from public sources. In 1978 and 1979 Yugoslavia was able to negotiate, on favourable terms, substantial new multilateral credits with the World Bank and the European Investment Bank, and the average rate of interest on new loans from public sources fell. But from 1980 interest rates on public loans took the same path as private sectors rate, though they never went nearly so high.

The crisis looms

At the beginning of 1981 the IMF approved a three-year credit of $2.2m for Yugoslavia. At that time it was the biggest IMF loan ever, and it represented a milestone in Yugoslavia's relations with the international financial community. Now, finally, Belgrade was realizing to what a dangerous degree she had become involved with the private multinational banks, as credit flows began to dry up in the wake of the Polish debt-service crisis of 1981. Now the IMF was giving a substantial token of the commitment of the public international financial community to do something to help Yugoslavia. In return, of course, the IMF laid down conditions – the Yugoslav authorities would have to impose restrictive monetary and fiscal policies, take measures to reduce the rate of growth of public expenditure, introduce more realistic exchange and interest rates, and generally use the breathing space to get on with belated adjustment policies. The Stabilization Programme promulgated by the Yugoslav government itself in 1983 espoused broadly similar policy lines.

The 1981 credit stretched Yugoslavia's indebtedness to the Fund to 400 per cent of her quota, as against a limit of 450 per cent. Even so, it was barely enough to cover the current account deficit for 1980, and by October 1981 the governor of the National Bank was in London discussing a loan of some $0.4bn with a number of Western banks. At that point the Western banks were demanding 1.5 percentage points above LIBOR, subsequently reduced to 1.25 per cent on appeal from the Yugoslav side. It was now, perhaps, that a real sense of crisis began to filter through to the Yugoslav public, already hit by steady falls in levels of real personal income since 1979. People were surprised to learn about the meeting only from the BBC World Service; were, perhaps, even more surprised to realize how reluctant some countries were to lend more money to Yugoslavia ('Informisanje' 1981). By this time the problem was beginning to assume an explicitly political dimension, with Belgrade using diplomatic channels to try to persuade governments to put pressure on their banks to look favourably on

Yugoslavia's requests. In the end, one way or the other, the loan was arranged.

By the middle of 1982, however, things were worse than ever. With debt service due for that year of $5bn+, it became increasingly clear that Yugoslavia would not be able to meet her international commitments without large-scale new credits. The Yugoslav economy was already suffering from serious external liquidity problems, with imports of materials being cut back and stocks falling to a dangerously low level. By the end of November nine Yugoslav ships were stuck at the entrance to the Suez Canal, unable to pay the fee to get through ('Paragraf – torpedo' 1982). A syndicated loan from private banks for another $200m was clinched towards the end of 1982, but this was a drop in the ocean, and gold and hard currency reserves were drawn down to the extent of $1.4bn over 1982 as a whole. As of December 1982 the black-market rate for the dinar was down to 270 dinars to the dollar, as compared to an official rate of 89 dinars to the dollar ('Pravi rečnik' 1982). Meanwhile, the full extent of the mismanagement of the situation was finally becoming apparent:

> One member of the government's international financial negotiating team, for example, revealed to the party's Central Committee in September 1982 that 'we still today do not have exact data with respect to our foreign obligations'. Earlier in the month, 'at an international financial meeting', he reported, there had been 'various explosions about some earlier, unregistered loans', and he admitted that 'we could not establish in advance, before we went to the meeting, where these unpaid obligations are hiding [and] learned this from our foreign partners instead.' One Western official privately characterized the situation as 'chaotic', with instances of the same collateral having been used for more than one loan. (Burg 1986: 174)

But Yugoslavia's lines of communication with the international financial community were still open, and in November 1982 Tom Clausen, president of the World Bank, visited Yugoslavia. Clausen seemed to go out of his way to speak soothing words, complimenting the Yugoslavs on how well their country had used World Bank funds (we will come back to that question in Chapter 8), and voicing general approval of the domestic stabilization measures introduced by the federal government. He advised the Belgrade government to concentrate on export stimulation rather than import substitution, and promised World Bank support for restructuring policies to the tune of $300–350m of new credits annually over the following five years ('Zajmovi . . . ' 1982). The message did, then, seem to be very much 'business as usual', and it was perhaps not surprising when negotiations spanning 1982 and 1983 managed to produce a massive rescheduling package, finally announced in April 1983.

The package was indeed a complex one, involving 15 countries and 583 creditor banks (80 per cent of the outstanding private debt was accounted for by the biggest 20 of those – Dujšin 1987: 7), with the Manufacturers Hannover Trust of New York leading the private consortium. Terms were two-year grace period and a rate of interest of 1.875 percentage points above LIBOR. (That, certainly, was what the consortium was asking for as late as March 1983. But the Yugoslavs were demurring, and the rate of interest may have been shaved slightly in the final agreement – 'Lagano napredovanje' 1983.) Reports vary on the exact breakdown of the deal, but the main elements seem to have been as follows:

1 The refinancing of some $2.8–3.2bn of long-, medium- and short-term liabilities owed to financial institutions or national governments.
2 A consortium loan of $0.6bn to the National Bank.
3 A $0.5bn bridging loan from the Bank for International Settlements, repayable by the end of 1983.
4 A structural adjustment loan and further project loans totalling $400m from the World Bank.,
5 Standby credit to the extent of $0.6 from the IMF. (This was actually just the last tranche of the 1981 IMF loan.)
6 New bilateral public loans totalling $1.2bn, $0.6bn to be disbursed in 1983 and the rest during 1984–5.

The impact on the domestic economy

Table 6.8 summarizes movements in the key macro-economic variables for the Yugoslav economy over this painful period.

Table 6.8 Income and price movements 1981–5 (annual percentage changes)

	1979	1980	1981	1982	1983	1984	1985
National Income	7.1	2.2	1.4	0.5	−1.2	1.7	0.4
Real personal incomes	−0.3	−8.1	−5.7	−3.3	−10.9	−5.7	3.0
Retail price index	22	30	46	30	39	57	76

Source: SGJ 1986

In-depth analysis of these trends must await the conclusions of the next chapter. But the general impact of the debt-service crisis is clear enough. It resulted in stagnation in levels of aggregate production, and a sustained fall in living standards which had cumulated to around 30 per cent by 1984. It was accompanied by an apparently inexorable escalation of the inflation problem. As of the end of 1984, according to the estimates of the Trade Union Congress, some two-thirds of the Yugoslav work-force were taking home wages 'inadequate to sustain a normal life' (Korošić 1985).

Why did the crisis hit living standards so much harder than aggregate production? And why, indeed, did living standards start to fall sharply as early as 1980, when Yugoslavia was still able to run a massive deficit on current account? There can be little doubt that the constant price National Income figures for the late 1970s and early 1980s do contain a significant degree of concealed inflation. This relates mainly to the padding of figures for increases in stocks, as stocks were revalued to take account of the rapidly rising rate of inflation (*Uslovi* . . . 1985: 123). With the reported gross fixed investment ratio still as high as 31.7 per cent in 1980 (cf. 34.5 in 1979 – Gnjatović 1985: 65), and assuming no significant elements of concealed inflation in the fixed investment figures themselves, it is possible that the real burden of fixed investment expenditure on Yugoslav National Income did actually increase in 1980 as the economy took the strain of attempted completion of the key investment programmes. Beyond that, the 'early turn' of the real personal income figures seems to reflect the extent of the impact of the Second Oil Shock on Yugoslavia's terms of trade. From 1980 onwards there was almost certainly a substantial amount of exporting at a loss, as Yugoslavia' sought to raise hard cash by hook or by crook, resulting in a continued deterioration in the terms of trade. Between 1982 and 1985 the index of Yugoslavia's export prices fell by 8 per cent (SGJ 1986: 320).

Yugoslavia's international debt problem in comparative perspective

Yugoslavia was, of course, by no means the only country to get into foreign debt difficulties in the early 1980s. Table 6.9 summarizes the position of the main debtor countries around the world in 1982. There is a clear family resemblance between most of the members of the club. The typical debtor-country is a medium-developed non-oil producer with a level of GNP per capital of $2,000 plus, reflecting a good post-war growth record. Most of the countries in the table could be classified as NICs, and in the majority of cases, capitalist and socialist, governments have adopted more or less explicit growth plans and targets. There are exceptions to all these generalizations – Venezuela is an oil-exporter, Argentina a case of deindustrialization rather than new industrialization, Egypt and the Philippines still very much poor developing countries, though not the poorest.

When we come to the crucial issue of *debt service*, however, we find striking differences between the members of the club. It was countries like Brazil, Mexico, Argentina and Poland, with debt-service ratios of

Table 6.9 Principal debtor countries: their vital statistics in 1982

	Debt outstanding ($m)	Debt per capita ($)	GNP per capita ($)
Brazil	91.6	722	2,240
Mexico	86.1	1.178	2,270
Argentina	43.6	1,536	2,520
South Korea	37.8	961	1,190
Venezuela	31.9	1,912	4,140
Poland	25.2	696	5,088
Philippines	24.3	480	820
Israel	22.2	5,561	5,090
Egypt	21.9	494	690
Yugoslavia	19.9	881	2,800
Turkey	19.7	423	1,370
Chile	17.3	1,509	2,210
Algeria	16.7	838	2,350
Greece	11.3	1,149	4,290
Ireland	10.6	3,029	5,150
Romania	9.4	418	4,370
Hungary	7.0	654	6,277

Source: World Bank, OECD and ECE statistics

over 50 per cent or even over 100 per cent, that found themselves forced to seek massive rescheduling in 1982. Other countries like South Korea – with a debt per capita figure higher than the Brazilian – experienced no crisis because export performance continued to be sufficiently buoyant to keep the debt-service ratio well below 25 per cent. Yugoslavia obviously falls in with the former rather than the latter category.

There are obvious specific resemblances between the Polish and Yugoslav cases – both socialist countries, both having pursued identifiably import-led growth strategies in the 1970s, both presenting manifold instances of the negative impact of political factors on economic efficiency, particularly investment efficiency. But we must take care not to press the comparison too far. There was no dramatic socio-political crisis of the Polish type in Yugoslavia at this time, no Yugoslav Solidarity, no complications with the Soviet Union, no imposition of martial law and concomitant difficulties with the West.

For Yugoslavia, then, a country with a serious debt problem in 1982 but by no means the most serious, a look round the world scene provided lessons, negative and positive. The worst of the Latin American cases showed just how bad a debt-service problem could become in a short period of time – Argentina's debt-service ratio, for instance, doubled between 1981 and 1982. The Polish case showed just how perversely the political factor could operate – in this case a major cause of the crisis and the major obstacle to its resolution. Finally, the South Korean case illustrated a very simple, and much more optimistic lesson – as long as an economy can consistently generate large-scale foreign exchange flows, there is no need to worry about stocks of debt, or levels of debt per capita. Looked at from a dynamic, policy-making angle, debt is not a problem as long as your adjustment mechanism is in order. As we saw in the last chapter, Yugoslavia's had, during the 1970s, been palpably out of order. Let us now see how things developed after 1982.

Chapter seven

Adjustment Policies in the 1980s:
Plus ça Change . . .?

The Balance of Trade and the Balance of Payments since the debt shock

Let us start with the good news. As Table 7.1 shows, the Balance of Payments on current account was back into surplus by 1983, with the deficit on Balance of Trade cut to less than half its 1981 level. The current account has remained in surplus ever since, and by 1986 the suficit totalled nearly $1bn, as the Trade Balance deficit fell to just $0.6bn. For hard-currency trade taken by itself the picture is less favourable, but the period 1983–6 probably yielded a cumulative surplus on that trade of around $1.5bn (WEFA 1988: 3, 139). Thus by 1983 Yugoslavia was earning enough from commerce with the rest of the world to pay the interest on her international loans, and have a little left over for repayment of principal or consolidation of reserves. But perhaps the most striking figures from Table 7.1 are those for exports. Exports in 1986 were at exactly the same level as they had been in 1982. The very substantial improvement in the Balance of Trade and the Balance of Payments between those two years was almost wholly due to a sharp cut in the level of imports. The bare figures seem to suggest, then, a continued failure to turn export-propulsion policies into hard export earnings, but some success on the import substitution side. Before going further with our analysis, however, let us look at how the Yugoslav government formulated its ideas about adjustment priorities in the post-debt shock period.

The report of the Kraigher Commission

In June 1983 the Commission formed in 1982 under the chairmanship of Sergej Kraigher to study the problem of 'adjusting the economic system to the demands of stabilization' submitted its findings. The main points of the report were as follows:

Table 7.1 The Balance of Payments 1982–6, in millions of dollars[1]

	1982	1983	1984	1985	1986
Current account					
Trade balance	−1833	−1152	−770	−579	−598
Exports	9475	9273	9889	10461	9448
Imports	−11308	−10425	10659	−11041	−10046
Balance of services					
Transport (net)	919	794	825	905	850
Travel (net)	1308	805	883	937	1027
Interest (net)	−1895	−1599	−1790	−1857	−1648
Other services (net)	−2928	−2005	−1940	−1814	−2043
Balance of goods and services	−4428	−3157	−2792	−2409	−2413
Transfers (net)	3998	3414	3259	3230	3351
Remittances from emigrants and Yugoslavs working abroad	3792	3206	3090	3059	3180
Other	206	208	169	171	171
Balance of current transactions	−430	257	467	820	937
Capital account					
Errors and omissions	74	−279	201	82	295
Net new credits	−938	−232	−572	−744	−522
Long-term (net)	−84	880	−259	78	−1198
Short-term (net)	−854	−1112	−313	−822	676
Change in reserves	1184	155	−238	118	−424

Note: The coverage of some of the sub-headings in these IMF statistics differs significantly from the coverage of the sub-headings in the Gnjatović statistics, on which tables 3.3 and 5.2 are based. Imports are reported f.o.b. rather than c.i.f. In addition, there are large discrepancies in relation to the 'remittances from Yugoslavs working abroad' and 'other services' categories, and to the breakdown between long-term and short-term capital. Care should therefore be taken in making direct comparisons between absolute figures in this table and in the preceding Balance of Payments tables. The OECD (1987: 14) gives incomplete figures which are more (though not completely) comparable to the Gnjatović figures, *viz.* –

	($ bn)			
	1982	1983	1984	1985
Trade balance	−3.1	−2.1	−1.8	−1.6
Exports	10.2	9.7	10.1	10.6
Imports	13.2	11.8	11.9	12.2
Remittances from emigrants and Yugoslavs working abroad	1.9	1.6	1.7	1.6

[1] Strictly in SDRs. The relevant exchange rates are (US dollars per SDR): 1982: 1.0401; 1983: 1.06900; 1984: 1.02501; 1985: 1.01534; 1986:1.17317 (IMF, *International Financial Statistics*). *Source*: IMF *Balance of Payments Statistics*.

1 Convertibility of the dinar should remain the ultimate aim in the sphere of foreign economic relations, and that means a single, realistic rate of exchange for the dinar.
2 Investment decision-taking and investment risk-taking must be brought closer together. Workers' councils should play a more active role in

the investment sphere, and the central authorities must ensure that funds are available to enterprises for investment purposes.

3 The taxation system, which had been fragmented and territorialized like so many other things during the 1970s, should be recentralized and rationalized, and the emphasis shifted back from indirect to direct taxation.

4 The definition of net income should be tightened up, as a basis for attacking the problem of fictional income (cf. discussion of concealed inflation Chapter 6). Procedures for the distribution of net income should also be tightened up, with a view to ensuring that a given job cannot be paid at widely different rates in different organizations.

5 'Under present conditions prices are not an economic category.' Reform of the price system is a key instrument for changing profitability, and hence investment patterns, particularly in relation to exports. Administrative control of prices has been totally ineffectual, whether in macro- or micro-terms, and should be abandoned. The proper criteria for prices in the future should be world prices and development/investment priorities. There must be a single price system for the whole of Yugoslavia, and that means that any subsidization must be of the consumer, not of the producer.

6 The procedures for rescuing or liquidating enterprises in financial difficulties should be tightened up.

These findings were neither surprising nor controversial. The Kraigher Commission paid lip service to the principles of the self-management system, but laid primary emphasis on the need to reform the price and investment vectors within the Yugoslav economic system. The most concrete immediate result of all this was the adoption of a new 'realistic rate of exchange' policy, which sought to effect the substantial real devaluation of the dinar which the 1970s had often promised, but never delivered.

Exchange rate policy after the debt shock

As we saw in Table 5.3, 1983 witnessed the first substantial effective devaluation of the dinar since the 1960s. The new policy line held for a couple of years, and a Zagreb Centre for Marketing Research study found that in February 1982 over 60 per cent of business organizations questionnaired thought that it was at least as easy to export as to sell on the home market (Vuger 1985). But by the middle of 1985, as the inflation rate accelerated, export profitability was again coming under threat (Ilijin 1986), and the dinar remained overvalued through 1986. By October of that year the black-market rate for the dinar against the dollar was some 50–100 per cent higher than the official ('Posao stoleća'

1986). At the end of 1986 72.3 per cent of industrial exports were going through at prices lower than domestic, compared to 55.8 per cent at the end of 1985 ('Kod kuće . . .' 1987). But the dinar depreciated faster than the rate of inflation rose during the first half of 1987, and the rate of effective export stimulation was reported to be many times higher in May 1987 than it had been in May 1986 ('Kurs bez tržista' 1987). As the rate of inflation kicked once more, however, in the later part of the year, export profitability was again squeezed. In May 1988, as part of the package associated with the new stand-by arrangement with the IMF (see Chapter 8), the dinar was devalued to the level of the black-market rate (Zimić 1988c).

The history of post–1983 exchange-rate policy has, then, been the history of a desperate race by the authorities to keep the rate of devaluation ahead of the rate of inflation. That represents a little bit of an oversimplification, because as we shall see later on, the authorities must themselves bear a large part of the responsibility for the escalating inflation rate. But we have certainly no reason to doubt the sincerity of the commitment to the realistic rate of exchange policy. In practice, however, the real rate of exchange has bobbed around so much that it has given enterprises little in the way of lasting incentives to export, though enough has probably been achieved to get rid of the permanent export-disincentive effect of pre-crisis exchange rate policy. As we saw in Chapter 5, there is in any case every reason to question the centrality of the exchange rate in explaining Yugoslav export trends. A government report published in January 1986, in reviewing the effect of the realistic exchange policy, expressed scepticism as to how much exchange-rate policy could be expected to produce an export-directed reorientation of investment in much the same terms as we did in Chapter 5. The policy may have helped with the task of cutting back imports, but given the predominance of direct controls over imports, that help could have been at most marginal. Exchange-rate policy, therefore, probably neither helped nor hindered import-substitution and export-propulsion policies to any great extent. Let us now try to pin-point what were, indeed, the dominant factors that conditioned the import and export trends documented in Table 7.1.

The import bill and the crisis: restriction and substitution

Given the severity of the debt service crisis as it broke in 1982, it is hardly surprising that the Yugoslav government adopted emergency short-term measures of an essentially administrative nature. Imports of consumer goods were cut by 18 per cent between 1981 and 1982, and by the end of 1982 rationing had been introduced for key consumer goods, including petrol, sugar, detergent, cooking oil and coffee. A survey done by the Business Chamber of Yugoslavia for 1982 found a 50 per cent aggregate deficit in detergent supply, with corresponding figures for coffee and lard of 70 per cent and 25 per cent. Milk, butter and meat were in serious shortage, and coal and tyres were totally unavailable ('Potemkinova sela' 1982). (Note that some of these specific shortages were caused by diversion of supplies from domestic to export markets, rather than directly by import restrictions.)

But import restrictions hit production just as hard as consumption, and by the summer of 1983 the leather, fur and shoe industry, a major exporter, was facing a serious shortage of hides as imports were cut just as exports of live animals were being forced ('Šagrinska koza' 1983). By the autumn of the same year 220,000 pigs had died on socialized-sector farms in Vojvodina as a result of import restrictions. Shortage of imported protein elements in their feed had lowered their resistance to infection, and petrol rationing had preventing veterinary surgeons from getting to the animals in time to save them ('Status' 1983).

None of this, it may be said, is surprising. The Yugoslavs did, after all, have a crisis on their hands, and the best-conceived import-substitution schemes in the world can only be introduced as quickly as new capacity can be laid down. Even so, the import restriction programme left much to be desired. In time-honoured fashion, the intensification of direct control over imports highlighted the problem of bureaucratic ineptitude. The Vojvodina pigs died partly because veterinary stations had been classified as 'administrative' rather than 'public' services, and had accordingly been denied access to extra petrol coupons for emergency purposes. In 1983 300 tons of crude phosphate was dumped in the sea as a result of customs red tape. The phosphate represented the 'sweepings' from the hold of a ship as it was cleaned out in the course of a routine re-fit. The shipowners wanted to give the phosphate to any agricultural organization that would pay to have it taken away. No, said the customs authorities: under the regulations only two things can be done. If the phosphate has commercial value, it must be bonded, pending application for an import licence. If it has no commercial value, it must be destroyed under customs supervision, and at the expense of the shippers. The captain decided that there was nothing else to do but throw the phosphate overboard ('Bolje u moru' 1983). All of this was taking place just as Yugoslavia's international rescue package was being finalized.

It was perhaps inevitable that administrative pressure to reduce imports should result in a burgeoning of barter deals. Over the first three months of 1983 alone, compensation deals worth a total export value of $890m and an import value of $740m had been put to the Business Chamber of Yugoslavia for approval ('Kompenzacioni poslovi . . .' 1983). By 1987 barter deals were accounting for 38 per cent of total trade turnover

(Zmijarević 1988). Clearly there was a good deal to commend this approach, in difficult circumstances. It guaranteed imported supplies, and created a direct incentive to export. But it did often also mean paying up to 25 per cent more for particular imports ('Kompenzacioni poslovi . . .' 1983). Thus while barter deals eased Yugoslavia's international payments problem, they did so in a wasteful and inefficient way.

Worst of all, 1987–8 found the situation, five years on from the debt-service crisis, little changed. Production was still being disrupted owing to shortage of imported raw materials, and in a 1987 interview Dragana Gnjatović predicted that a continuation of restrictive policies would stop technology transfer altogether, and condemn Yugoslavia to long-term economic decline (Gnjatović 1987). A curious case from 1987, reported as 'yet another victory for domestic know-how', highlighted just how perverse the interaction between import substitution and technology transfer can be. Local electrical engineers at a Tuzla milk sterilization plant had finally managed to get a troublesome imported control system to work. By so doing they saved the enterprise the cost of sending the system back to Holland, where it was made. But how much money had really been saved? The system had already been installed for several years, but had never worked properly. Dutch specialists had subsequently been called in to have a look at it, but only after the guarantee period had run out. They got the system working, but it broke down again as soon as they left ('Kasno paljenje' 1988). This story seems to illustrate three key points in relation to technology transfer:

1 The time factor is always crucial.
2 The wording of contracts must leave nothing to chance, or to charity.
3 Training of local cadres must be an integral part of the technology transfer deal, so that user-enterprises can maintain technical efficiency without the presence of donor-enterprise personnel.

The real problem in the Tuzla milk sterilization plant case is that none of these conditions were observed: it was only that state of affairs that permitted domestic technology to come and score its (from the technical point of view) perfectly laudable victory. Thus had the technology transfer process been conducted efficiently, the issue of import substitution would *never have arisen*.

A survey conducted by the Zagreb Centre for Marketing Research in February 1985 found that only 15 per cent of respondents thought that the effect of new (mostly imported) technologies had been 'very high' over the period 1980–4. Significantly, similar surveys conducted about the same time in the USA and West Germany produced corresponding figures of, respectively, 42 per cent and 44 per cent (Vuger 1985). Clearly, then, the Tuzla case of ineffectual technology transfer is by no means an isolated one. Yugoslavia has signally failed to obtain good value for money from its purchases abroad of equipment and know-how. On the other hand, as Gnjatović points out, if you persist with crudely restrictionist import policies, you may end up with no technology transfer at all. Either way, you will provide plenty of scope for 'victories for domestic know-how', but will only create further obstacles to the kind of rationalized, coordinated import substitution pattern which some Yugoslav economists seek.

The export drive and the crisis: improvization and strategy

As we saw in the last section, some of the consumer shortages that over-took the Yugoslav economy from the end of 1982 were caused by diversion of supplies to export, and there can be no doubt that Yugoslav exporting organizations did respond to the call for a special effort as the country stood on the brink of financial disaster. Between 1983 and 1984 exports for hard currency increased by 4.6 per cent (SGJ 1987: 317). But they grew by a total of only 2.2 per cent over the succeeding two years, to rise again by 7 per cent in 1987 (Zmijarević 1988). Changes in the real exchange rate may help to explain fluctuations around the trend, but it is the trend that we are primarily interested in, and the trend is essentially stagnatory. There is every general indication, then, that attempts to reorientate domestic investment patterns more towards exporting for convertible currency met with as little success in the early 1980s as they had in the late 1970s. Let us try to put some micro-economic flesh onto this general proposition.

No one expects agriculture to solve all of Yugoslavia's economic problems. We saw in Chapter 5, however, that Yugoslavia enjoys comparative advantage in a number of areas of specialized, quality food lines. Yet the record in this area through the early 1980s was dismal. Yugoslav exports of cold meats and sausages to the USA fell, and those of cheese and wine ceased altogether. Yugoslav exporters of canned fruit and vegetables found themselves constrained to switch out of West European markets. In both cases falling quality was the problem, in both cases back of quality problems we find investment deficiencies. Meat-processing capacities have become increasingly obsolete, despite the costly import of substantial volumes of slaughterhouse equipment, some of it financed by the World Bank. In the case of canning facilities, old and new capacities alike share defects, some purely technical, some more related to the human capital dimension, which make the attainment of top quality impossible. In the case of fruit production the case is further complicated by an ageing stock of trees, which cannot guarantee consistently good harvests (Ivanović 1984; *Proizvodna Orijentacija . . .*, 1985: 69–132). Yet when the American side of the Yugoslav–US

Committee for Scientific and Technical Cooperation proposed a conference for 1986 on the subject of transfer of food-processing technology, they met with few responses ('Komparativna prednost . . .' 1985). Maybe the Yugoslav organizations which might have responded were simply too despondent about the prospects of raising the hard currency involved.

Perhaps the most striking example of the complex nexus of price, quality, investment and technology factors is provided by the tourist industry. In 1987 foreign tourism was accounting for around 40 per cent of total net inflow of hard currency into Yugoslavia. But this reflected the weakness of the rest of the Yugoslav economy rather than the strength of the tourist industry, which has been steadily losing ground to its European competitors in terms of income over the past 15 years, and which suffered a catastrophic decline in receipts *precisely in 1983*. But while it took the industry until 1987 to regain the level of income from foreign tourism achieved in 1982, numbers of foreign tourists visiting Yugoslavia rose by some 30 per cent between those two years. So clearly the problem is not in the number of tourists, but rather in how much, or rather how little they spend when in Yugoslavia.

To some extent the collapse in tourist receipts in 1983 was a direct result of the emergency measures taken to reduce imports. Foreign tourists were not immune from the shortages affecting the Yugoslav population as a whole, and there were additional irritations like the embargo on the import of foreign newspapers. But behind this lay more deep-seated problems relating to the whole approach to the development of the tourist industry. When Mirko Ilić, the distinguished Zagreb graphic designer now working in the United States, returned to Yugoslavia to receive an award for services to the international promotion of Yugoslav design, he remarked on the state of design and quality in the domestic Yugoslav economy in the following terms: 'In a country where you can only get milk up to 10 a.m., who needs a good design to sell milk?' (Ilić 1988).

Of course the Yugoslav market socialist economy does not suffer from quality problems to the extent of the centrally planned economies of Eastern Europe, but producers for the domestic market are certainly not capable of taking the *lead* in quality and design matters. Yet at the same time we observe an almost perverse resolve on the part of the tourist industry that no special provisions should be made for foreign tourists. A 1987 report, for instance, tells us of one Yugoslav food company which insists on putting on sale in tourist areas products which are banned in the majority of European countries. Meanwhile some foreign tourists are actually bringing their own potatoes with them, on the basis that Yugoslav potatoes are 'unfit for human consumption' (Djuričić 1987).

We can use this kind of anecdotal evidence as a starting point for a more precise picture of the relationship between price, quality and investment variables in tourism. Clearly the main immediate cause of the sharp fall in tourist earnings in 1983 was a failure of demand to respond to the lower prices created by devaluation. In 1987 hotel prices and rates for other tourist services in Yugoslavia were some 30–65 per cent lower in Yugoslavia than elsewhere in Europe ('S glavom . . .' 1987). Yet around the same time one leading Dubrovnik hotel tourist organization was very successfully following a policy of 'world quality – world prices' – refusing to follow the official recommendation to cut dollar prices as much as possible, and managing to increase hard-currency revenue all the same ('Jeres . . .' 1986).

Clearly, then, quality is more important than price in determining income from tourist services, narrowly defined. But what about total tourist expenditure? A survey conducted in 1985 ('Uslov za devize', 1985) posed the question: with the dinar so low against foreign currencies, why do foreign tourists spend so little on quality and speciality articles like clothes, leather goods, crystal and jewellery? Why does only 13.1 per cent of total daily tourist expenditure go on non-food shopping (by 1987 the figure is said to have dropped to 6 per cent – Djuričić 1987), and of that the bulk on cigarettes, newspapers, films, small souvenirs and beverages? One reason is certainly deficiencies of design, quality and marketing in the speciality lines. An independent source tells us that in the same year Yugoslavia was selling gold jewellery to the United States for a price, in terms of gold content, 34 per cent lower than the world price of gold ingots, mainly because of shortcomings in styling and quality ('Cena sirovosti' 1985). Beyond that, the major constraint is simply lack of retail capacity. The tourist regions of other Mediterranean countries have 19 times as many retail outlets per tourist as the Yugoslav Adriatic. (Significantly, such outlets are, in Yugoslavia as elsewhere, predominantly privately owned. The difference is that they pay penal rates of taxation in Yugoslavia.) Whichever way we look at it then, the answer is the same. Yugoslav receipts from foreign tourism are unresponsive to changes in the exchange rate because Yugoslavia has never invested in the capacity, production and distributive, to give tourists something to spend their extra money on.

We may add that failure to develop Yugoslavia's estimable traditional fare into a high-value *haute cuisine* on the French model has deprived Yugoslav agriculture of one of the easiest ways to expand agricultural exports in a world dominated by CAPs and the like – through the stomachs of tourists. In the words of vice-governor of the National Bank, Boris Konte,

> every analysis shows that Yugoslavia has the least polluted agricultural lands in Europe, among the cleanest in the world . . . And agricultural produce is the alpha and omega of tourism. It is inconceivable that

tourism can make a big step forward without an abundance of varied agricultural produce.

(Konte 1987)

Yugoslav tourism expert Predrag Djuričić sees at the root of the problem a fundamentally misconceived strategy for investment and development in the sector over an extended period of time (Djuričić 1985). Too much money has been put into the 'heavy industry' side of tourism – big hotels with an average number of beds of around 300 (in other Mediterannean countries the average is 22–38), designed as 'oases' which can provide the tourist with absolutely everything. In practice, provision is often deficient, and in any case modern tourists want to 'shop around' more. While investment in general infrastructure has been neglected, investment in small, private hotels and in bed and breakfast facilities has been positively discouraged by high taxation and oppressive legislation. In 1981, just a year before the foreign debt crisis broke, a law was passed forbidding private individuals to rent out rooms except through a socialized sector organization. By 1987 there was a serious shortage of tourist beds which Yugotours was hoping to ease by bringing in more accommodation in private houses (Djuričić 1987). Whether we are looking at the accommodation issue, then, or that of retail outlets, the key systemic issue of the *balance of socialized and private sectors* is obviously of crucial importance in assessing the current prospects for increasing tourism revenue. We shall return to this question later.

We can point up the essential problem of Yugoslav export performance in the post-debt shock period by looking at one of Yugoslavia's comparatively successful export initiatives of the 1980s – the Yugo car. Developed by the Crvena Zastava firm in technical cooperation with the US concern, Mabon-Nuget, the Yugo was able to carve a niche for itself in Western markets, especially in the US, as a cheap second or third car. In 1983 Yugo exports totalled around $250m, and sales to the US grew steadily up to 1987. As of around 1984 Yugos were selling, on international markets, for 40 per cent less than comparable top-quality cars, 25 per cent less than comparable medium-quality cars, 15–17 per cent less than vehicles produced by less popular firms, or firms just coming onto the market like SEAT of South Korea, but up to 20 per cent more than other East European vehicles (*Proizvodna Orijentacija* 1985: 55–6). Now the evidence from Yugoslav experience with the tourist industry and the food-processing industry, and indeed from East European exporting experience in general, is that there is no straightforward trade-off between price and quality, that cheap, low-quality goods are often simply unsaleable on export markets. The Yugo is certainly cheap, and it is certainly not a class car. So why is it an exception?

The steps taken by Crvena Zastava in relation to quality control for the American market provides a precedent which could serve as an example for other producers. Through an integrated programme of action Crvena Zastava were able to mobilize all factors affecting the marketing of the product, from the production stage right through to transporting the cars and loading them onto the ship. All along the production line, including ancillary suppliers, a red alert regime was instituted which specified measures and deadlines for the execution of every task. The quality of every component delivered by ancillary suppliers was checked. Where it was not up to standard, the components were bought in from abroad. The quality control service was stiffened up from a manpower point of view, and the new, stricter and more comprehensive quality control procedures applied to all output, not just to that going for export. Special selection and training procedures were introduced for those working on the assembly line, and a special incentive scheme adopted.

(*Proizvodna Orijentacija* 1985: 43)

The most important point to emerge from all this is that it is less the absolute level of quality that matters in export markets as the reliability of a product in a given quality range. The Yugo may be a down-market car, but you know what you are getting when you buy one. Precisely one of the key problems in the Yugoslav tourist industry is that the foreign guest is never quite sure when the next unpleasant surprise will come. The Yugo material also illustrates a number of important, subsidiary points. If you want quality control, it has to be for everyone, not just for the export markets even if exporting is your priority goal. If you want to keep domestic ancillary suppliers on their toes, you have to be prepared to use the threat of switching to foreign suppliers. One is left wondering how that policy fared for Crvena Zastava through the period of extreme restriction on imports in the mid-1980s.

Of course the Yugo case illustrates problems as well as successes. The Crvena Zastava management are clear that if they want to expand exports they will have to move up-market, which means even tighter quality control. They are equally clear that the future for the vehicle industry lies in the introduction of robotization and flexible production systems. That means bringing in technology from abroad, but with Yugoslavia a relatively low-wage, labour-abundant economy, robotization patterns would have to be adjusted to suit local conditions. This is where domestic Research and Development should come in. With large-scale expansion of vehicle exports it would become economical to set up import-substituting capacities to produce basic inputs into vehicle manufacture like float glass, cold-rolled steel, plastics, synthetic rubber, paints, etc. (*Proizvodna Orientacija* 1985: 48–9), though that again would in most cases involve technology transfer from abroad. It would at the same time integrate Yugoslavia, for the first time, into the kind of micro-specialization patterns which have come increasingly to dominate international trading in the post-war period.

Over the first six months of 1988 Yugo exports to the US fell by 39.6 per cent. This partly reflected a general switch-back on the part of American buyers to home-produced cars. Significantly, however, Hyundai of South Korea still managed to increase sales by 16.9 per cent (Simović 1988b). These developments brought a fresh urgency to the question of new models, and in the autumn of the same year Zastava announced that production had started on a new 'Florida' range of cars. With an initial capital cost of $400m, the production line will be turning out at least ten variants on the basic model by 1989. Simultaneously work will proceed on the development of new models, with a horizon going up to 1995. Initially about 40 per cent of parts will be imported, but this should be reduced to just a few per cent with the development of new models in the 1990s. When the production line reaches full capacity in 1990 it should be turning out 60,000 cars a year. Zastava hopes to export 1,000 Floridas in 1989, half of them to the USA, where the car will sell for around $10,000 ('Automobili' 1988). These plans obviously raise as many problems as they solve. A major breakthrough on the American market, and a dramatic reduction in dependence on foreign parts will have to be seen to be believed. But at least someone in Yugoslavia is doing some strategic thinking on exports.

While the Yugo saga certainly holds out some hope for the future of Yugoslav exports, it has, nevertheless, to be set against a background on which Yugoslavia often seems to be falling further behind. For international markets are not static, and the trend in recent years has been for them to become even more demanding on precisely the points where the Yugoslav economy is weakest. One of the main quality control innovations on Western markets of recent years, for example, is product coding. The EAN system of coding was introduced for the first time in 1976, and currently covers about half the categories of goods traded in the EC. There are now more than 60,000 EAN code numbers, but only 0.06 of them have been taken up and used by Yugoslav organizations, and less than 5 per cent of the types of food product exported by Yugoslavia are coded. Yugoslavia formally adopted the system in 1982, but had done little to develop it up to 1986, by which time obstacles to the export of uncoded goods were becoming increasingly formidable. Business Chamber experts reckoned at the beginning of 1987 that within a few years Yugoslavia's backwardness in this area could turn into a 'critical foreign-trade barrier for our country' (Djuričić 1987a). One of the problems lying behind the coding bottleneck is lack of the necessary information technology, once again illustrating how crucially dependent exporting is on efficient technology transfer.

We find the same widening gap in relation to the whole dimension of international marketing. The history of the one-sided conquest of European and North American markets by Far Eastern exporters is, *inter alia*, the history of the development of Japanese, Korean, etc. technical representation in the West, and the failure to develop Western technical representation in the Far East. In the early 1980s, for instance, there were more Japanese representatives in Dusseldorf than EC representatives in the whole of Japan. Now technical representation abroad has never been a Yugoslav strong point, but one of the pennywise side-effects of the 1982 debt-service crisis was something of a campaign to economize on representation, a campaign which has, for instance, threatened the development of a Yugoslav presence in the potentially enormous Chinese market ('Tudja briga' 1987). But as with so many things, efficient marketing abroad does not necessarily mean doing it all yourself. Thus when the Yugoslavs tried to sell tyres in the US through their own marketing company they came a cropper, while the South Koreans, going through an American dealer, prospered ('Poslovni rizik' 1986).

Post-debt shock productivity trends

One of the most striking things about developments since the breaking of the crisis is the way that trends in the domestic economy have paralleled those in the external sector. In a word, the failure to produce a change of gear in the trading profile has been mirrored exactly by a *deepening* of the reversion to extensive growth patterns which began in the mid-1970s. Labour productivity in the socialized sector fell by 1.8 per cent in 1981, 2.1 per cent in 1982, 3.2 per cent in 1983, grew by just 0.4 per cent in 1984, and fell again by 2 per cent in 1985 (Karakašević 1986). It grew by 0.6 per cent in 1986 (*SGJ* 1987: 92). As of 1986 the general level of overmanning in the socialized sector was still of the order of 20–30 per cent, despite an increase in unemployment of some 200,000 1982–86; in 1986 it was estimated that even in fully employed Slovenia (just 14,836 people out of work at the end of September 1985 – Karakašević 1985) there were still some 100,000 surplus workers (Karakašević 1986).

We can fill out this picture of widespread under-employment by looking at some micro-economic data. Subotica professor of economics Stjepan Han calculated in 1983 that workers in relatively high-productivity enterprises in the more advanced republics of Yugoslavia were doing an average of 3 hours and 6 minutes actual work a day (Han 1983). A 1985 Business Chamber survey covering 3,264 specialists working in 305 enterprises found that 1.8 per cent were, by their own account, 'busy' only 25 per cent of their working time, 14 per cent were busy less than half their time, 36.6 per cent up to 75 per cent and just

14.8 per cent busy 90–100 per cent of the working day. If this was the view of the specialists themselves, the *Ekonomska Politika* reporter asks, what would their colleagues say about them? ('(Ne)iskorišćenost . . .' 1985) Muriš Osmanagić of the Technology Faculty at Tuzla sharpens the picture when he compares two salt works built in the 1960s, both with an annual production capacity of 200,000 tons, one in Yugoslavia, one in the USA. In 1987 the Yugoslav plant was employing 1,200, the US plant 120 (Sitarski 1987). Member of the Presidency of the Central Committee of the League of Communists Nikola Stojanović summed up the problem in 1985 when he said that 'employment of a social character which holds back productivity [is the most important] negative factor disturbing the general political situation and hindering the battle for development and progress' ('Izuzetak' 1985).

The same picture emerges when we look at energy consumption. Between 1982 and 1986 industrial production grew by 13.5 per cent, while industrial energy utilization increased 29.6 per cent (*SGJ 1987*: 265). Once again, then, the damaging trends which set in in the late 1970s simply continue into the post-debt shock period. But this recalcitrant profligacy in the utilization of power in industry must be set against a background of critical shortage of energy, as the annual level of oil imports was cut by over 27 per cent 1979–85, while the problem of shortage of generating capacity inherited from the late 1970s remained unsolved. In the first half of 1984 there was a deficit of 7.6 per cent on the total energy balance (Horvat 1984), and regular, daily power-cuts to the domestic consumption sector had to be introduced.

Yugoslavia's politico-economic structure continued to manifest its extreme unsuitability to the resolution of these energy problems, and by 1988 the republics and provinces were still unable to reach agreement on 1) the time-scale on which energy resources should be exploited; 2) the basis on which amortization funds should be allocated to new investment; 3) the basis on which rental payments and compensation for exploitation of non-renewable resources should be calculated; 4) the procedure for repaying 'associated' (*udruženi*) funds, i.e. compulsory loans. In addition there was still no accord on more specific issues like, for example, whether the vast lignite deposits of Kosovo 'belong' to the autonomous province, or to the republic of Serbia, or to Yugoslavia (Nedeljković 1987, 1988). In a word, there was agreement on nothing, and Serbia was preparing to cut investment in the electricity industry and cut deliveries outwith the republic.

We can give concrete illustration of the impact of these planning failures by looking at the experience of particular fuel industries. Policy on investment in coal-mining, for example, has remained in disarray, with price relatives radically out of step with investment plans. As a result, investment in Serbian pits through the middle 1980s was running

141

at just one-third its planned level (Lakićević 1985). Meanwhile political complications going far beyond abstract notions of ownership have continually hampered the formulation of policy on the Kosovo lignite fields (Nedeljković 1985).

Not all Yugoslav economists are convinced of the wisdom of trying to develop import-substituting coal production on a large scale. The really striking thing about the recent evolution of the coal situation is the apparent inability of the institutions charged with the management of the energy balance to provide any kind of consistent strategic orientation, or even to generate the data on which such an orientation could be based. In this, sadly, the experience with coal has merely reflected a more general malaise of energy planning from which the system seems unable to free itself.

Reference to the official statistics indicates that the *ratio of gross fixed capital formation to National Income* dropped sharply after the crisis. Having stood at 28 per cent as late as 1981, it fell to an average level of 21 per cent over the three years 1984–86 (*SGJ 1987*: 92). It has been argued that, when proper account is taken of elements of concealed inflation, the rate of net fixed production investment turns out to have been negative since 1979 (*Uslovi . . .* 1985: 123). This conclusion may appear extreme, but there can be no doubt that the rate of effective new investment had fallen to a very low level by the early/mid-1980s. Now it is true that one of the reasons for widespread inefficiency in the investment process during the 1970s had been excessive investment demand. We might have expected that cut-backs in the volume of fixed capital formation would at least have permitted the authorities to impose higher standards of cost-effectiveness in the investment sphere. In practice, the *means* the authorities chose to implement emergency investment measures were such as to exacerbate rather than alleviate efficiency problems.

Perhaps understandably, in the context of critical difficulties relating to foreign borrowing, the National Bank declared a freeze on investment finance on 30 June 1982. The stand-still was strengthened by new measures promulgated on the last day of 1984. Now the trouble with investment freezes, as other East European countries including Hungary have discovered, is that while they may save investment funds, they inevitably prolong average gestation periods and increase unit capital costs. In the Yugoslav case they also had a very deleterious impact on labour productivity in construction, with construction output falling by some 50 per cent through the period 1980–7, and the building labour force falling hardly at all ('Što manji . . .' 1987) Of course exceptions were made to the 1984 freeze for 'priority' projects, but how were the priorities to be determined?

In 1985 the drafting of a series of 22 sectoral joint programmes for production and development in the period up to 1990 and beyond was initiated. These programmes were to constitute the 'blood and meat' of the 1986–90 five-year plan. But as of September 1985 little progress had been made in generating concrete concerted programmes, with the energy saga recounted above only the most extreme illustration of a general problem. For the government, this series of joint programmes represented 'the most important instrument of affirmation of the intensive function of planning'. For sceptical Yugoslav economists it just sounded like the key investment programmes of 1976–80 all over again (Ilijin 1985). Some progress was made in the middle 1980s towards a more active and export-oriented pattern of transfer of funds by association (*udruživanje*) from richer to poorer regions. But it continued to be hindered by attempts on the part of the authorities in the less developed republics to divert the money away from restructuring into shoring up the existing industrial structure (Pjević 1987). At a colloquium organized by the Investment Bank in 1987 Yugoslav economists listed the underlying problems in the investment field as follows:

1 'A system in which the workers decide their own wages cannot be rational or guarantee normal economic development.'
2 'The Basic Organization of Associated Labour is a social, rather than a business organization, while the banks operate as "services" rather than on a commercial basis.'
3 There is no 'single Yugoslav market'.
4 There is no proper procedure for founding new enterprises.
5 There is no mechanism for chanelling private savings into small investments ('Imati i . . .' 1987).

We might wish to argue about the relative importance of these five points, but the overall conclusion of the colloquium is as indisputable as the echo of the Kraigher Commission report of four years earlier is unmistakable. In a word, the failure to effect a qualitative change in the nature of the investment process after 1982 is intimately tied up with general systemic factors. Precisely the same argument can be advanced in relation to external trading patterns and to the pattern of energy production and consumption. Let us turn now, therefore, to an examination of these systemic trends.

The crisis and the system

We saw in Chapter 6 how the rate of increase of the retail price index started to rise in 1984. By 1986 it had reached 88 per cent and in 1987 it topped 100 per cent. In February 1988 the annual rate of inflation stood at 157 per cent, and by January 1989 it had reached nearly 300 per cent.

Now a certain degree of cost-of-living inflation was no doubt a necessary condition for the reduction in real wages which crisis conditions demanded. But after 1982 the rough, Phillips-curve inverse relationship which had existed between inflation and unemployment in the 1960s and 1970s disappears completely. The post-debt shock trend is for unemployment to rise, and for inflation to go through the roof. This clearly suggests some fundamental problem of monetary control. Table 7.2 shows how in practice the authorities have found it increasingly difficult to plan and control the supply of money. The relationship between the supply of money and the total level of economic activity in nominal terms also continued to be troublesome, as it had been in the late 1970s and the early 1980s, and the velocity of circulation was still rising as late as 1985. It is, indeed, only from 1986 that we are able to impute the totality of annual inflation rates to the increment in the supply of money. The monetary sector presents, arguably, a unique focal point for all the problems and dilemmas of system adjustment which the crisis brought to the fore. So let us begin our systemic review by studying in greater depth the evolution of the money supply situation in the 1980s.

Table 7.2 The supply of money (M1) 1980–86: targets and outcomes (annual percentage change)

	1980	1981	1982	1983	1984	1985	1986
Target	22.0	22.0	17.1	18.5	32.5	42.0	43.0
Revised target	26.0	28.0	16.5	15.5	42.7	36.9	82.0
Outcome	23.1	26.6	26.6	20.1	43.1	46.5	109.1

Source: OECD 1987: 53; Statistički Godišnjak Jugoslavije 1987: 214

In Chapter 4 we pin-pointed a number of peculiarities of the Yugoslav monetary sector which left the system vulnerable to cost-inflationary pressures – the absence of a capital market, the importance of trade credit as near-money, the role of selective credits. Reports on individual industries through 1986 and 1987 confirm to a striking degree the survival into the post-debt shock period of the tendency which had been so marked in the 1970s for producers automatically to pass on any increases in their costs. Perhaps we should not be surprised at this, since nothing had happened in the meantime to make the structure of the Yugoslav economy more competitive – indeed emergency restrictions on imports did, of course, reduce further any pressure of competition from abroad. Again, the sharp fall in the price of oil in 1985 which helped Western countries to finish off the inflation problems inherited from the 1970s once and for all had little impact on domestic Yugoslav cost structures because of tax changes. Even so, the pricing behaviour of Yugoslav firms in the mid-1980s indicates firm expectations that monetary policy would ultimately be accommodating. Let us see whether anything was happening on the monetary policy front that might have proved those expectations to be unfounded.

By 1984 selective credits were accounting for some 97 per cent of annual emissions of primary money (Bjelica 1985: 150). The great bulk of selective credits were supposed to go to agriculture and exports, but there is substantial evidence that the tendency to divert these funds to other purposes grew stronger in the early 1980s. Thus by the mid-1980s

> the key factor reducing the effectiveness of monetary and credit policy in the sense of controlling the money supply and credit policy, was the rigidity, the extreme inelasticity of the system of approval of selective rediscounted credits to banks from primary emission. This rigidity flows from established practice, customary rights, social conventions, compromises, pressures, and not from basic legal prescriptions . . . Selective credits are now . . . the main factor influencing the formation of the credit potential of the business banks.
>
> (Golijanin 1985: 25)

The pressure for increased diversion of selective credit funds did, of course, ultimately come from the explosion of near-money in the late 1970s and early 1980s. By the end of 1986 there was more than 3,000bn dinars worth of 'grey' bills of exchange in circulation in Yugoslavia, in addition to about the same total value of properly guaranteed bills (Grličkov 1987b). With credit rationing a permanent feature of central bank policy from 1978 onwards (Goljanin 1985: 26), the more powerful banks tended to accumulate excess liquidity. They quickly developed the practice of using this blocked liquidity to guarantee inter-enterprise credits of various kinds (OECD 1987: 53), thus effectively nullifying the purpose of credit rationing.

Still, as we saw in Chapter 4, holders of near-money will always want to convert it into actual money sooner or later, and with an increasingly severe problem of enterprise liquidity as the 1980s progressed (by 1987 total enterprise deposits on giro account were covering just over 20 per cent of the total volume of bills of exchange in circulation – Grličkov 1987b), the demand for money was bound to intensify, as it had done in the early 1970s in similar circumstances. It is this that mainly explains the way that the growth rate in the supply of money abruptly shoots ahead of that for National Income in nominal terms in 1986. The rest of the explanation is less peculiarly Yugoslav in nature. The authorities were forced to have recourse to primary emissions to balance the federal budget in 1985 (Bogoev 1985), this in turn reflecting a continued failure to develop any kind of a bond market.

We can illustrate the relationship between near-money and the money supply under Yugoslav conditions by reference to what was, perhaps, the greatest financial scandal ever to hit the country – the Agrokomerc affair. In September 1987 the giant Bosnian food/agriculture combine declared itself insolvent to the extent of 377bn dinars, including 192bn dinars worth of bills of exchange ('Alajbegova . . .' 1987; Čehajić 1987). At that point total debts exceeded the capital value of the entire combine. The bills of exchange were spread around some 60 banks throughout Yugoslavia, and the immediate impact of the crash was to send Agrokomerc's local bank, the Bihać branch of the Business Bank of Sarajevo, into liquidation. Beobanka also found itself in serious trouble over its Agrokomerc exposure. By October the débâcle had brought the inter-bank market in bills of acceptance to an almost complete standstill, creating serious liquidity problems throughout the commercial banking sector (Grličkov 1987c). By late 1987 the National Bank was under intense pressure to increase primary emissions to ease the liquidity situation in the banking sector, and to 'rescue' Agrokomerc, just at a time when it was struggling to keep escalating inflation under some kind of control.

Technical questions of the money supply aside, the Agrokomerc story illustrates how closely interrelated the monetary and investment dimensions are in the Yugoslav case. Stricter appraisal of Agrokomerc's projects would surely have prevented a crash on such a scale from happening in the first place. Proper receivership procedures might have made it feasible for Agrokomerc to be 'put on the market', possibly dismembered, with a view to re-establishing profitable production on the basis of a 'clean slate'. Under Yugoslav conditions, politically-motivated cross-subsidization through the take-over of ailing enterprises by strong enterprises remains the only regular form of industrial reorganization. It is, of course, a form inimical to the interests of efficient use of capital stock. By the same token it is a form which can only be financed through the diversion of selective credits.

There were other ways in which the peculiarities of the monetary sector continued to impinge on the investment sphere. Credit rationing, ineffectual in macro-economic trends, was damaging in micro-economic trends, because it penalized strong banks, which we can presume to be those best fitted to appraise potential projects, and because it left the system even more vulnerable to investment favouritism, as exceptions to the credit limits were made for 'special projects' (Grličkov 1987a). Real rates of interest were consistently negative throughout the late 1970s and early 1980s, and as the rate of inflation escalated after 1982, the gap between nominal rate of interest and rate of change in the price level increased to record levels (see Table 7.3).

In a situation dominated by soft budget constraints we should not, perhaps, lay primary stress on negative rates of interest as a factor on the investment scene. But double-figure negative interest rates must have made it a lot easier for would-be investors who did *not* enjoy special political status to take a cavalier attitude to the future amortization of present loans.

Table 7.3 Rates of interest and the rate of inflation 1976–84

	Average bank interest rates		Annual percentage change in retail price index
	Passive	Active	
1976	5.48	7.93	9
1977	5.43	7.23	13
1978	4.73	5.89	13
1979	3.81	5.65	22
1980	3.83	5.49	30
1981	3.94	6.42	46
1982	4.32	7.51	30
1983	5.93	10.18	38
1984	8.11	13.43	57

Source: Radmilović 1985: 45; *SGJ 1987*: 220

Finally, there was the international monetary dimension. We can perhaps just put it down to lack of experience that the National Bank failed to take account of the inflationary impact of the Balance of Payments surpluses of the mid-1980s. The stubborn problem of so-called 'losses arising from foreign exchange movements' (*kursne razlike*) is a more deep-seated, systemic one. It takes two forms. First, because Yugoslav citizens hold large volumes of foreign exchange in special hard-currency accounts, and because these are, quite properly, counted as part of the money supply, accelerating inflation in terms of the dinar creates a recurring problem of revaluation, and of 'positive exchange rate differences'.

> [Monetary] targets are defined net of valuation effects, i.e. the foreign-exchange component of the aggregates is calculated in foreign exchange at the exchange rate ruling at the time when targets are set. As depreciations of the domestic currency lead to an equivalent revaluation of the foreign-exchange component of targets, any depreciation in excess of that originally anticipated and implicit in the formulation of objectives is automatically accommodated. Over the period 1980–5 such revaluations have been responsible for between 40 and almost 70 per cent of the growth of targets, depending on their precise definition.

(OECD 1987: 53).

Even graver, from the point of view of the efficiency of the banking system as an allocator of resources, was the problem of *negative* exchange rate differences. As we saw, one of the main factors lying behind the rapid growth in external debt in the 1970s was an increasing tendency for Yugoslav commercial banks to borrow abroad in order to finance expansion of *dinar* credits. Again, as the rate of inflation of the dinar got increasingly out of hand, as interest rates became increasingly negative, and as these hard-currency loans matured, the banks involved found themselves faced with the prospect of massive losses, even in cases where debt service on their *dinar* claims were in perfectly good order. The inevitable result was intense pressure on the authorities to cover these losses by primary emission. At the end of 1985 it was agreed that 50 per cent of all foreign exchange losses should be covered by the National Bank (Dumezić 1986a), and in early 1988 the federal government agreed to cover all losses arising from exchange movements in connection with the import of oil, and the import of equipment for construction organizations doing work abroad. Leading economic journalist V. Grličkov, argued in the pages of *Ekonomska Politika* that the decision was in flat contradiction to the policy of real exchange rates, which *aims* to impose losses on those who do not adjust to changing conditions (Grličkov 1988b). In more general terms, we can see how the problem of soft budget constraints ramifies *within* the banking system, as well as on the interface between banking and production sectors, and how these ramifications did, indeed, become more rather than less problematic after 1982. It was admitted at the end of 1988 that the extra-budgetary balance, supposedly abolished in the 1970s, was alive and kicking, and indeed bigger than the regular budget. It was being spent on covering exchange-rate losses and 'intervention' in the economy, and was, presumably, being financed mainly from primary emissions ('Ni programa . . . ' 1988)

It would be unfair to suggest that absolutely nothing had been achieved by 1988 in the direction of tightening up on some of these systemic weaknesses. A new law on the reporting and allocation of income promulgated at the end of 1985 sought to improve receivership procedures and make it simpler to liquidate unprofitable enterprises, and to limit the use of bills of exchange. But it seemed if anything to make it easier for enterprises to overvalue their stocks, and was equally soft on the issue of primary emissions (Dumezić 1986a). In 1986 a limitation was placed on the right of banks to guarantee promissory notes. Again, however, we are still waiting for this move to have any significant impact on the problem of grey emissions. In the same year a law was passed which limited the right of workers' councils to dispose of their funds for personal income purposes, thus effectively depriving the organs of self-management of the right to decide on the key issue of the division between consumption and investment (Dumezić 1986b). This law was largely an *ex post* formalization of an existing situation, and its main significance may lie in the exoneration it offers the Yugoslav working class for any further blame in connection with cost-inflationary pressures. It certainly had no effect whatsoever on the trend in the rate of inflation. Indeed a 1988 report demonstrated just how tenuous the link between enterprise income and individual remuneration has been in pointing out that there is generally an inverse relationship between loss-making and personal incomes. Thus, for example, workers in the deeply troubled oil industry remain among the most highly paid in the country ('Koga država . . . ' 1988). The interpretation placed on these facts in the report is simple enough. Losses are concentrated in heavy industry – in oil, chemicals and ferrous metallurgy. The organizations involved are created, financed, and finally bailed out [back to primary emissions] by a state still obsessed with the construction of economic giants as part of a mythical heavy-industrial fundament for the economy, and as a guarantee of future prosperity. High personal incomes in these organizations are just a way in which the state ensures that 'its' employees do not suffer the consequence of its mistakes. So much for industrial restructuring.

Systemic adjustment and the private sector

The onset of the crisis inevitably redirected the attention of policy-makers back to the private sector. Individual farmers and small entrepreneurs had, after all, always managed to survive, if not to flourish, in conditions where the state took out a good deal more than it put in. As the molly-coddled socialized sector reeled in 1982, the lesson in terms of a more pragmatic approach to the balance of collective and individual enterprise was there for all to read. The major policy memorandum produced by the influential Institute for Economic Sciences in 1985 (*Uslovi . . .* 1985) for the federal government based its estimates for future Yugoslav economic growth on the assumption that the private sector would grow faster than the socialized. By 1988 some analysts were reckoning that private business outside agriculture (*mala privreda*) could increase employment from a current 373,772 to around 1.8 million (Ostojić 1988). Yugoslav economists were increasingly impressed by the key role played by small firms, in cooperation with large, precisely in the dynamic, high-tech sectors of the US and Japanese economies, including electronics, aerospace and vehicle production. Indeed they could read the lesson in going no further than their own Slovenia, where policy has always been more liberal on the private sector. There the pattern was already well established by the mid-1980s, with small private firms involved in tightly-knit division of labour with Iskra, the big international electronics firm based in Ljubljana (Lakićević 1987).

Beyond that, they simply sought ways of accommodating and rationalizing the massive retreat into the second economy which the post-debt shock erosion of 'official' wages had induced.

In agriculture, a series of conferences from 1985 onwards pin-pointed the surviving obstacles to a full realization of the potential of a sector crucial for the external balance of the country, viz. –

1 Price and tax policies which continued to conspire to impose an excessive fiscal burden on the peasant and inhibit private agricultural investment.
2 Continued inadequacies in the supply of industrial inputs to agriculture.
3 The perennial land maximum, not perhaps of enormous operational significance in itself, but 'surviving as a political fiction, as a psychological guarantee that we still "rule" the peasant (LCY activist Dragan Veselinov, quoted in Živkov 1985).
4 More generally, a continued tendency for the government to lapse into command-planning habits with respect to agriculture, to 'plan in tons, rather than planning or foreseeing behaviour, the interests of people and producers' (LCY activist Čedo Grbić, quoted in Živkov 1985), with campaigns against 'agrobusiness', sowing plans, priorities for particular crops, price controls, selective credits, and import-export bans (Ilijin 1987).

Still, it was encouraging to hear these points being made so forcibly by the kind of people – party activists and government officials – who might have qualified and prevaricated in the 1970s. With public opinion strongly in favour of abolishing the land maximum (Jambrek 1987), there seemed every chance that agriculture would finally come out of the shadows of second-class citizenship.

In the event, there had been a less than total clarification of the situation by 1989. In 1985 a law was passed establishing that any land in private possession not sown to some crop in two years out of five would be confiscated and transferred to the socialized sector. Once again, then, the problem of uncultivated land was being attacked in obstinate isolation from the central issue of the land maximum. In the following year the regulations compelling private peasants to offer the socialized sector first refusal before selling land to another private peasant were tightened up in Serbia ('Ništa bez . . . ' 1986). Meanwhile socialized sector agricultural organizations continue, with the connivance of local authorities, to bully private peasants into selling their produce only to them ('Zaustavljeni . . . ' 1986), while ideologues write loftily about the continued importance of association between socialized and private sectors. Perhaps not unconnectedly, agriculture's terms of trade worsened by some 17 per cent 1983–6 in terms of the cost-of-living index (*SGJ* 1987:

220). At the end of 1988 the land maximum was finally increased from 10 to 30 hectares. This is certainly a major step forward, though some may argue the the second-class citizen tag will never be removed as long as there is *any* land maximum at all.

But perhaps bigger things are afoot. In 1988 the peasants of Slovenia finally took the step of founding their own independent Peasants' Union. The outcome of this audacious initiative remains unclear at time of writing, but one crucial point is absolutely clear. Government and party may *proclaim* agricultural reform, but any attempt by them to *implement* it is as the kiss of death. Implementation must come from below, and that means permitting the private peasants to *organize* independently.

We find the same mixed picture when we look at developments in the *private sector outside agriculture*. Television programmes have been dedicated to showing that private enterprise is not a threat to the self-management system, and the 'Three Partners' – One Product' system developed by the Belgrade Dvadeset Prvi Maj motor parts enterprise, in cooperation with a number of small, private-sector enterprises and the Belgrade Bank ('Cetvrti . . . ' 1988), is a model of contemporary micro–specialization. Significantly, it is being developed in Serbia, often one of the more conservative republics on these matters. In mid-1988 the Commission of the Federal Executive Council for the Reform of the Economic System even had the temerity to suggest that socialized sector enterprises facing bankruptcy should be offered for sale, at the market price, to their workers, in cases where no socialized sector enterprise had shown interest ('Još da . . . ' 1988).

But the political establishment remains bitterly divided on the issue of private enterprise. There is still no general agreement as to whether the role of the private sector should be seen in terms of a short-term improvization in difficult times, or in terms of a permanent and enlarged function in the economy. There are still politicians, even in 'liberal' Croatia, who identify any hiring relationship with exploitation ('Mala privreda . . . ' 1987). The last few years have been marked by successive campaigns against particular elements within the private sector – usually on a local basis. Erstwhile Prime Minister Mikulić himself did not escape public criticism over the issue. Thus when he had a meeting at the beginning of 1987 with expatriate Yugoslavs who had made money abroad, he was severely taken to task by trade union leader Zvonimir Hrabar. Big entrepreneurs, Hrabar argued, could take over entire communes: what Yugoslavia wants is 'socially controlled small-scale private enterprise' [i.e. what she has got already] (Hrabrar 1987).

Most important, the private sector still labours under a mass of petty regulation, stipulating for instance that the boss of a private enterprise needs more formal qualifications than a socialized sector director in the same line of business (Ostojić 1988), and a tax regime which is oppressive in its provisions and the manner in which it is implemented. Rado Bergant, a highly successful 'high-tech' private entrepreneur from Slovenia, complains that:

> they look on our business, our income and our living standards with envy. The inspection of our books at the end of each year is a real massacre, a real bureaucratic massacre. And what's worse, they arrogate to themselves the power to decide which of our expenditures are necessary, and which are not, even when we are asking for tax allowances to which we are entitled by law.
>
> (Lakićević 1987)

Of course there never was a businessman who did not try to squeeze the maximum advantage out of the tax system. But existing regulations, e.g. in relation to the import of equipment, make it impossible for private entrepreneurs to carry on business without actually breaking the law. Again, the uncertainty of policy towards the private sector inevitably breeds an opportunistic, 'get rich quick' attitude amongst many private operators, and this in turn tends to reinforce the prejudices of conservative political elements. Perhaps most disturbing of all, the trend through the 1980s has been for the share of private sector employment in total employment to grow, but for its share in total National Income to fall. This reflects partly an increasing tendency for the private sector to concentrate on services – on the sectors which, indeed, have the weakest linkages with industry. Beyond that it reflects a continued failure to generate an adequate level of technological dynamism in private manufacturing. For all the triumphs of individual cooperation schemes on the 'Three Partners – One Product' model, the general pattern remains one of low levels of technology and poor, even falling productivity. Far from providing an antidote to the general reversion to extensive growth patterns, trends in the private sector have tended to fortify that reversion. For this state of affairs policy-makers must bear a good deal of the blame.

The crisis and the role of the party

We saw in the early chapters of this book how the reappraisal of the foundations of socialism had flowed from a rejection of the Soviet/Stalinist notion of the leading role of the party; how the implications of that reappraisal, in terms of the re-establishment of the market mechanism, had inevitably produced a fundamental change in the operational role of party activists within the Yugoslav economy. We saw further that one of the main underlying reasons for Yugoslavia's failures of adjustment policy in the 1970s was the continued dominance of party cadres, by this time usually regional cadres, in the areas of investment policy and high finance. In this area, as in others, then, the lesson of the external debt crisis of 1982 should have been clear enough – time to complete the process begun in 1950, and eliminate arbitrary party interference in *all* sectors of economic decision-taking once and for all. In the words of Slovenian Party leader Milan Kučan,

> holding other people responsible should mean, first and foremost, that the League of Communists should give those people room to exercise that responsibility – by keeping its involvement strictly within the limits set out by the constitution and statute of the LCY.
>
> ('Lakše je . . . ' 1987)

But that was not how things worked out. The immediate reaction of one city party presidency to the onset of the crisis was to call on party activists to campaign for increased exports and reduced consumption, and to get rid of people in responsible positions opposed to the Stabilization Plan ('U stabilizaciju' 1983). We can hardly doubt the good intentions of the Bosnian LCY leadership when, in 1985, it predicated that any member guilty of 'unjustified' price increases should be stripped of all political functions and expelled from the League ('Iz antiinflacione . . . ' 1985), or of the party organization of the Šipad-Šator timber complex, which in 1986 demanded a list of names of workers responsible for poor-quality production ('Partijski . . . ' 1986). Still, developments like these represent extraordinary atavisms in a country striving to make the final transition to a full-blooded market economy. Less lofty in motivation, but no less damaging systemically, were some of the *démarches* reported in 1987, with new campaigns against 'illegal enrichment' launched by party committees in some localities ('Krivica' 1987), and the party leaders in one commune taking legal action against an inspector of the Social Accountancy Services for divulging details of their personal incomes ('Partija . . . ' 1987).

In 1988, with Yugoslavia entering into new commitments to the IMF to liberalize and rationalize her economic system, things seemed to get worse rather than better. By the middle of the year president of the Belgrade city party committe Radoš Smiljković was calling on League activists to take the lead in restructuring the economy of the capital, touring local enterprises and telling management that they needed to sharpen up their advertising and marketing approach; otherwise they would be replaced! ('Besplatni saveti' 1988) Elsewhere we find party committees sacking directors, imposing 'emergency management' and interfering in inter-enterprise integration moves. A report on one such *casus* ended with the thought that, no doubt, in a few years' time, there would be another party conference at which the question would be asked: why is there so much lawlessness in Yugoslavia? ('Važi li . . . ' 1988). In another case the local party committee sacked the director of one of 'their' enterprises and stipulated that the new director should have no say on matters relating to the size of the work-force, on recruitment, even in relation to the management team, or on business strategy. Not surprisingly, it turned out to be extraordinarily difficult to fill the post ('Vruća . . . ' 1988).

These developments have taken place against a background of falling party membership, and indeed falling party prestige. Total membership has dropped steadily since 1987. More specifically, numbers of workers, peasants, engineers, teachers, artists, housewives, students and unemployed in the League have fallen, while those of state functionaries, managers, economists, lawyers, scientists and pensioners have risen ('Komplementarna . . . ' 1987). Increasingly, then, the party has tended to become a policy-makers' club, and to lose its standing with those without whose cooperation no policy can be implemented.

We should be careful not to overdraw this picture of the League of Communists as *diabolus ex machina*. It is natural for political activists to want, above all, to *do something* in a crisis. Certain of the political initiatives of recent years worthiest of condemnation in narrowly economic terms make a lot more sense in terms of maintenance of local employment levels. Nevertheless the specifically Bolshevik notion of political activism, inherited by the Yugoslavs from the Soviet Union and never sloughed off, has proved an encumbrance to the task of crisis-management, the more so that it has continued to manifest itself in that peculiarly fragmented, particularist Yugoslav way. If the point needs underlining, we need only glance back at the eminently sensible conclusions of that most distinguished committee of party activists, the Kraigher Commission. As of 1988 its goals, in terms of rationalization of the price and investment systems and reform of the tax and accounting systems, remained largely unachieved. We shall return to the political theme in the final chapter.

Chapter eight

Yugoslavia and the World – an Awkward Customer?

Yugoslavia and the international financial community

As we saw in our earlier chapters, the history of the Yugoslav economy, pre-war as well as post-war, could be written in terms of capital import. In the immediate post-war period in particular, capital import provided the nexus, not only of economic evolution, but indeed of political developments too. It was the promise of large-scale economic assistance from the Soviet Union which cemented the early alliance with Stalin; it was by cutting off that assistance that Stalin sought to bring Tito to heel; and it was through aid and 'soft' loans (repayable in dinars) that the United States in turn put muscle into its commitment to the maintenance of Yugoslav neutrality and independence in the 1950s. After the ending of US aid to Yugoslavia in 1961, Belgrade was able to build up a stable relationship with the IMF and the World Bank (the latter lent a total of $2.2bn to Yugoslavia 1961–82 for infrastructural investment alone – Gnjatović 1985: 111), and to maintain a high rate of capital import on generally favourable terms. From the standpoint of the early 1970s, indeed, it seemed that Yugoslavia had much to teach the developing world in terms of the tactics of securing finance for ongoing current account deficits, and of using the supplementary resources thus obtained to promote growth.

We see now, with the benefit of hindsight, that things went badly wrong; that the resources were not used efficiently, or at least not efficiently enough, that when external circumstances changed, the Yugoslav political economy was quite unable, for all its triumphs of extensive growth, to respond appropriately. Can we lay some of the ultimate blame for this on the nature of the relationship between Yugoslavia and the international financial organizations? To try to answer this question, let us look in greater detail at Yugoslavia's dealings with the World Bank in the 1970s and early 1980s.

IBDR activity in Yugoslavia in the early 1970s was dominated by a number of transport projects – road, pipeline and rail, and these projects seem generally to have been implemented with a reasonable level of efficiency. There was, however, some difficulty with the 1974 railway loan. The Bank was initially unhappy about the financial state of Yugoslav Railways, and about its tariff policy, and, having provisionally agreed the loan in 1973, was still seeking 'strong guarantees' at the beginning of 1974 (Grubić 1974). But the loan did eventually go through later on that year.

Rather more serious were the difficulties that arose with the first World Bank loan for the development of Yugoslav agriculture. It was in 1971 that the bank, jointly with the Food and Agriculture Organization of the United Nations, offered Yugoslavia a loan of $30 million for the development of stock-raising in the private sector. They asked for a reply by 1972. The situation as of early 1973 was that the federal government had passed on the project to the republics, as it was obliged to do under the constitutional amendments, and that the Bank and the FAO had heard nothing from them (Mejovšek 1973). By 1974 the position was as follows: Macedonia had dropped out of the project, having negotiated a separate loan of $31m with the World Bank. Slovenia and Croatia were hoping to do the same. There was still, therefore, no integrated proposal to put to the Bank, nor was there any response to the Bank's insistence on a single, Yugoslav guarantor for the whole project. In addition, the FAO was unhappy about the lack of commitment to 'infrastructural' work to improve the quality of pastures (Urošević 1974). Finally, however, a 'programme for the production of meat and milk on private farms' was unveiled at the end of 1974 ('Projekat . . .' 1974). It envisaged the creation of 22,600 private cattle stations with 5–10 cows apiece, and 1,250 sheep farms. The World Bank would provide 50 per cent of the finance. The loan was eventually approved at the beginning of 1976, with a further loan for the same purpose going through in early 1978.

After all that trouble, Yugoslav agriculture proved slow in taking up the loans. As of September 1978 the take-up rate rate for the first loan was still under 75 per cent, and for the second loan under 50 per cent ('Zeleni kredit' 1978). That did not, however, stop the bank from lending Yugoslavia a further $86m at the end of 1979 for agricultural development in the period 1980–4. About half this third loan was earmarked for the private sector ('Zajam' 1979).

In June 1980 the World Bank ratified its ninth loan to Yugoslavia for road-building. But by April 1982 the four regional road transport SIZ-ovi involved – from Serbia, Croatia, Slovenia and Vojvodina – had still not agreed on the allocation of the $2m set aside for the purchase of equipment to be used on the *autoput* (the Ljubljana–Zagreb–Belgrade motorway), with the Federal Committee for Transport and Communications standing by helpless ('Vladina veza' 1982). A similar story unfolded with a loan of $32m from the International Financial Corporation, a subsidiary of the World Bank, for the development of small-scale economic activity, including private enterprise outside agriculture. Originally approved in 1980, the loan lay totally unused for more than a year ('Sto babica . . .' 1981). As of mid-1982 the take-up rate was still very low ('Neiskorišćene . . .' 1982).

A number of points emerge from these case histories, viz. –

1 We can hardly fault the Bank or the IFC on its project selection. Transport – agriculture – small businesses – the private sector – these are all sectors whose development has been pin-pointed by Yugoslav economists and policy-makers as crucial for the effective restructuring of the Yugoslav economy.
2 Much of the trouble in the negotiation and utilization of the loans flowed from the constitutional and organizational peculiarities of the period of the sovereignty of associated labour.
3 For the rest, the special difficulties surrounding private enterprise in Yugoslavia created further obstacles to rapid take-up. Sheer political prejudice apart, there were specific technical difficulties. In a situation where the World Bank was offering only a part of the necessary finance, it was very difficult for private peasants, under prevailing conditions, to raise the other part without going into association with the socialized sector, which on the whole they did not want to do. Part of the trouble with the IFC loan for small businesses was the fact that it was denominated in dollars. In Yugoslavia private businessmen are not allowed to borrow foreign exchange.
4 There is a suspicion that the Yugoslav authorities may, *ex post*, have been quite happy to leave balances from some of these loans idle. In this way project-specific finance could, in difficult times, be diverted to general Balance of Payments support purposes.
5 Whatever the exact truth of that matter, the ultimate impact of project-specific multilateral foreign lending to Yugoslavia over the crucial pre-crisis decade, was, in *micro-economic* terms, clearly well below maximum.

But it would be unfair to lay the whole blame for that on the Yugoslav authorities. One of the most prominent and constant leitmotifs of post-war Yugoslav history has been the on-going US commitment to Yugoslavia's independence of the Soviet bloc. The ending of American aid as such to Yugoslavia in 1961 did, as we saw in Chapter 3, have a major impact on the Yugoslav international economic position, but there can be no doubt that the dominant American position within the IMF, and particularly within the World Bank, helped to ensure that the flow of capital import would not be seriously interrupted.

Successive arrangements with the Fund and the Bank, from 1961 onwards, made finance available on a conditional basis – conditional on the liberalization of the foreign trade regime and price regulations, conditional on the all-round improvement of investment project appraisal procedures. Time and time again, Belgrade was unable to deliver the goods in terms of those conditions, time and time again the international financial organizations forgave and forgot. As we saw in Chapter 6, Tom Clausen visited Yugoslavia in the dark days of November 1982 to comfort rather than upbraid, to promise new funds rather than threaten foreclosure.

We see the pattern repeated in 1986–8. In 1986 Yugoslavia abandoned its stand-by arrangement with the IMF after disagreements over policy. The Fund was unhappy about escalating inflation rates and still heavily negative interest rates. The new government of Mr Mikulić was inclined to take a critical view of the international financial commitments of the previous government of Mrs Planinc, and in September 1986 a high official of the National Bank stated publicly that Yugoslavia had made a big mistake when it had allowed itself to be 'tied hand and foot' by the IMF for a 'paltry' $300m (Bošković 1986). For the time being, then, the slogan was 'stand-by, goodbye'.

Mr Mikulić's government was soon to discover that things were not so easy, and that the IMF's paltry $300m was less important than the IMF's good offices with the rest of the international financial community. Thus when the World Bank turned down a Yugoslav request for a structural adjustment loan in early 1987, one of the sticking points, continued policy disagreements apart, was the fact that Yugoslavia did not at that point have a stand-by arrangement with the IMF.

The crunch came in June and July 1987, when Yugoslavia found herself unable to meet debt repayments totalling $240m. This was no reflection of the Balance of Trade or current account positions, which remained healthy. Rather it reflected an unfortunate bunching of maturities, itself a result of the emergency borrowing of 1983, with nearly $2bn of repayments, in addition to $2bn of interest payments, falling due during 1987. To make matters worse, the rate of withdrawals from private citizens' hard-currency bank accounts in Yugoslavia was rising rapidly, as confidence in the rapidly-depreciating dinar drained away. Yugoslavia initially sought to solve the problem by negotiating an emergency bridging loan with the Bank for International Settlements. Again, however, the sticking point was the relationship with the IMF. The BIS normally stipulates a stand-by arrangement with the Fund and an IMF guarantee as conditions for such a loan.

Still, it did not prove too difficult to negotiate this new debt-service crisis. After two days of discussion with Fulvio Dobrich, the Yugoslav–American Senior President of the Manufacturers Hannover Trust Company and chief coordinator for Yugoslavia's creditor banks, agreement was reached on rescheduling the June and July payments for September. Around the same time the Yugoslav–American Council was meeting in Cavtat, near Dubrovnik (Dobrich was there), and US bankers were making a point of assuring the Yugoslav side that they were in principle prepared to help Yugoslavia regain access to international credit markets. But they wanted to see Belgrade mend its fences with the IMF first.

All this gave much food for thought to the policy-makers in Belgrade, and in August 1987 Boris Konte, vice-president of the National Bank, admitted in an *Ekonomska Politika* interview that it was very hard for Yugoslavia, in difficult times, to make arrangements with its international creditors in the absence of an IMF stand-by credit. In September 1987 negotiations were re-opened with the IMF, and those finally bore fruit in April 1988, when a new stand-by agreement was negotiated. This in turn provided the basis for the further rescheduling of around one-third of Yugoslavia's total foreign debt, and the clinching of a \$330m World Bank structural adjustment loan.

It would be quite wrong to suggest that IMF conditionality has had no impact whatsoever on Yugoslav economic policy-making. For better or worse, for example, collective consumption fell from 42.2 per cent of Gross Social Product in 1979 to 31.5 per cent in 1984 (Bogoev 1985: 124). The new stand-by package of April 1988 committed Belgrade to an unfreezing of domestic prices and a substantial liberalization of the import regime (see below). Successive attempts by fund and bank to persuade the Yugoslav authorities that positive real interest rates must be established met with stubborn resistance, which often found justification in the argument that, in the context of already very high rates of inflation, positive real rates of interest tend themselves to act as a powerful cost-inflationary pressure because of the degree of 'front-loading' they introduce into amortization patterns. At the end of 1987, however, the Gordian knot was cut through the introduction of indexation for bank credits, and the principle that interest rates should be explicitly fixed at so many percentage points above the rate of inflation. By September 1988, however, domestic political difficulties (see next chapter) had forced Prime Minister Mikulić to compromise on some of the elements in the IMF package.

What we miss in all this is any concerted, explicit pressure by the international financial bodies on Yugoslavia *to improve her resource allocation procedures*. The Fund has, perhaps quite properly, interpreted its brief in largely macro-economic terms, believing, it seems, that reductions in public expenditure, combined with strict monetary control and liberalization of imports would ensure a fall in the rate of inflation, which would in turn bring interest rates more or less automatically back into the black, and permit painless liberalization of domestic prices as tight money and foreign competition conspired to impose a new discipline on enterprises. The peculiarities of the political economy of Yugoslavia mean, however, that these linkages, plausible enough perhaps for a capitalist economy, simply do not exist in the given case. Following on the new agreement with the IMF in April 1988 we have seen Yugoslav inflation rates climb steadily higher (to a level of nearly 300 per cent by the beginning of 1989), real interest rates stay stubbornly negative, and the process of *concertation* of investment programmes remain as unsatisfactory as it was before.

But we should not assume that the IMF is deeply unhappy with this state of affairs. As we saw in the last chapter, Yugoslavia has been strikingly successful in putting its current account in order through restrictive (one can hardly use the word 'deflationary' in the Yugoslav context!) policies, and it is, indeed, one of the standard criticisms of the Fund that it

> lays too much emphasis on *rapid moves towards balance in the external sector*, at the cost of other important development objectives, such as investment and growth, . . . fails to differentiate between the causes of balance of payments disequilibria, thus failing to address changes in its criteria that might contribute to successful adjustment in the new international environment,
>
> (Griffith–Jones 1984:64)

Be that as it may, Yugoslav economists and policy-makers have been more than ready to accept that debtor countries are to a large extent to blame for their own problems. Thus J. Almuli writes, *a propos* of Latin America, that:

> there are no magic solutions, either for the others or for Brazil . . . [The Brazilian experience] has confirmed that the debt burden is the fault, not only of exploitative foreigners, but also of Brazilian nationals, of their policies, their habitual and disastrous weaknesses, of sectional interests, egoism and incompetence.
>
> (Almuli 1987)

We must presume that Almuli sees this also as a fitting text for Yugoslavia. Thus the Yugoslav commitment to debt service, and to ultimate repayment, has never been in serious doubt. The essential short-term international problem for Belgrade since 1983 has been one of *liquidity*, and the international financial organizations have been able to help out with that problem without really squaring up to the underlying structural and systemic problems which bedevil the Yugoslav economy.

The essence of Yugoslavia's relations with the international financial powers was summed up when *Ekonomska Politika* interviewed US ambassador in Belgrade John Scanlon, just after the clinching of the new deal with the IMF. Like Clausen five years earlier, Scanlon was at pains to soothe and encourage. No, Yugoslavia was not a bad debtor. But when she abandoned the old stand-by arrangement with the IMF in 1986, international doubts as to her ability to meet her commitments began to mount, and the stand-still on debt service of mid-1987 only seemed to confirm those doubts. Once Belgrade had recognized its error, however, recognized the need for reprogramming and recognized that the first step towards that was a new stand-by arrangement, the rest was only a formality (Scanlon 1988). The message, then, seems to be 'Stay with us, and we will always see you through, whatever you get up to at home, as long as you keep trying to repay your debts. Try to go it alone, and you will come unstuck.'

We should, certainly, exercise some caution in criticizing the Fund for the incompleteness, sometimes inappropriateness of its conditionality, and the Bank for the fragility of its control over project-specific efficiency. After all, precisely the reason why Yugoslavia had increasing recourse to the private multi-national banks in the 1970s was that she wanted, like so many other medium-developed countries, to avoid conditionality altogether. Precisely the biggest weakness of the approach of the private banks to lending was their exclusive concern with political stability and the ability to repay, irrespective of how efficiently the money lent might be used. Still, we can justifiably criticize the West, and in particular the United States, for being excessively concerned with the essentially geo-strategic issue of Yugoslav independence and neutrality. In the end, it seems to have been more important to keep Belgrade facing West, while keeping the international bankers happy, than to find a way of keying international finance into the essential restructuring tasks the Yugoslav economy faces.

As Yugoslavia started to negotiate with the IMF at the end of 1987, hopes began to rise that a new stand-by arrangement might open the way for the assembly of a package of multilateral, bilateral and commercial credits which would give Yugoslavia billions rather than millions of dollars, and provide a solid basis for a new investment and modernization drive. Doubts about the capacity of the Yugoslav system to deliver the goods in terms of investment decision-taking apart, it seems unlikely, under present conditions, that this package will be forthcoming. Inevitably, then, the thoughts of economists and bankers, Yugoslav and foreign, turn to the possibility of attracting private equity capital to Yugoslavia. Before looking at the prospects for a radical new initiative in this area, let us catch up on how the structure of financial regulation for the external sector has developed since 1982.

The development of the foreign exchange system since the debt shock

In July 1982 the Commission of the Federal Social Councils for Economic Stabilization Problems reached agreement on a 'Long-Term Conception of the System of External Economic Relations'. This document set out as a strategic goal the reversal of the trend towards increasing internal inconvertibility of the dinar, and the recovery of the dinar's position as the single means of payment within Yugoslavia. While enterprises should continue to enjoy the right to maintain balances of foreign currency, they should only be able to use these balances within Yugoslavia after conversion into dinars at the National Bank. Around the same time we find emerging an increasing consensus amongst Yugoslav federal policy-makers that the republicanization of the Balance of Payments in the 1970s had, indeed, been a disastrous error, and should be reversed as a basic condition for improving the whole approach to the international division of labour.

The republics, needless to say, were reluctant to accept that logic, and it was not until the beginning of 1986 that a new law on foreign exchange came into force. The law allotted to the National Bank the following functions:

1 To monitor the development of the Balance of Payments of Yugoslavia as a whole.
2 To manage the foreign currency reserves.
3 To issue regulations on the settlement of external claims and liabilities.
4 To re-activate the foreign currency market on the basis of a 'dirty float'.
5 To ensure, with the cooperation of the commercial banks, that the foreign currency market worked on an integrated, all-Yugoslav basis.
6 To borrow money abroad within the framework of the planned projection of the Balance of Payments for the given year (subject to the restriction that long-term loans from anyone else except the IMF should require passage of a special law).
7 To monitor the foreign exchange dealings of the registered banks, and take the necessary measures against those breaking the regulations.

Beyond that, the new regulations established in law the principle that the dinar was the only instrument for the settlement of claims within Yugoslavia (Nedeljković 1986).

In practice, the revitalized foreign exchange market proved a weak reed. Its operation was riddled with quotas and priorities right from the start (Pejović and Zmijarević 1986), and the basic legislation was not supported by appropriate detailed regulations.

Under these conditions the work of the unified foreign exchange market was reduced to an absurd situation where banks which . . . were supposed to supply surpluses of foreign exchange to the unified Yugoslav market were in fact coming onto the market as buyers.

(Nicović 1986)

Perhaps, under the given conditions of supply and demand, that result was in any case inevitable. For the key to the success of the new foreign exchange market lay in the effective re-establishment of the dinar as the primary instrument of payment within Yugoslavia. That was not achieved, and was not achievable except through an effective assault on the inflation problem. In the last analysis, then, the reconvening of the foreign exchange market failed as a secondary result of the failures of domestic monetary policy.

It would be wrong to suggest that the 1986 legislation achieved nothing at all. The National Bank has been able to reassert a degree of control over the national Balance of Payments and has been able to impose a regime under which the foolhardy borrowing practices of the late 1970s could never be repeated. But it came as no surprise when the Belgrade authorities had another go at the foreign exchange market issue in the wake of the new accord with the IMF in 1988. Following on the liberalization of some 40 per cent of imports in April 1988, a refurbished foreign exchange market, free of the old quotas and priorities, was established. The principle was clearly enunciated that the demand for foreign exchange should be limited through strict control over the supply of dinars to the domestic economy, and the high price of foreign exchange. (By May 1988, after a succession of devaluations, the official rate for the dinar had been brought into equality with the black-market rate for the first time for many years.) This sounds fine in principle, and there is no reason to doubt the commitment to a proper international valuation for the dinar. But as we have seen, there is little reason to believe the exchange rate by itself can have a major impact on import and export demand schedules in Yugoslav conditions. As far as strict control over the money supply is concerned, we need only refer back to the sorry tale of ineffectuality told in Chapter 7. Early reports of the operation of the re-established market indicate a surprising absence of excess demand, but this seems to be essentially related to short-term factors – illiquidity problems in industry, and a rush by private citizens to convert hard-currency savings into dinars, as real wages fall and the dinar depreciates (Grličkov 1988c).

Like so much legislation and regulation in the Yugoslav system, the foreign exchange regime, as it has developed over the years, seems to have generated more paperwork than effective policy implementation. In the ironic words of Ivan Ribnikar:

> After giving much thought to the matter, we came to the conclusion that we did not know what was meant by 'foreign-exchange system'. So we sought help in the foreign literature. But we were unable to find the concept there. Thus 'foreign-exchange system' is one of our original ideas . . . And if it is our original idea, this may be symptomatic of serious flaws in our currency, and in our financial system in general . . . We have specialists in the foreign-exchange system, even special subjects at Higher Schools, and these specialists present the 'foreign-exchange system' in the first place in terms of regulations, what you are allowed to do, and , more important, what you are not allowed to do. And that again is symptomatic – in fact of our economic system as a whole.
>
> (Ribnikar 1986: 9–10).

In essence, then, the foreign-exchange system has been part and parcel of the weakness of the Yugoslav economic system, but also a defence mechanism against the possible effects of that weakness on the Balance of Payments. The biggest problem with the current effort to simplify and liberalize the system is that the underlying trading position may simply be too weak to stand liberalization.

> Today the Yugoslav economy has fewer goods than ever which it can export competitively, in terms of price and quality, to the hard-currency market. This is, of course, a consequence of the whole structure of contemporary domestic economic policy, and the result of often incomprehensible initiatives on the part of the federal government in the domain of prices and money supply, and of the lack of independence on the part of economic subjects.
>
> (Zimić 1988c)

It is precisely this concern with export competitiveness, and with systemic rationalization, which has generated the renewed controversy in Yugoslavia over the role of foreign capital.

Prospects for joint ventures

As we saw in Chapter 6, Belgrade had introduced some rather unsatisfactory joint venture legislation in 1967, and had done nothing during the 1970s and early 1980s to make it more satisfactory. Minor amendments introduced in 1985 and 1986 produced a marginal improvement in conditions, and in 1987 36 new agreements were signed. Nevertheless by 1987 conditions for joint ventures in Yugoslavia were rather less attractive than they were in the Soviet Union. In early 1988, the total value of foreign investment in Yugoslavia was around $250m, some 1.2 per cent of the total capital stock, and substantially less than it had been in 1980. At the same time, the joint-venture sector currently accounts for 5.1 per cent of total Yugoslav exports, and just 2.7 per cent of total imports. More than 60 per cent of joint ventures export above 20 per cent of their output to the hard-currency area (Zimić 1988b: 10).

Jakšo Barbić has check-listed the difficulties with the joint-ventures regime as of mid-1988 in the following terms:

1 The foreign investor has practically no property rights, even over his share in the joint investment.
2 He has practically no control over the composition or decision-taking of management in the joint venture.
3 He has practically no say in relation to the size and composition of the work-force.
4 He has great difficulty in repatriating profits.
5 He fears the instability of the domestic market, and the unpredictability of the element of political interference.
6 He worries about the continuous depreciation of the dinar (Zimić 1988b: 9).

Barbić might have added, as a seventh point, a tax policy 'so restrictive that it would put anyone off' (Zimić 1987, quoting Davor Savin).

After much hesitation, a new law on joint ventures was finally passed on 8 January 1989. But the law is a disappointment. It leaves many points unclarified, many issues awaiting further legislation. Of the list of difficulties above, it really only addresses the first, in that it provides for genuine joint ownership of mixed companies. It does nothing to make profit repatriation more certain, it actually makes the tax position more unfavourable, at least for the time being, and fails to clarify the relationship between foreign investment and self-management. Perhaps most important, it is so inadequately drafted that it can only deepen the sense of institutional uncertainly (Kovačević 1989).

One of the central points that remains at issue is the territorial coverage of the new legislation. Some policy-makers have favoured a 'Chinese' approach, whereby foreign capital is given completely free rein in clearly delimited Special Economic Zones. But Yugoslavia is a small country – smaller than some of the Chinese Special Zones – and any attempt to chop up the country in this way would likely end up with ludicrous results. On the other hand, if the whole country is to be one big Special Economic Zone.

it would be quite impossible to conceive of a system whereby one part of the economy, the part with foreign investment, could function on the basis of some economic and market-based laws which would provide guarantees to foreigners, if the rest of the economy were not under the same regime. But this regime, in the opinion of specialists and economists, cannot be achieved . . . *without a redefinition of social ownership*.

(Zimić 1988b: 11, emphasis added)

Going one step further:

> the fact is that without the *fundamental resolution of the question of social ownership* . . . there can be no effective escape from the vicious circle of inefficiency and unchanging socio-economic relation-ships . . . Capital is a synonym for economic efficiency . . . Behind capital should stand only the banks – but not the kind of banks they have in Bihać. [See discussion of Agrokomerc affair in Chapter 7]

(Zimić 1988b: 10, emphasis added)

At time of writing the issue of Special Zones was still one of those awaiting legislative clarification.

We seem, then, to be back with the basic systemic problems which have been the central theme of much of this book. But there is, perhaps, another element here. The Belgrade Institute for Foreign Trade – a leading Yugoslav think-tank with close governmental links – found, when asked by a foreign government to investigate the possibility of foreign investment in four sector of the Yugoslav economy, that it could only take on the job with the express permission of every republican and provincial government. The clumsiness of Yugoslav institutions apart, there is a hint here of a difficulty which goes beyond the purely systemic dimension. Many Yugoslav politicians remain fundamentally suspicious of foreign capital, suspicious that free rein for foreign capital could spell the end of what is left of socialism in Yugoslavia. Many Yugoslav economists, on the other hand, feel that unless a significant positive gesture is made soon, an unbridgeable credibility gap will open up between Yugoslavia and potential investors. Even with the new legislation, Yugoslavia is arguably still 'the least attractive country in the world to invest in' (Zimić 1988c).

Yugoslavia and the European Community

In 1980 a trade and cooperation agreement was concluded between Yugoslavia and the EC. Its main provisions were:

1 The EC should help Yugoslavia to develop and diversify production, and to build up infrastructure.
2 Cooperation in exporting to third markets should be developed.
3 About 70 per cent of the nomenclature of Yugoslav industrial goods would be allowed into the EC duty-free. The rest (amounting to just 29 products) would be wholly of partly exempt from duty within quotas.

The Yugoslav side remained less than satisfied with the arrangements on Yugoslav agricultural exports to the Community. The accession of Greece to the Community in 1980 created particular problems in relation to regional Balkan trade, especially with regard to Yugoslav beef exports to Greece. Criticism also emerged, after the signing of the agreement, of the high incidence of restrictive clauses affecting cooperation and technology-transfer deals. For Yugoslavia, after all, the overwhelming priority in the early 1980s was to develop hard-currency exports, precisely the thing that many of these restrictive clauses aimed to inhibit ('Pretpostavke. . .' 1980; 'Zasedanje. . .' 1980).

As Yugoslavia's payments position became more critical, further discussions produced some progress in the key area of cooperation. In 1983 it was agreed that meetings between Yugoslav industrial associations and EC groups of experts should be arranged to discuss development plans for specific sectors of the Yugoslav economy. It was also agreed that there should be an exchange of energy missions, and that a seminar on EC–Yugoslav cooperation on Third World markets, with particular regard to engineering services, should be arranged. The possibility of direct EC investment in Yugoslavia was not high on the agenda at this point, though Brussels was showing some interest in Yugoslav agriculture in that connection ('Novi planovi' 1983).

By 1988 Yugoslavia could look with satisfaction on the elimination of her trade deficit with the Common Market, quotas or no quotas. On a more strategic dimension, however, things had not moved much further forward. As the Community progressed towards 1992, as Comecom announced its own plans for moving towards a single socialist market and the Soviet Union finally recognized the EC, there was a feeling in Belgrade that only Yugoslavia and Albania remained outside the major currents of European integration (Zimić 1988a). At time of writing the EC remains positively disposed towards Yugoslavia, and responsive to Yugoslav hopes for a closer relationship with the Twelve. In concrete terms, however, Community goodwill extends as far as helping with rescheduling, some further short-term credits and loans from the European Investment Bank, and no further. Beyond that, there is general scepticism amongst Community activists about the progress of systemic reform in Yugoslavia. Some Yugoslavs have cherished the hope that EFTA might provide an avenue for Yugoslav entry into the main stream of European integration. In practice, EFTA seems if anything more sceptical about Yugoslavia than the Community (Zimić 1988a).

In June and July a number of EC dignitaries visited Yugoslavia, including Claude Cheysson, member of the Commission responsible for Mediterranean and North–South affairs, and Jean Joseph Schwed, head of division within the Directorate-General for External Relations responsible for links with the Mediterranean and the Middle and Far East.

It was confirmed on the occasion of Schwed's visit that the EC was prepared to offer Yugoslavia a short-term bridging loan of $400m, subject to general agreement between Belgrade and the Club of Paris on rescheduling. There is also talk about another ECU500m of long-term credits for road construction. But Schwed highlighted the price Yugoslavia has paid for getting its trade balance with the Community into the black when he defended the invocation of EC anti-dumping regulations against Yugoslavia, especially with regard to steel exports. He also made it quite clear that Yugoslavia could expect no significant increases in private investment from the Community until satisfactory new legislation was in place (Schwed 1988). General Secretary of EFTA Per Kleppe made exactly the same point when he visited Yugoslavia at the end of February 1988 (Kleppe 1988). Whether the legislation of December 1988 will fill that bill or not remains to be seen.

Perhaps Schwed's most important message for Yugoslavia was on the implications of the Single European Act.

> Given that you are effectively integrated into the EEC from a trading point of view, you will have to bear all the consequences of standardization in the EEC. If you want to keep on exporting to the EEC you will have to accept these standards, and take account of the unification of all the relevant regulations. But there is a good side to this. Instead of having to get to know the standards of each national market individually, you will now have just one set, which will represent a big saving in time and money.
>
> (Schwed 1988)

The message from Brussels is, therefore, in principle encouraging enough. Give us a proper legislative basis for private investment in Yugoslavia, attack the problem of standards and standardization head-on, and there is no reason why Yugoslavia should not prosper as a country 'effectively integrated into the EEC from a trading point of view'. As we have seen, however, these are precisely amongst the most problematic areas of policy-making in Yugoslavia.

Yugoslavia and the world – the future

The difficulties and dilemmas of Yugoslavia's current economic situation present a picture which in many ways is all too familiar amongst the medium-developed countries of the world. The basic problem is this: having borrowed a great deal in the past, and used these borrowings with an indifferent degree of effectiveness, Yugoslavia now finds herself in a situation where she is forced to try to reduce her total volume of international debt. The fact that she has been able, in recent years, to run a positive balance on current account testifies to her success in this

168

Table 8.1 Perverse flows – net resource transfer 1982–6

	Total net interest and capital flow ($bn)	As percentage of total exports
Argentina	−16.8	43.5
Brazil	−37.1	30.6
Chile	−3.1	16.4
Mexico	−49.9	46.9
Venezuela	−26.8	37.8
Yugoslavia	−2.1	24.3

Source: Griffith-Jones 1987: Table 7.1

connection. Thus Yugoslavia has, since 1983, been *exporting capital to the developed West*, quite apart from interest payments. In so doing she has fitted in only too well with the pattern of 'perverse transfer of resources' from the poor to the rich which has dominated the profile of relationships between creditor and debtor countries since 1982, as Table 8.1 shows. It is, indeed, the supreme irony of the international debt problem that the countries which have made the greatest efforts to maintain correctness in debt service are the countries which have done their growth prospects the greatest damage. In the South and Central American case:

> The export of Latin American savings required to service the debt has been reflected in a significant drop in the ratio of investment, which . . . declined from 26 per cent of GNP in 1981 to 20 per cent in 1983. It has also been a major factor contributing to a dramatic decline in per capita GDP, which has implied a reversal of previously uninterrupted growth during the last thirty years.
>
> (Griffith-Jones 1985)

But things are, in a sense, even worse than that for Yugoslavia. We saw how in 1987 a bunching of maturities forced Belgrade into a request for rescheduling, despite the fact that the current account was showing a surplus. Table 8.2 demonstrates that this bunching problem is going to get worse rather than better in the period up to 1990. No doubt this pattern is partly a result of poor debt management on the part of the National Bank in the past. Its significance for the future is that Yugoslavia may find herself obliged to ask for repeated reschedulings, *even while she continues to be a net exporter of capital to the West*.

This is clearly an unsatisfactory situation for Yugoslavia, a developing country which could expect, in the normal course of economic development, to be able to continue to supplement domestic savings for investment purposes until levels of GNP per capital commensurate with those of developed countries had been reached. It is also unsatisfactory

Table 8.2 Actual and scheduled debt repayments 1985–93 ($mn)

	1985	1986	1987	1988	1989	1990	1991	1992	1993
Official	508	354	700	829	759	816	662	597	529
Private guaranteed	115	760	951	1192	911	1034	801	601	599
Private non-guaranteed	645	310	225	150	810	779	687	640	556
Total	1268	1424	1876	2171	2480	2629	2150	1838	1684

Source: World Bank Debt Tables; WEFA estimates

for the international banks. For as we were forcibly reminded by the Brazilian stand-still of 1987, it is usually the exporter of capital that calls the tune, even if he is a substantial net debtor.

There have been signs from the most recent accommodations made with the big Latin American debtors that the period of large-scale perverse transfer of resources may be coming to an end, that Western governments and banks may increasingly be coming round to the view that further lending to the developing countries is in the interests of world development and world banking alike. If the most optimistic scenario is confirmed, what are Yugoslavia's chances of getting their share and putting it to good use? At present, it must be said, rather poor. The contrast between Yugoslavia's brave Balance of Payments showing and her continued failure to restructure the domestic economic system is only too stark. As long as that failure persists, Yugoslavia will lack a mechanism for ensuring investment effectiveness, and potential foreign lenders will justifiably lack confidence in the ability of the country to generate the kind of export-led growth which is the best guarantee of ongoing hard-currency payments capacity. Specific areas of difficulty like the absence of satisfactory joint-venture legislation only serve to exacerbate the basic problem.

The tenor of much of the preceding analysis has been that it is on the political dimension that we must seek the root causes of Yugoslavia's inability to generate meaningful economic reform. It follows that in seeking possible solutions, we must look in the first place at the prospects for political reform. This is the theme which we shall address in our final chapter.

Politi[   ] .e Price of Reform

Party and state – a perverse pluralism?

'Democracy can be loosely defined as the right at least to ask – why are we living so badly?' ('Usko grlo', 1987) Thus an *Ekonomska Politika* leader on the eve of the March 1987 Plenum of the Central Committee of the League of Communists. The economic crisis has, indeed, generated a whole series of challenges to the Yugoslav political establishment. At the most fundamental level, it has called into question the very basis of Marxist–Leninist ideology – the notion that under post-revolutionary conditions a ruling Communist Party would play the role of midwife to a law-given process of continuous expansion of productive forces, continuous betterment of the material conditions of life. By the same token it has called into question the legitimacy of one-party role, of the political monopoly of a party which has never won an open election in Yugoslavia. At a more mundane level, it has raised the most serious doubts about the fitness of the leading cadres of the League of Communists to hold high office, about the wisdom of entrusting the economic destiny of the country to men and women who have made so many mistakes. Lastly, it has generated pressure for more open government. The scandal of the international debt is not just that it was contracted, but that information about it was systematically withheld from the public. Thus it was revealed in 1988 that while the Federal Skupština was adopting a plan in 1976 which envisaged no increase in indebtedness over the period 1976–80, a secret document from the same year talked of an ominous rise in the level of external indebtedness ('Javni i . . .' 1988). Whichever dimension we look at, then, the 1980s have witnessed the opening-up of a huge credibility gap between rulers and ruled in Yugoslavia.

> This resignation and lack of efficacy are most apparent among Yugoslav youth, who quite readily now confess that they view their political institutions and leadership as fundamentally irrelevant and that they perceive the major social problems to be inherently insoluble.

A major poll of Serbian youth conducted during the spring of 1986 illustrates this point; 65 per cent of the respondents reported little or no faith in the League of Communists . . . Among Slovenian youth the situation is even more alarming. In this, the most developed republic with the lowest rate of unemployment and objectively the greatest opportunities for youth, confidence in the political leadership is so low that only 4.5 per cent acknowledge a willingness to join the League of Communists.

Pessimism about the future is also apparent . . . Only 1 per cent of the youth polled [in a major Serbian survey] thought that the current Yugoslav system performs well and does not need fundamental reform. Simultaneously, over 90 per cent reported little or no political involvement, and similarly high percentages expressed little or no interest in becoming personally involved with the political or social institutions . . . A recent national poll conducted by the Institute of Social Science in Belgrade found that only 2 per cent of respondents identified external factors as the primary determinants of the current social crisis; 29 per cent stated that responsibility must be shared at all levels of the system, while 59 per cent preferred to limit responsibility to the political and economic leadership.

(Seroka 1988: 84–5)

We need only add that contemporary oral reports from Slovenia say people are now commonly writing to the party headquarters in Ljubljana to ask for written confirmation that they have *never* been members of the party.

Does the fault simply lie with the one-party system in itself? There is certainly plenty of evidence from the rest of the communist world that one-party systems may impose a high price in terms of efficiency of policy articulation and implementation, even in cases where the credibility and legitimacy of the regime has not been called seriously into question. Perhaps the best contemporary example is that of the Soviet Union. Under the leadership of a dynamic, forceful and reform-oriented leader like Mikhail Gorbachev, the Soviet Union is making but hesitant steps in the direction of effective restructuring of the economy and economic system. The reasons for this are manifold, but one of them lies in the peculiar pattern of *co-optive oligarchy* which seems to be a universal characteristic of Communist Party leaderships. Thus powerful as the position of General Secretary of the Communist Party of the Soviet Union is, it does not carry with it the prerogative of *choosing your own team*. Throughout his term of office Mr Gorbachev has had to co-exist, *inside the Politburo*, the highest decision-making body in the Soviet Union, with men like Egor Ligachev, a conservative who has repeatedly and publicly voiced serious reservations about Gorbachev's economic policies and approach to the Stalinist legacy. Even after the changes approved at the September 1988 Plenum of the Central Committee of the Communist Party of the Soviet Union, which strengthened Gorbachev's position considerably, Ligachev remains a Politburo member.

The system of co-optive oligarchy creates difficulties while leaders are alive, but may create even greater difficulties when they fall ill or die. It cannot, by definition, accommodate any automatic rule of succession, since that would deny the prerogatives of the oligarchs. The history of the Soviet leadership since the mid-1970s shows just how damaging this can be to the cause of forceful policy-making. With Brezhnev's health failing increasingly in the late 1970s and early 1980s, economic policy drifted hopelessly, as performance indicators worsened dramatically. When Brezhnev finally died in October 1982, there was a brief recovery of policy impetus, with the able and astute Yurii Andropov taking over the key position. But by the middle of 1983 his health had broken down irrevocably, and we were back with policy drift. Mikhail Gorbachev was already in charge of economic policy-making under Andropov, and seemed the obvious heir apparent when the latter died in February 1984. Instead, however, the oligarchs went for Konstantin Chernenko, an old Brezhnevite. Chernenko was, in fact, already too ill at that point to fulfil the duties of General Secretary, and Gorbachev frequently took the chair at Politburo meetings during the former's tenure. But it was not until Chernenko's death in March 1985, at which point the oligarchs finally accepted Gorbachev as Number One, that the Soviet leadership really started to attack the economic problems inherited from the 'period of stagnation' again.

In Yugoslavia the picture is complicated to an immense degree by the regional dimension. For the co-optive oligarchy in the Yugoslav case is a motley collection of republican and provincial leaders, all with powerful regional power-bases, none, since the death of Tito, with much of a federal power-base. Thus the apposite parallel for the workings of the Yugoslav Politburo – the Central Executive Committee – may in some ways be the pre-Luxembourg Compromise Council of Ministers of the European Community, rather than the Soviet Politburo. 'National' leaders come together infrequently, and sometimes without great goodwill, to try to thrash out generally acceptable compromises on problematic issues. Each member can exercise the *liberum veto*, and the result is a decision-making process just about as efficient as that in operation in 18th century Poland.

We should be careful not to exaggerate the degree to which policy stance is uniquely determined by regional identity. Rather, the picture is of a range of policy orientations, each one of which tends to be strongly identified with particular parts of the country.

The Yugoslav leadership is . . . divided into tendency groups that might be labelled 'confederationalists', 'ideological conservatives', and 'liberal reformers'. The 'confederationalist' grouping comprises those regional leaderships engaged in expanding their political autonomy at the expense of the centre. It includes the Slovenian, Croatian, Vojvodinian, and at least some elements in the Bosnian leadership. The 'ideological conservatives' are the most heterogeneous grouping, comprising individuals in all regions who are generally sympathetic to a more centralistic, primitively egalitarian, and 'closed' model of society than has been established in Yugoslavia in the past two decades, and hostile to the establishment of a market economy and its integration into the world economy. They are found predominantly among the military and veterans, members of the revolutionary generation, and leaders of the underdeveloped regions. In addition, some prominent members of the Croatian and Serbian leaderships have on occasion expressed such views . . . 'Liberal reformers' are found primarily among the Serbian party leadership. At LCY Central Committee plenums and in meetings organized by the Serbian party, a new generation of Serbian political leadership has given outspoken support to implementation of the stabilization programme . . . Liberal reform measures have received the support of individual political figures in other regions, as well . . . 'Liberal reformers' have also received some support from the renaissance of Yugoslav social science in the period since the onset of crisis.

(Burg 1986: 187–8)

The spectrum of views within the Yugoslav political establishment is not, then, so very different from what it is in other states. The problem lies in the degree to which this spectrum is overlayed by purely localistic tendencies. Thus many members of the republican political establishments in Slovenia and Croatia shares the views of the Serbian liberals on the best way to run an economy. But because they do not trust Belgrade to run *any* policy, because they believe that all Serbs, even liberal ones, are ultimately centralists and hegemonists, because, indeed, many necessary elements in a comprehensive package of economic reform would have to increase the power of the federal government, they align themselves with the confederationalists rather than the liberals. It is for this reason that the 'natural majority' of liberally minded activists at the more sophisticated and well-educated end of the Yugoslav political spectrum never makes itself felt, for this reason that the Serbian liberals remain isolated and weak, leaving confederationalists and ideological conservatives in a stalemate where each blocks systematically what the other wants to do.

The pattern of co-optive stalement is repeated at the personnel level.

The rigid system of regional quotas governing the composition of the central organs 'negates the criterion of demonstrated productivity, capability and expertise' ('Pašić letter' quoted in Burg 1986: 186), the more so that it is overlayed by a strong element of 'negative selection', with Croats and Slovenes in particular showing, perhaps, even greater reluctance than in the past to move to Belgrade. The automatic rotation rule for key posts has inevitably created a 'Buggins' turn' system of succession, with each region waiting in line, even at the level of the premiership. Mr Mikulić may, arguably, have been the best available candidate for the prime ministership in 1986, but he got the job mainly because it was Bosnia's turn. That fact surely made it much more difficult for Mikulić to bring his undoubted administrative ability to bear on the problems of the federation. His resignation in December 1988 in protest against lack of support for his policies amongst the political elites may ultimately do the Yugoslav political system more good than harm, in that it has broken the Buggins' turn rule. Whether the new premier, Ante Marković, can do better than Buggins did is another matter.

The call for democracy

It has not been difficult for Yugoslav intellectuals to articulate a critique which focuses on the one-party system as it has developed in Yugoslavia, with its fragmented arbitrariness and quasi-pluralism, as the main obstacle to concerted reform and reconstruction. At the general economic level:

> The Yugoslav concept of organization of the economy lacks the dimension of an independent and responsible enterprise, and lives in an illusion of association of labour and capital. The operation of the market is restricted, and planning agreements are propagated as a substitute for it. In essence we have a system of informal direction of the economy by state and para-state institutions . . . As a result, income as a pure macro-economic category is mechanically transferred to micro-economic quasi-subjects . . . National Income is spent ever more quickly, is ever more difficult to generate.
>
> (Kovačević 1988)

In more specific terms:

> All this leads to the substitution of every economic parameter by a political one – from economic decision-taking, choice of rational business strategy, content of extended reproduction and distribution of Social Product, to substitution of the law of political agreement and association for the operation of economic laws.
>
> (Maksimović 1988: 2)

But the negative impact of the one-party system goes beyond the dimension of quality of decision-taking. The absence of meaningful pluralism at the level of the state makes it very difficult for the authorities to cope with the *objective* pluralism of economic interests. This problem was cast into sharp relief in 1987, when a wave of strikes hit the Yugoslav economy at the worst possible time. The workers were certainly striking as a protest against falling living standards, but were they striking against their 'own' management, their own workers' council? When *Ekonomska Politika* put the question to a number of distinguished academics, the answer was a clear 'no' ('Ni rat . . . ' 1987); strikes in Yugoslavia are usually aimed at 'the authorities, ultimately the League of Communists, and their instruments, the Trade Unions. The League, in fact, is faced with an impossible situation, since it cannot in practice operate as a transmission belt for worker's demands. In the words of Bogomir Kovač:

> The Labin [a big coal mine] strike demonstrates a quite normal division of social functions under socialism: the workers strike because they are still only workers who work in bad conditions and for low wages; the communists break the strike because that is what their leading social role demands.

Kovač goes on to argue in favour of independent unions, and an 'institutionalization of industrial conflict'. The current situation whereby strikes are neither allowed nor forbidden is wholly unsatisfactory, because it excludes by definition any proper mechanism for settling disputes. Time and resources are wasted, and at the end of it all people are still dissatisfied – not the ideal pattern for an economy struggling to raise labour productivity. But if the institutionalizaton of conflict is a necessary condition for economic efficiency, asks the League activist, what are the political implications? If you allow independent, branch unions, is that not the first step towards institutionalized *political* pluralism, and the end of the one-party system? Exactly the same issue arose over the formation of the independent Peasants' Union in Slovenia in 1988. Two views of this development emerged. Party activists saw it as a direct consequence of the collapse of the agricultural policy of the League of Communists, as a reflection of inadequate ideological work amongst the peasantry, and as the first step towards a multi-party system. Economists saw it in terms of a hard-working and efficient group of farmers creating an autonomous organization which would better represent their particular interests ('Idejni . . . ' 1988). Is there any way these two views could be made compatible?

There has certainly been an enormous change in public attitudes to the democracy issue in Yugoslavia since the crisis. A public opinion survey conducted in Slovenia in 1987 found 53.5 per cent of the sample in favour of direct elections. (The existing Yugoslav arrangement is a complex and clumsy system of indirect elections.) Just 37 per cent were explicitly in favour of a multi-party system, with about the same proportion against. But 93 per cent said they thought new socio-political movements were necessary, and 44 per cent thought that those movements should be completely independent of the League and its cognate organizations. When asked a slightly different question about the position of the League of Communists a 1986 sample showed itself 65 per cent in favour of political pluralism. The majority of the 1987 sample was also in favour of the repeal of legislation limiting freedom of speech (Jambrek 1987).

But Slovenia is not Yugoslavia, and once we move onto the broader stage, we have to content ourselves with the views of scholars, writers and politicians – important enough in their own right, but not necessarily the views of the masses. The basic issues and arguments were put forward with commendable clarity in a leader in *Ekonomska Politika* in 1987. Why, the leader asked, should not at least some of the fundamental dilemmas facing Yugoslavia be settled by national referendum, with different programmes being put forward by different groups of authors? It is time to recognize, it went on, that the 'technology' of democracy, is *a priori*, neither bourgeois nor socialist. 'Direct elections with multiple candidates and programmes . . . are not "class" categories, but the inheritance of civilization.' The only obstacle are the politicians, who are likened to oligopolists. Like other oligopolists, they are always trying to hive off a bit of the market, so that they can effectively become monopolists. They have no need fear the consumer (the citizen), but only their competitors (other politicians) ('Profesija . . .' 1987).

The message is again unmistakable. Just as you cannot have a market economy without genuine competition, so you cannot have a political system running a market economy without genuine competition. And the competition must apply to policies as well as people. The League of Communists has to start off by admitting that 'unacceptable ideas' may sometimes be less damaging than 'generally accepted' ones ('Usko grlo' 1987).

But does that mean that Yugoslavia should risk the proposition that there are *no* ideas that are in principle unacceptable? Svetozar Stojanović, a prominent Serbian liberal, is quite clear that the answer is 'no'.

Even if it were possible, [the creation of new parties] would not be good political programme, for it would entail very undesirable consequences. The brief social experience of a multi-party set-up in pre-war Yugoslavia, the national conflicts within the League of Communists, particularly over the last fifteen years, show that parties in Yugoslavia – this time round as well – would most probably be formed on predominantly national and confessional lines, and with that kind of political pluralism much older and stronger political units than Yugoslavia would break up. Apart from that, Yugoslavia's geo-strategic situation is still such that a multi-party system would also legalize the operation of groups which at a moment of crisis could serve as a bridgehead for foreign intervention.

(Stojanović 1986: 96–7)

Stojanović goes on to suggest that a form of 'guided' pluralism might be introduced through the vehicle of existing political institutions:

The proper political environment for the operation of the Communist Party in our country should be the formation of a *new* Socialist Alliance [traditionally a League of Communists tool for the mobilization of the masses], and the existing Trade Union Congress, if it is really democratised . . . The Socialist Alliance would represent a voluntary association of individuals and groups committed to the building of democratic socialism in Yugoslavia . . . The new organization would accept the leading role of the League of Communists *only if* it democratized itself . . . The democratic-communist potential is significantly broader than the reforming wing of the League of Communists: there are many former members of the Party, dis-illusioned or squeezed out, who would support well thought-out, progressive social changes. In all this, League activists would in the first place practice *democratic tolerance*, and socialists *political realism*, but accepting the leading role of the League of Communists . . . The League of Communists, the Socialist Alliance and the Trade Union Congress would commit themselves to the principles that Yugoslavia should remain a federation, decentralized in an administrative and cultural sense.

(Stojanović 1986: 98–9)

Stojanović's formulation is cautious. It was published in the proceedings of a conference organized by the Serbian Academy of Sciences, an organization often at odds with the authorities, from which a number of contributions were censored out. But it differs only in detail from a proposal put forward by two leading Croatian liberals:

The League of Communists . . . should renounce its role as 'the party of power', and become leader in the development of a multi-programme (pluralistic) socialist democracy. It should give up its monopoly over cadres policy, and stop thinking of itself as everyone's and everything's controller and the supreme arbiter in all situations. It should open the way to a democratic pluralism of ideas and programmes.

(Goldstein and Korošić 1987: 11)

These proposals, taken to their logical conclusion, are for a multi-party system, constrained only by the rule that all parties must be 'socialist', and must be committed to the continued existence of Yugoslavia. Inevitably, the 'leading role' of the League of Communists would ultimately have to go.

What can we hope for in the short to medium term? The concept of 'guided democracy' does not have a very happy ring. It smacks of the less repressive of Third World dictatorships, or simply of window-dressing to keep foreign friends happy. But there is little evidence that Yugoslav communists, beleaguered as they are, are any happier about giving up their monopoly of power than other East European or East Asian communists. What we can perceive is that Yugoslavia's primary need at present if for a more *efficient* form of government, a form of government in which specific programmes can be clearly identified with specific leaders and specific political groupings, where policy failures can likewise be clearly attributed, and where unsuccessful leaders can be removed by due electoral process. As one distinguished Yugoslav political scientist asked:

> Would the debt crisis and the Kosovo crisis [see below] have been possible, at least in the dangerous form that we have them, if decisions on borrowing and nationality relations in Kosovo over the past decade or so had been taken on a democratic, rather than a sham, quasi-democratic, oligarchical basis?
>
> (Popović 1988: 44)

It is only at first sight surprising that many League of Communists radicals, perceiving the essential problem of *political blockage* in Yugoslavia, profess great admiration for Margaret Thatcher – no friend of socialism, to be sure, but a leader who can always be clearly identified, who does not make U-turns (well, not many), and is always ready to stand or fall by her policy outcomes.

Can Yugoslav political culture accommodate reform?

It is, then, the interaction of the traditional monopoly of political power of the League of Communists and the ethnocentrism of regional leaderships which represents the main specific obstacle to meaningful political change. But regional leaderships did not invent ethnocentrism. As we saw in Chapter 1, national particularism has always been an essential element of Yugoslav political culture, and the post-war political history of Yugoslavia could be written in terms of a (rather unsuccessful) attempt to come to terms with this. But let us imagine for a moment that we have a strong government with a clear programme and a will to implement it installed in Belgrade. Most Yugoslav political activists accept the proposition that the quasi-market economy of associationism has been a disaster, that Yugoslavia must move to a more full-blooded market system. But how would ordinary people react to such a programme?

As ever, we find that their attitudes are always complex and varied, often ambivalent. The Slovenian public opinion survey from 1987 we quoted earlier found that 81 per cent of the sample wanted to see the agricultural land maximum abolished, 91 per cent thought that loss-making enterprises should be liquidated [there is, of course, very little unemployment in Slovenia], and that a majority were in favour of significantly extending the scope for private enterprise. Against a background where ideologues continue to suffer public anguish over the question of the role of private ownership of the means of production under self-management, one factory in Pula, Croatia, has been borrowing from its own workers since 1970, so that 'the worker feels himself to be in some sense a shareholder in his own enterprise' ('Akcije' 1987).

At the same time Yugoslav policy-makers ignore at their peril the strength of egalitarian sentiment amongst the masses. That sentiment may be strongest in the poorer, southern and eastern regions, but it is certainly not absent from the north and west. Thus distinguished sociologist Josip Županov found, on the basis of a public opinion survey done in Croatian 1983, that the average Croatian worker was hardly ready, in attitudinal terms, for the 'social market economy'. Respondents showed themselves still generally unwilling to gauge their own work effort in terms of the evaluation of the market, and the overall conclusion was that 'for our people it isn't a terrible thing if they live badly – but it's a tragedy if someone else lives better.' Most interestingly, only one in five workers considered the right to strike to be a basic human right (Županov 1983). They may have changed their opinions since 1983, but if not, it is bad news for reformers who seek the institutionalization of industrial conflict.

The same picture emerges when we look at general patterns of income distribution. The official line since the breaking of the crisis has been that 'levelling' is a bad thing, that 'you can't get out of a crisis with half-empty stomachs all round.' From 1985 this began to impact on the distribution of income, as inter-job, inter-sectoral and inter-regional differentials all began to widen ('Prestaje . . . ' 1985). But with average real wages still falling, the authorities encountered substantial grassroots opposition to the trend. At many enterprises piece-work rates were padded and overtime stints artificially extended in order to fudge the principle of payment by results ('Vreme . . . ' 1985). By 1986, indeed, Trade Union officials were publically showing increasing sympathy with egalitarian sentiments ('Sindikat u . . . ' 1986).

But perhaps the most striking thing to emerge from recent public opinion surveys is the general pattern of attitudes to working harder. A survey done by the Zagreb Centre for Marketing Research in 1988 found that 73 per cent of the sample would only be prepared to work harder if they were going to be paid more, with as much as 25 per cent looking for a doubling of incomes to provide an adequate incentive ('Motiv više' 1988). Given the current state of the Yugoslav economy, it is clear that such expectations could not possibly be fulfilled in the short run, even on the best possible policy scenario. Significantly, it was the Slovenes and Croats who showed themselves least prepared to work harder. Thus we find at the level of popular attitudes an interesting echo of attitudes at the level of regional political elites – Belgrade got us into this mess: let Belgrade get us out of it, and don't expect *us* to make any special efforts.

What price a re-alignment of political forces?

Is there a way out of the deadlock? Steven Burg suggests one scenario which is certainly within the bounds of the possible, and which holds out some prospect for an effective majority:

> Ideological conservatives, although the most powerful tendency at present and seemingly in the majority in the current Presidency, could not [push through an effective reform] alone. They do not appear to offer any programme that would be broadly acceptable either at home or among the country's international creditors. Liberal reformers, on the other hand, while the least powerful tendency, have formulated a comprehensive programme. Moreover, that programme contains centralizing elements attractive to ideological conservatives. While the difficulty of establishing a stable majority of any kind at this time, in support of any policy, should not be underestimated, a coalition between ideological conservatives and liberal reformers, based on a shared belief that 'something must be done', might establish the requisite conditions for a strategy of 'governance by temporary measure'.
>
> (Burg 1986: 189)

We witnessed in 1988 dramatic developments in Yugoslav politics which do, indeed, promise or threaten finally to break the mold of post-war politics. The catalyst is Serbian League of Communists leader Slobodan Milošević. Against a background of almost total loss of confidence in the federal government (a NIN public opinion survey found that in 1987 just 16 per cent of respondents felt that the prime minister had completely fulfilled their expectations, as compared to 47 per cent in 1986 (Grizelj 1987)), Milošević has succeeded in establishing a degree of charismatic popularity not seen in Yugoslavia since the death of Tito. In his mobilization of mass pressure against the party leadership of Vojvodina, culminating in their collective resignation, he has shown a quality of political muscle which, if put to the right purpose, could stand Yugoslavia in good stead.

But will it be put to the right purpose? Milošević is above all a populist, even a rabble-rouser. He has built up tremendous support in Serbia through blatant exploitation of Serbian sensitivities in relation to Kosovo, an autonomous province of the Serbian republic, but 85 per cent Albanian in population. The historic heartland of Serbia, Kosovo has seen its Slav population dwindle to a beleaguered minority over a period of centuries. By far the poorest region of Yugoslavia, Kosovo was run as a repressive police state within a state up until the ouster of police chief Aleksander Ranković in 1966. The post-1966 policy of allowing Kosovo autonomous republican status in all but name did something to soothe Albanian resentments, but fell short of providing Yugoslav Albanians with total security of civil rights. Economic development policies since the mid-1960s have had little impact on Kosovo's poverty, partly because of the very high rate of natural increase of the Albanian population, partly because of mistakes made by the provincial government, now substantially Albanian in membership, particularly in relation to the utilization of development grants.

By the mid-1980s this combination of factors had produced an explosive situation. Gory reports of intimidation of Serbian and Montenegrin Kosovars fanned the flames of national indignation in Serbia proper, while Albanian Kosovars continued to feel the sense of second-class citizenship as keenly as ever. it was against this background that Milovšević was able to stage a dramatic take-over of the Serbian Party leadership, on a platform which committed him to seeking an end to Kosovo's quasi-republican status, and a reintegration of the two autonomous provinces of Vojvodina and Kosovo back into Serbia proper.

Is Milošević the man to give Yugoslavia a new lead? Almost certainly not. His brutal assault on the Vojvodina leadership, in response to their alleged failure to give him proper support over the Kosovo issue, is in a sense a side-show. The substantial Hungarian minority in Vojvodina is prosperous, within the limits of the Yugoslav situation, and quite untroublesome. It is Kosovo that Milošević is hunting, but because Vojvodina has the same constitutional status as the more southerly province, any move to end Kosovo autonomy would inevitably have the same effect on Vojvodina – clearly an unsatisfactory solution for local Vojvodina leaders. More importantly, Vojvodina, despite its Serbian majority, has tended to line up with the confederationalists of Slovenia and Croatia on broader policy issues. Inevitably, then, the western republics have been Milošević as a potential threat to *their* constitutional position.

But perhaps the most striking characteristic of the Milošević phenomenon is its lack of a serious economic policy dimension. There is no reason to doubt the capacity of ex-banker Milošević to cope with economic policy matters. It is difficult not to feel, however, that in focusing so obsessively on what is, by international standards, a rather minor problem of inter-community tension, Milošević has sought quite intentionally to divert public attention from national economic difficulties. In the 1987 NIN public opinion survey, 79 per cent of respondents said that they believed that Yugoslavia's economic problems might never be solved. In such a climate of public opinion, economic policy is likely to be the least rewarding theme for the demagogue. There is no hint here of the kind of broadly-based, businesslike conservative-liberal coalition that Burg saw as a possibility a few years ago. And because Milošević has been so abrasive in his dealings with regional leaderships, the credibility of such a coalition – which would inevitably be Serbian-dominated – may have gone for ever.

The current prospects for a political realignment such as would significantly facilitate economic policy articulation and implementation are, therefore, rather bleak. We have seen large sections of the Yugoslav population, through 1987 and 1988, turning their faces away from the real problems of the day, retreating into an atavistic ethnic sectarianism which can only create new barriers to the national consolidation which Yugoslavia so desperately needs. To republican leaders in Zagreb and Ljubljana, Milošević looks like just another Greater-Serbian hegemonist, a throw-back to the pre-war period, and therefore by definition of doubtful legitimacy as a potential national leader. If Milošević should ever succeed in capturing the federal government we can be sure that he will enjoy minimal cooperation from the western republics. Yet Milošević may yet render Yugoslavia a signal service. If the bogeyman of Greater-Serbian hegemonism can jolt the Slovenes and Croats out of their *own* ethnocentric particularism, he may do more than his liberal colleagues have been able to do to forge their 'natural majority' into a national political force strong enough to push through the kind of 'Single Yugoslav Act' without which full economic recovery is impossible.

There is, one must add, a more sombre scenario. It was revealed in 1988 that the Yugoslav army has a contingency plan for taking over control of Slovenia, should party authority collapse there altogether. Whether they have a similar contingency plan for Yugoslavia as a whole is not known, but if the party fails to sort out the Milošević crisis, the military might be tempted to try to impose their own kind of national unity. Any such *putsch* would, however, involve an extraordinary political irony. For historical reasons, the officer corps of the Yugoslav army is predominantly Serbian. For demographic reasons, the rank and file of national servicemen includes an extraordinarily high proportion of Albanians from Kosovo.

Conclusions – crisis and conditionality

We argued in the last chapter that IMF conditionality packages and World Bank project assessment procedures have largely failed to have the expected impact on the Yugoslav economy because they have been designed for market economies. Yugoslavia is not a market economy. We argued at the same time that there is every reason, from an economic development point of view, to try to reverse the perverse resource flow out of Yugoslavia, to try to ensure that Yugoslavia regains access to international capital markets. But reform of the domestic economic system is a *sine qua non* of any such development. That reform would not necessarily involve transition to a Thatcherite economy, but it would have to be based on a clearly defined and major role for the market. As we have just seen, however, there are no prospects for meaningful economic reform as long as the present political deadlock continues.

Is there *anything* the West can do to help in these circumstances? Should national and international leaders take the view that internal Yugoslav affairs are absolutely none of their business, that Western interest in Belgrade's economic policy-making should essentially stop at the question of debt service, that a Milošević or army takeover would only be of interest if it threatened to take Yugoslavia back into the Soviet bloc? Of one thing we can be sure. Any Western attempt to take sides in the political dramas now unfolding would almost certainly have a perverse effect. But there may be scope for trying to evolve a new kind of conditionality, a kind of conditionality which would take as its starting point the fact that Yugoslavia is not a market economy, but rather a fragmented para-statist economy, and that realistic programmes of economic rationalization would almost certainly have to include substantial elements of state intervention, ranging from a possible renationalization of the electricity industry to the selective use of price and income controls, in addition, for instance, to a much more radical and consistent policy on the private sector and a much tougher approach to the whole question of financial and monetary discipline. That is the kind of package most of the Serbian liberal reformers are looking for, and it could be saleable to confederationalists suitably chastened by the Milošević experience. The presence of significant elements of price and income control might be enough to ensure a degree of acceptance from ideological conservatives.

To get even that far would obviously require a lot of political changes. But once in place, a credible policy configuration would itself help to stabilize the political situation. The need to maintain credibility amidst constantly changing conditions, not least in the world economy, would ensure unremitting pressure for the development of a new kind of pluralism which would offer the Yugoslav people alternative policies rather than alternative shibboleths, give them a basis for facing the future rather than retreating into the past. It would be foolish to suggest that this outcome is likely. But it is possible, and it is worth a sporting bet.

References

'Akcije' (1987) *Ekonomska Politika*, 5 October, p. 6.

Aktuelna Monetarna Politika i Politika Kamatnih Stopa (1985) Belgrade.

'Alajbegova slama' (1987) *Ekonomska Politika*, 31 August, p. 5.

Almuli, J. (1987) 'Nova ponuda poveriocima', *Ekonomska Politika*, 29 June, p. 46.

'Automobili' (1988) *Ekonomska Politika*, 10 October, pp. 15–16.

Babić, M., and Primorac, E.(1986) 'Some causes of the growth of the Yugoslav external debt', *Soviet Studies*, 38 (1).

Bašić, S. (1981) 'Sve je to Jugoslavia', *Ekonomska Politika*, 23 March, pp. 6–7.

Bakarić, V. (1960) *O Poljoprivredi i Problemima Sela*, Belgrade: Kultura.

—— (1971) Speech to Second Congress of Self-Managers, Sarajevo, 5–8 May, 1971, reported in *Vjesnik*, 7 May, pp. 4–5.

Bergson, A. (1978) *Productivity and the Social System – the USSR and the West*, Cambridge, Mass.: Harvard University Press.

'Besplatni saveti' (1988) *Ekonomska Politika*, 30 May, p. 6.

Bićanić, R. (1973) *Economic Policy in Socialist Yugoslavia*, Cambridge: Cambridge University Press.

Bjelica, V. (1985) 'Rigidnost selektivne politike i politike visokih kamatnih stopa', in *Aktuelna Monetarna Politika*. . . .

Blagojević, S. (1968) *Odnosi Fiksnih Fondova i Proizvodnje u Jugoslovenskoj Privredi*, Ekonomski Institut, Narodne Novine, Zagreb.

Bogoev, K. (1985) 'Uslovljenosti efikasne stabilizacione monetarno-kreditne politike' in *Aktuelna Monetarna Politika* . . .

'Bolje u more' (1983) *Ekonomska Politika*, 30 May, p. 7.

Bošković, D.(1986) 'O caru i premijeru', *Ekonomska Politika*, 8 September, p. 11.

Burg, S.L. (1986) 'Elite conflict in post-Tito Yugoslavia', *Soviet Studies*, 38, (2).

Čehajić, R. (1987) 'Blockade se nastavljaju', *Ekonomska Politika*, 19 October, pp. 14–15.

Čemović, M. (1969) statement in *Borba*, 6 February.

'Cena sirovosti', *Ekonomska Politika*, 30 December, p. 6.

'Četvrti partner' (1988) *Ekonomska Politika*, 15 February, p. 6.

Čičin-Šain, A. (1982) 'Strukturne slabosti platne bilance Jugoslavije i mogućnosti njihova prevladavanja mjerama dugoročnog programa ekonomske stabilizacije', in *Aktuelni Problemi Privrednih Kretanja i Ekonomske Politike*

Jugoslavije, Zagreb: Informator.
'Cijena novih rokova' (1978) *Privredni Vjesnik*, 23 October, p. 6.
Čkrebić, D. (1975) statement in *Privredni Vjesnik*, 20 January, p. 3.
Čobeljić, N. (1959) *Jugoslavije, Politika i Metodi Privrednog Razvoja*, Belgrade: Nolit.
Dedijer, V. (1953) *Tito*, New York: Simon & Schuster.
Dimitrijević, D. and Macesich, G. (1973) *Money and Finance in Contemporary Yugoslavia*, New York, Washington and London: Praeger.
'Direktorijumi' (1976) *Borba*, 23 May, p. 4.
Dirlam, J. and Plummer, J. (1973) *An Introduction to the Yugoslav Economy*, Columbus, Ohio: Charles E. Merrill.
Djilas, M. (1969) *The Unperfect Society*, London: Methuen.
Djodan, Š. (1971) 'Gospodarski položaj Hrvatske', *Kritika* (Zagreb), 4 (17).
Djuričić, P. (1985) 'Od ''radinosti'' do privrede (II)', *Ekonomska Politika*, 2 September, pp. 21–4.
—— (1987a) 'Izvozna prepreka – EAN', *Ekonomska Politika*, 19 January, p. 12.
—— (1987b) 'Neturistički faktori 87', *Ekonomska Politika*, 19 October 1987, pp. 18–20.
'Dosledno' (1980) *Ekonomska Politika*, 26 May, pp. 6–7.
Društveni Plan Privrednog Razvoja Jugoslavije 1957–61 (1957) Belgrade: Kultura.
Dujšin, U. 'Les relations entre les pays endettés et les banques commerciales internationales: le cas Yougoslave'. Paper presented to the *Congrès International des Economistes de Langue Francaise*, Fribourg, 1–3 June, 1987.
Dumezić, T. (1986a) 'Saniranje po površini', *Ekonomska Politika*, 27 January, pp. 10–11.
—— (1986b) 'Šta je ostalo od samoupravljanja', *Ekonomska Politika*, 18 August, p. 11.
'Dvostruki život' (1983) *Ekonomska Politika*, 7 February, p. 7.
Dyker, D. A. (1974) 'The Yugoslav deficit on Balance of Payments', *European Economic Review*, 5 (4).
—— (1977) 'Yugoslavia: unity out of diversity?', in A. Brown and J. Gray (eds) *Political Culture and Political Change in Communist States*, London: Macmillan.
—— (1983) *The Process of Investment in the Soviet Union*, Cambridge: Cambridge University Press.
—— (1985) *The Future of the Soviet Economic Planning System*, London: Croom Helm.
Ellman, M. (1979) *Socialist Planning*, Cambridge: Cambridge University Press.
Estrin, S. *et al.* (1988) 'Market imperfections, labour management, and earnings differentials in a developing country: theory and evidence from Yugoslavia', *Quarterly Journal of Economics*, 103 (3).
Fleming, J.M. and Sertić, V.R. (1962) 'The Yugoslav economic system', *International Monetary Fund Staff Papers* 9 (2).
Gavrović, M. (1979a) 'Sankcije i akcije', *Privredni Vjesnik*, 28 May, p. 5.
—— (1979b) 'Jedanaesta teza o reformi', *Privredni Vjesnik*, 12 November, p. 5.
—— (1980) 'Aduti i teškoće', *Privredni Vjesnik*, 28 March, p. 5.
Gerl, F. (1968) statement in *Ekonomska Politika*, 16–22 December.

References

Giannitsis, T. (n.d.) 'International specialization of the European newly industrialised countries. Evolution and differentiation in the period of crisis', paper presented to the *Collogue UNITAR: Stratégies pour le Futur de la Région Mediteranéenne*.

Gnjatović, D. (1985) *Uloga Inostranih Sredstava u Privrednom Razvoju Jugoslavije*, Ekonomski Institut, Belgrade.

—— (1987) interview reported in 'Kako uspostaviti neto računicu', *Ekonomska Politika*, 21 September, pp. 27–9.

Goldstein, S. and Korošić, M. (1987) 'Vrijeme radikalnih poteza', *Danas*, 1 December, pp. 10–11.

Golijanin, M. (1985) 'Za uravnotežniji odnos restriktivnih i stimulativnih elemenata u monetarno-kreditnoj politici', in *Aktuelna Monetarna Politika*.

Grdjić, G. (1972) *Dve Decenije Razvoja Privrede SR Srbije*, Ekonomski Institut, Belgrade.

Gregory, P. and Stuart, R. (1986) *Soviet Economic Structure and Performance*, 3rd edn, New York: Harper and Row.

Griffith-Jones, S. (1984) *International Finance and Latin America*, London: Croom Helm.

—— (1985) 'It's now time for a debtors' initiative', *The Guardian*, 26 June.

—— (1987) 'Perverse flows and the poverty trap', *South*, November, pp. 3–4.

Grizelj, J. (1987) 'Koliko ste zadovoljni radom SIV–a', *NIN*, 17 June, p. 10.

Grličkov, V. (1987a) 'Sve po starom', *Ekonomska Politika*, 12 October, pp. 11–12.

—— (1987b) 'Nemoć politike', *Ekonomska Politika*, 19 October, pp. 13–14.

—— (1987c) 'Tržište – bez novca', *Ekonomska Politika*, 19 October, p. 14.

—— (1988a) 'Pokrića kao povod', *Ekonomska Politika*, 15 February, pp. 20–1.

—— (1988b) 'Strah od deviza', *Ekonomska Politika*, 5 September, pp. 10–11.

Grubić, J. (1974) 'Sto prijeći četvrti inozajam', *Privredni Vjesnik*, 5 April, p. 12.

—— (1976) 'Ustavna preobrazba uvjet ekspanzije', *Privredni Vjesnik*, 12 January, pp. 4–5.

Hamilton, F.E.I. (1968) *Yugoslavia, Patterns of Economic Activity*, London: Bell.

Han, S. (1983) statements reported in 'Radno–neradni dani', *Ekonomska Politika*, 4 July, p. 6.

Hoffman, G.W. and Neal, F.W. (1962) *Yugoslavia and the New Communism*, New York: Twentieth Century Fund.

Holmes, P. and Estrin, S. (1983) *French Planning in Theory and Practice*, London: Allen and Unwin.

Horvat, B. (1969) *Privredni Ciklusi u Jugoslaviji*, Belgrade: Institut Ekonomskih Nauka.

—— (1984) 'Problemi finansiranja razvoja eletroprivrede', *Ekonomist*, (2).

Hrabrar, Z. (1987) statements reported in 'Iznevereno prezime', *Ekonomska Politika*, 26 January, p. 6.

'Idejni rad na selu' (1988) *Ekonomska Politika*, 23 May, p. 6.

Ilić, M. (1988) interview reported in 'Ko je kome potreban', *Ekonomska Politika*, 1 February, p. 6.

Ilijin, M. (1985) 'Hajde da rastemo', *Ekonomska Politika*, 23 September, pp. 10–11.

—— (1986) 'Ulepšavanje balasta', *Ekonomska Politika*, 20 January, pp. 18–19.

—— (1987) 'Imitacija ekonomije', *Ekonomska Politika*, 16 February, pp. 25-6.

'Imati i uložiti' (1987) *Ekonomska Politika*, 18 May, pp. 14-15.

Industrial Relations Counsellors Inc. (1972) 'Group wage incentives: experience with the Scanlon Plan', in T. Lupton (ed.) *Payment Systems*, London: Penguin.

'Informisanje' (1981) *Ekonomska Politika*, 9 November, p. 13.

'Iskustva i pouke DINE: (1982) *Ekonomska Politika*, 1 March, pp. 19-22.

Ivanović, S. (1984) 'Izvoz poljoprivrednih proizvoda', *Ekonomski Misao* (4).

'Iz antiinflacione prakse' (1985) *Ekonomska Politika*, 3 June, p. 7.

'Izuzetak' (1985) *Ekonomska Politika*, 19 August, p. 6.

Jambrek, P. (1987) 'Šta hoće Slovenci', *Ekonomska Politika*, 19 October, p. 9.

'Javni i tajni dug' (1988) *Ekonomska Politika*, 1 February, p. 6.

' "Jedinstvo" koje razdvaja' (1970) *Privredni Vjesnik* , 26 November, p. 4.

Jelić, B. (1962) *Sistem Planiranja u Jugoslovenskoj Privredi*, Belgrade: Ekonomska Biblioteka.

Jelić, M. and Cvetković, R. (1956) 'Razvitak privrede izmedju dva svetska rata', in *Razvoj Privrede FNRJ*, Belgrade.

'Jeres – u ceni ili kvalitetu' (1986) *Ekonomska Politika*, 18 August, p. 6.

Johnson, A.R. (1972) *The Transformation of Communist Ideology: the Yugoslav Case, 1945-53*, Cambridge, Mass.: Harvard University Press.

'Još da ih ubede' (1988) *Ekonomska Politika*, 6 June, p. 6.

Jovanović, M. (1980) 'Izmedju poželjnog i mogućeg', *Ekonomska Politika*, 3 November, pp. 25-8.

Jugoslavia 1945-64 (1965) Savezni Zavod za Statistiku, Belgrade.

Kamišar, I. (1972) 'Recept za "duboko oranje" ', *Privredni Vjesnik*, 28 December, p. 11.

Karakašević, V. (1985) 'S one strane ekonomije', *Ekonomska Politika*, 30 December, pp. 17-18.

—— (1986) 'Uspesi i neuspesi Društvenog dogovora', *Ekonomska Politika*, 20 October, pp. 14-15.

—— (1987) 'Nove mere ili preduzetništvo', *Ekonomska Politika*, 25 May, pp. 28-33.

Kardelj, E. (1960) *Socializam i Rat*, Belgrade: Kultura.

—— (1974) statement in *Privredni Vjesnik*, 18 October, p. 2.

'Kasno paljenje' (1988) *Ekonomska Politika*, 11 January, p. 7.

Kidrič, B. (1951) 'O nacrtima novih ekonomskih zakona', *Komunist*, 5 (4-5).

Kleppe, P. (1988) Interview reported in 'Irgovina otvara vrata kapitalu', *Ekonomska Politika*, 7 March, pp. 14-15.

'Kod komšije po devize' (1981) *Ekonomska Politika*, 24 August, p. 6.

'Kod kuće je najbolje' (1987) *Ekonomska Politika*, 9 February, p. 14.

'Koga država voli' (1988) *Ekonomska Politika*, 30 May, p. 7.

Kolarić, D. (1979) statement in *Privredni Vjesnik*, 18 September, p. 3.

'Komparativna prednost – zainteresovanost' (1985) *Ekonomska Politika*, 2 September, p. 7.

'Kompenzacioni poslovi u porastu' (1983) *Ekonomska Politika*, 9 May, p. 12.

'Komplementarna objašnjenja' (1987) *Ekonomska Politika*, 12 October, p. 6.

Konte, B. (1987) Interview reported in 'Iščekivanje septembra', *Ekonomska Politika*, 10 August, pp. 21-3.

References

Koprivica, V. (1973) 'Selidba kreditne politike', *Privredni Vjesnik*, 6 December, p. 6.

Korošić, M. (1985) 'Nejednakost u stvarnosti', *Ekonomska Politika*, 3 June, pp. 26–8.

Kovačević, M. (1982) 'Novi propisi – nova ograničenja', *Ekonomska Politika*, 8 November, pp. 20–2.

—— (1988) 'Preduzeće i poslovni uspeh', *Ekonomska Politika*, 6 June, pp. 24–6.

—— (1989) 'Nedovoljno uloženo u zakon', *Ekonomska Politika*, 16 January, pp. 20–2.

Kovačić, Z. (1985) 'Inflacija i lični dohoci', *Ekonomska Analiza*, 19 (2).

'Krivica' (1987) *Ekonomska Politika*, 16 February, p. 7.

'Kurs bez tržišta' (1987) *Ekonomska Politika*, 25 May, p. 5.

Kuznets, S. (1954) *National Income and its Composition 1919–1938*, vol. 1, NBER, New York.

'Lagano napredovanje' (1983) *Ekonomska Politika*, 21 March, pp. 10–11.

Lakićević, M. (1985) 'Od prioriteta do likvidacije', *Ekonomska Politika*, 24 June, pp. 13–14.

—— (1987) 'Storija za CK', *Ekonomska Politika*, 1 June, pp. 28–30.

'Lakše je reći' (1987) *Ekonomska Politika*, 5 October, p. 6.

Ledić, M. (1984) 'Debt analysis and debt related issues – the case of Yugoslavia', *Ekonomska Analiza* (1).

'Licitacija' (1982) *Ekonomska Politika*, 31 May, p. 6.

Maddison, A. (1976) 'Economic policy and performance in Europe 1913–1970', in C.M. Cipolla (ed.) *The Fontana Economic History of Europe*, vol. 5(2).

Maksimović, I. (ed.) (1986) *Ekonomika i Politika*, Belgrade: Srpska Akademija Nauka i Umetnosti.

Maksimović, I. (1986) 'Ekonomska nauka – izraz odnosa ekonomi je i politike', in Maksimović (ed.) *Ekonomika i Politika*.

'Mala privreda – veliko ogledalo' (1987) *Ekonomska Politika*, 16 February.

Marković, P. (1973) *Aktuelna Pitanja Ekonomskog Položaja i Daljeg Razvoja Jugoslovenske Poljoprivrede*, Belgrade: Eksport.

McGlue, D. (1979) *Regional Economic Policy and Regional Economic Development: the Case of Yugoslavia*, D.Phil thesis, University of Sussex.

Meade, J.E. (1975) 'The theory of labour-managed firms and of profit-sharing', in J. Vanek (ed.) *Self-Management. Economic Liberation of Man*, London: Penguin.

Mejovšek, B. (1973) 'Milijuni čekaju na odgovor', *Privredni Vjesnik*, 8 February, p. 6.

Mencinger, J. (1980) 'Činjenice protiv zemlijišnog maksimuma', *Ekonomska Politika*, 1 September, pp. 31–2.

Mencinger, J. and V. Bole (1980) *Ekonometrični Model Jugoslovenskega Gospodarstva*, Ekonomski Institut Pravne Fakultete, Ljubljana.

Mesarić, O. (1973) statement in *Privredni Vjesnik*, 1 March, p. 3.

Mihailović, K. (1977) *Rasprave o Razvoju Jugoslovenske Privrede*, Ekonomski Institut, Belgrade.

Mihailovic, P. (1969) 'Tržište finansijskih sredstava u Jugoslaviji', *Ekonomist* (1).

Mijatović, K. (1974) statement in *Privredni Vjesnik*, 26 April, p. 3.

Milenkovitch, D. (1971) *Plan and Market in Yugoslav Economic Thought*, New Haven and London: Yale University Press.
Milić, S. (1972) statement in *Privredni Vjesnik*, 16 March, p. 13.
Mirković, M. (1968) *Ekonomska Historija Jugoslavije*, Zagreb: Informator.
Momtchiloff, N. (1944) *Ten Years of Controlled Trade in South-Eastern Europe*, Cambridge: Cambridge University Press.
Montias, J.M. (1959) 'Economic reforms and retreat in Yugoslavia', *Foreign Affairs*, 37 (2).
'Motiv više' (1988) *Ekonomska Politika*, 20 June, p. 6.
'Naftovod' (1975) *Privredni Vjesnik*, 10 November, p. 2.
'Naličje rizika' (1980) *Ekonomska Politika*, 20 October, pp. 6–7.
Nedeljković, D. (1985) 'Dogovaranje o Kosovu', *Ekonomska Politika*, 19 August, pp. 18–19.
—— (1987) 'Planiranje manjkova', *Ekonomska Politika*, 19 January, pp. 20–1.
—— (1988) 'Papirnati plan', *Ekonomska Politika*, 22 August, pp. 23–4.
Nedeljković, T. (1986) 'Narodna Banka Jugoslavije i novi devizni sistem', *Jugoslovensko Bankarstvo*, March.
'Neiskorišćene devize' (1982) *Ekonomska Politika*, 10 May, p. 8.
'(Ne)iskorišćenost kadrova' (1985) *Ekonomska Politika*, 9 December, p. 8.
Nejašmić, I. (1973) 'Nezaposleni postaju sve stručniji', *Privredni Vjesnik*, 19 April, p. 10.
Nicović, Dj. (1986) 'Funkcije ovlašćenih banaka po zakonu o deviznom poslovanju', *Jugoslovensko Bankarstvo*, March.
Nikolić, D. (1976) 'Stare zadruge koče razvoj', *Borba*, 24 July, p. 4.
'Ni programa ni ljudi' (1988) *Ekonomska Politika*, 26 December, p. 5.
'Ni rat – ni mir' (1987) *Ekonomska Politika*, 1 June, pp. 10–14.
'Ništa bez potvrde' (1986) *Ekonomska Politika*, 18 August, p. 7.
'Nisu samo sredstva problem' (1981) *Ekonomska Politika*, 29 June, pp. 23–5.
Nötel, R. (1986) 'International credit and finance', in M.C. Kaser and E.A. Radice (eds) *The Economic History of Eastern Europe 1919–75*, vol. II, Oxford: Clarendon Press.
Nove, A. (1969) *An Economic History of the USSR*, London: Penguin Press.
'Novi planovi' (1983) *Ekonomska Politika*, 1 August, pp. 14–15.
OECD (1983) *Economic Outlook 33*, July.
—— (1987) *Yugoslavia. Economic Survey 1986–87*.
Oršanić, V. (1973) 'Slavonija: požurivanje s razlogom', *Privredni Vjesnik*, 6 December, pp. 5–6.
Ostojić, B. (1988) 'Sve po spisku programa', *Ekonomska Politika*, 20 June, p. 16.
'Paragraf – torpedo' (1982) *Ekonomska Politika*, 15 November, p. 7.
'Partija VS SDK' (1987) *Ekonomska Politika*, 14 September, p. 7.
'Partijski spisak' (1986) *Ekonomska Politika*, 27 January, p. 6.
Paver, M. (1973) 'Hrvatska u JNA', *Vjesnik u Srijedu*, 2 May, p. 3.
Pečar, N. (1970) *Sistem Družbenih Računov SR Slovenije za Leto 1967*, Ljubljana.
Pejović, S. and Zmijarević, D. (1986) 'Na granici konfuzije', *Ekonomska Politika*, 27 January, pp. 12–13.
Perišin, I. (1972) Speech to the Croatian parliament, published in *Privredni Vjesnik*, 20 January, p. 2.

References

Pertot, V. (1971) *Ekonomika Medjunarodne Razmene Jugoslavije*, Zagreb: Informator.

Petrašinović, P. (1980) 'Karakteristike ciklusa 1976–80', *Ekonomska Politika*, 1 September, pp. 22–6.

Petrović, A. (1974) 'Partner samo u dobru', *Borba*, 11 December, p. 4.

Pjević, J. (1987) 'Sukobljeni interesi', *Ekonomska Politika*, 25 May, pp. 10–12.

'Poen za bolju upravu' (1969) *Privredni Vjesnik*, 20 April, p. 2.

Poležina, V. (1973) *Prelivanje Narodnog Dohotka u Primarnoj i Sekundarnoj Raspodeli, Njegovi Efekti i Kvantifikacija*, Ekonomski Institut, Skopje.

Popov, S. and Jovičić, M. (1971) *Uticaj Ličnih Dohodaka na Kretanje Cena*, Belgrade: Institut Ekonomskih Nauka.

Popović, M. (1980) 'Ucjena, dogovor ili nesto treće', *Privredni Vjesnik*, 28 August, pp. 4–6.

Popović, Milan (1988) *Dileme Političkog Pluralizma*, Univerzitetska Riječ, Nikšić.

Popović, Milentije (1964) *Društveno Ekonomski Sistem*, Belgrade: Kultura.

'Posao stoleća' (1986) *Ekonomska Politika*, 20 October, p. 6.

'Poslovni rizik' (1986) *Ekonomska Politika*, 25 August, p. 6.

'Potemkinova sela' (1982) *Ekonomska Politika*, 13 December, p. 6.

'Pravi rečnik' (1982) *Ekonomska Politika*, 20 December, p. 6.

'Pravo prvenstva' (1982) *Ekonomska Politika*, 15 March, p. 13.

'Prestaje li pad zarada' (1985) *Ekonomska Politika*, 17 June, p. 5.

'Pretpostavke šire suradnje' (1980) *Privredni Vjesnik*, 29 February, p. 1.

'Profesija – političar' (1987) *Ekonomska Politika*, 21 September, p. 5.

Proizvodna Orijentacija Privrede SR Srbije van Teritorija SAP u Funkciji Povećanja Izvoza u Periodu 1986–1990 (1985) Institut za Ekonomiku Industrije, Belgrade.

'Projekat za mini-farme' (1974) *Ekonomska Politika*, 30 December, pp. 17–18.

Prokić, D. (1966) 'Radnici – seljaci', in *Društveno-Ekonomska i Politicka Pitanja u Razvoju Poljoprivrede i Sela*, Belgrade: Zajednica Naučno-Istraživačkih Ustanova Jugoslavije za Ekonomiku Poljoprivrede.

Prout, C. (1985) *Market Socialism in Yugoslavia*, Oxford: Oxford University Press.

'Pruga Beograd – Bar spremna za saobraćaj' (1976) *Borba*, 5 May, p. 1.

Račić, Dj. (1955) *Nauka o Novcu*, Školska Knjiga, Zagreb.

Radmilović, S. (1985) 'Problemi kamate, kamatnih stopa i revalorizacije sredstava', in *Aktuelna Monetarna Politika* . . .

'Razlog za suglasnost' (1980) *Ekonomska Politika*, 4 August, p. 11.

'Reč ili misao' (1981) *Ekonomska Politika*, 21 September, p. 6.

'Repatrijacija na slovenski način' (1970) *Privredni Vjesnik*, 24 September, p. 3.

Ribnikar, I. (1986) 'Deviza nasuprot deviznim i dinarskim ulozima (depozitima) kod banaka', *Jugoslovensko Bankarstvo*, March.

Rogić, Z. (1985) 'Monetarno-kreditna politika u 1985 godini', in *Aktuelna Monetarna Politika* . . .

Rukavina-Šain, M. and Ćirić, Z. (1975) 'Nova pozicija udruženog rada u drustvu', *Privredni Vjesnik*, 24 February, p. 4.

'Šagrinska koza' (1983) *Ekonomska Politika*, 16 May, p. 7.

Scanlon, J. (1988) interview reported in 'Jugoslavija nije loš dužnik',

Ekonomska Politika, 20 June, pp. 13–14.

Schrenk, M. *et al.* (1979) *Yugoslavia. Self-Management Socialism: Challenges of Development*, World Bank, Baltimore and London: Johns Hopkins University Press.

Schwed, J.J. (1988) Interview reported in 'Ulaganja čekaju jasne zakone', *Ekonomska Politika*, 18 July, pp. 17–18.

Seroka, J. (1988) 'The interdependence of institutional revitalization and intra-Party reform in Yugoslavia', *Soviet Studies*, 40 (1).

'S glavom u "korpi" ' (187) *Ekonomska Politika*, 12 October, p. 7.

Simović, M. (1988) 'Vrtlog američkog tržišta', *Ekonomska Politika*, 15 August, pp. 15–16.

Šimunić, J. (1979) 'Dokle pod tutorskom zakona', *Privredni Vjesnik*, 2 April, p. 5.

'Sindikat u visokom letu' (1986) *Ekonomska Politika*, 15 September, p. 8.

Sirc, L. (1979) *The Yugoslav Economy Under Self-Management*, London: Macmillan.

Sitarski, P. (1987) 'Izazov za politiku', 16 February, pp. 9–10.

Sojić, M. (1984) 'Uzročnici i kontrola inflacije kod nas', *Ekonomika Udruženog Rada* (12).

Spiljak, M. (1974) statements reported in 'Uzleti i padovi', *Ekonomska Politika*, 9 September, p. 8.

Štahan, J. (1972) 'Inflacija i životni standard', *Ekonomist* (2)

Stambolic, I. (1974a) statement in *Privredni Vjesnik*, 7 March, p. 2.

—— (1974b) statement in *Privredni Vjesnik*, 6 September, p. 2.

Staničić, M. (1972) 'Pouke velikog izvoznog uspjeha', *Privredni Vjesnik*, 23 November, pp. 5–6.

'Stanje duhova' (1981) *Ekonomska Politika*, 17 August, p. 8.

Stanojlović, S. (1974) 'Od Nove godine bez državnog kapitala', *Privredni Vjesnik*, 10 January, p. 6.

—— (1976) 'Stvarnost na pruzi snova', *Privredni Vjesnik*, 12 January, pp. 6–7.

—— (1979) 'Suštinska primjena ZUR-a na početku', *Privredni Vjesnik*, 1 October, pp. 5–6.

'Stari kadri' (1982) *Ekonomska Politika*, 5 April, pp. 14–15.

Statistički Godišnjak Jugoslavije (various years) Savezni Zavod za Statistiku, Belgrade.

'Status' (1983) *Ekonomska Politika*, 1 August, p. 6.

'Sto babica . . .' (1981) *Ekonomska Politika*, 5 October, p. 8.

Stojanović, S. (1986) 'Sadašnja jugoslovenska kriza i neophodnost političkih reformi', in Maksimović (ed) Ekonomika i Politika.

'Što je to samoupravni odnos?' (1970) *Privredni Vjesnik*, 24 September, p. 4.

'Što manji promet – to veće cene' (1987), *Ekonomska Politika*, 15 June, pp. 9–10.

Strukturne Karakteristike. Dinamika Rasta i Akumulativnosti Privrede SR Hrvatske do Godine 1985 (1977) Ekonomski Institut, Zagreb.

'Stvar prestiža' (1980) *Ekonomska Politika*, 14 July, p. 6.

Šublja, S. (1980) statement in *Privredni Vjesnik*, 28 March, p. 3.

Tito, J. (1972a) Speech to the Croatian Party leadership, published in *Vjesnik u Srijedu*, 10 May, pp. 4–5.

—— (1972b) Speech in Rijeka, published in *Borba*, 6 September, pp. 1 and 6.

References

—— (1972c) Speech to Serbian LCY leadership, published in *Borba*, 18 October, pp. 1 and 5.

'Transformator u delovima' (1981) *Ekonomska Politika*, 2 November, p. 6.

'Treća revizija najvećeg projekta' (1981) *Ekonomska Politika*, 5 October, pp. 24–5.

'Tudja briga' (1987) *Ekonomska Politika*, 8 June, p. 6.

Urošević, M. (1974) ' "Mini-farme" dočekale programe', *Privredni Vjesnik*, 12 April, p. 12.

'Usko grlo' (1987) *Ekonomska Politika*, 16 February, p. 5.

Uslovi, Mogućnosti i Pretpostavke Razvoja Jugoslovenske Privrede za Period 1986–1990 godine, sa Posebnim Akcentom na Analizi Uvozne Zavisnosti i Pravcima Investicionih Ulaganja (1985) Institut Ekonomskih Nauka, Belgrade.

'Uslov za devize' (1985) *Ekonomska Politika*, 9 December, pp. 6–7.

'Usporeno kretanje' (1981) *Ekonomska Politika*, 21 December, p. 14.

'U stabilizaciju' (1983) *Ekonomska Politika*, 5 September, p. 6.

'Usvojen sporazum o podsticanju izvoza' (1980) *Ekonomska Politika*, 14 April, p. 12.

'Uvoz uz dozvolu – predah za prestrojavanje' (1975) *Privredni Vjesnik*, 7 July, p. 1.

Vanek, J. (1975) 'Introduction', in J. Vanek (ed.) *Self-Management. Economic Liberation of Man*, London: Penguin.

Vasić, V. (1984) 'Izvoz se mora selektivno stimulisati', *Ekonomska Misao*, (4).

'Važi li zakon za partiju' (1988) *Ekonomska Politika*, 30 May, p. 6.

'Veće proizvodjača' (1983) *Ekonomska Politika*, 5 September, p. 7.

Vinski, I. (1965) *Procjena Rasta Fiksnih Fondova po Jugoslovenskim Republikama od 1946 do 1960*, Ekonomski Institut, Zagreb.

—— (1970) *Klasna Podjela Stanovništva i Nacionalnog Dohotka Jugoslavije u 1938 godini*, Ekonomski Institut, Zagreb.

'Višak nezaposlenih – i zapóslenih' (1982) *Ekonomska Politika*, 12 April, pp. 16–18.

Vizek, Z. (1974) 'Sporazumi zapeli na uravnilovki', *Privredni Vjesnik*, 16 August, p. 4.

'Vladina veza' (1982) *Ekonomska Politika*, 19 April, p. 7.

Vlaho, B. (1975) 'Obvezuje li odluka Komore organizaciju udruženog rada', *Privredni Vjesnik*, 2 June, p. 4.

—— (1978) 'Što je pokazala analiza investiranja?', *Privredni Vjesnik*, 16 September, p. 4.

—— (1979a) 'Za dvije i pol godine – dva i pol puta veće', *Privredni Vjesnik*, 22 January, pp. 5–6.

—— (1979b) 'Žilavi korijeni potrošnje' *Privredni Vjesnik*, 13 August, pp. 4–5.

—— (1979c) 'Investiranje mimo plana' *Privredni Vjesnik*, 3 September, p. 9.

—— (1979d) 'Nedovoljno udruživanje rada i sredstava', *Privredni Vjesnik*, 13 September, p. 9.

—— (1979e) 'Roba za svoju republiku', *Privredni Vjesnik*, 21 September, p. 4.

—— (1979f) 'Devize za svoje tržište', *Privredni Vjesnik*, 8 October, p. 9.

Vodopivec, M. (1986) 'Opredelitev funkcij zunanjetrgovinskih tokov za jugoslovensko gospodarstvo', *Ekonomska Revija*, 37 (1).

'Vreme je novac' (1985) *Ekonomska Politika*, 16 September, pp. 6–7.

'Vruća sedla' (1988) *Ekonomska Politika*, 18 January, p. 7.

Vuger, R. (1985) 'Nije za prodaju', *Ekonomska Politika*, 27 May, p. 11.

Vukmanović-Tempo, S. (1964) *Privredni Razvoj i Socialistička Izgradnja*, Belgrade: Rad.

Ward, B. (1958) 'The firm in Illyria: market syndicalism', *American Economic Review*, 18 (4).

Waterson, A. (1962) *Planning in Yugoslavia*, Baltimore: Johns Hopkins University Press.

WEFA (1988) *CPE Outlook for Foreign Trade and Finance*, July.

World Bank (1983) *Yugoslavia. Adjustment Policies and Development Perspectives*, Washington DC.

'Zabluda' (1980) *Ekonomska Politika*, 4 August, p. 6.

'Za dlaku' (1982) *Ekonomska Politika*, 19 April, p. 8.

'Zajam' (1979) *Privredni Vjesnik*, 24 December, p. 2.

'Zajmovi kao i dosad' (1982) *Ekonomska Politika*, 13 December, pp. 12–13.

'Zasedanje Mešovite komisije' (1980) *Ekonomska Politika*, 17 November, p. 10.

'Zaustavljeni transport' (1986) *Ekonomska Politika*, 21 July, p. 9.

'Zeleni kredit' (1978) *Privredni Vjesnik*, 22 September, pp. 2–3.

Zimić, F. (1987) 'Novi izgledi, stare prepreke', *Ekonomska Politika*, 17 August, pp. 22–3.

—— (1988a) 'Koliko je daleko Evropa?', *Ekonomska Politika*, 1 February, p. 14.

—— (1988b) 'Od kredita ka vlasnistvu', *Ekonomska Politika*, 11 April, pp. 9–11.

—— (1988c) 'Dinar kao jedino sredstvo plaćanja', *Ekonomska Politika*, 6 June, p. 11.

Živkov, Lj. (1985) 'Ko se plaše bogatog seljaka', *Ekonomska Politika*, 24 June, pp. 12–13.

Zmijarević, A. (1980) 'Ko i o čemu da se dogovara', *Ekonomska Politika*, 27 October, pp. 20–3.

Zmijarević, D. (1986) 'Šta je doneo realan kurs', *Ekonomska Politika*, 20 January, pp. 11–12.

—— (1988) 'Nastavak 1986. godine', *Ekonomska Politika*, 1 February.

Znanstvene Osnove Dugoročnog Razvoja SR Hrvatske do 2000 Godine. Koncepcija Dugoročnog Privrednog Razvoja SR Hrvatske (1984) Ekonomski Institut, Zagreb.

Žulj, S. (1970) 'Nesporazumi oko budućnosti petrokemije' (1970) *Privredni Vjesnik*, 9 April, p. 10.

Županov, J. (1983) statements reported in 'Inteligencija i radništvo', *Ekonomska Politika*, 8 August, p. 7.

Žuvela, M. (1974) statement in *Privredni Vjesnik*, 15 March, p. 3.

Index